# The Elements of Style

# THE
# ELEMENTS
## OF
# *Style*

BY
# WILLIAM STRUNK Jr.

*With Revisions, an Introduction,*
*and a Chapter on Writing*

BY
# E. B. WHITE

THIRD EDITION

MACMILLAN PUBLISHING CO., INC.
*New York*
COLLIER MACMILLAN PUBLISHERS
*London*

COPYRIGHT © 1979, MACMILLAN PUBLISHING CO., INC.

PRINTED IN THE UNITED STATES OF AMERICA

Earlier editions © 1959 and © copyright 1972 by Macmillan Publishing Co., Inc.

The Introduction originally appeared, in slightly different form, in *The New Yorker,* and was copyrighted in 1957 by The New Yorker Magazine, Inc.

*The Elements of Style,* Revised Edition, by William Strunk Jr. and Edward A. Tenney, copyright 1935 by Oliver Strunk.

MACMILLAN PUBLISHING CO., INC.
866 Third Avenue, New York, New York 10022

COLLIER MACMILLAN CANADA, LTD.

*Library of Congress Cataloging in Publication Data*

Strunk, William, 1869–1946.
   The elements of style

   1. English language—Rhetoric.   I.   White, Elwyn Brooks,   (date)   II.   Title.
   PE1408.S772   1979        808          78-18444
   ISBN 0-02-418190-0
   ISBN 0-02-418200-1 pbk.

PRINTING        10   YEAR        789

ISBN   0-02-418190-0

ACKNOWLEDGMENT

The coauthor, E. B. White, is most grateful to Eleanor Gould Packard for her assistance in the preparation of the second edition.

# *Contents*

# *Introduction*

AT THE close of the first World War, when I was a student at Cornell, I took a course called English 8. My professor was William Strunk Jr. A textbook required for the course was a slim volume called *The Elements of Style*, whose author was the professor himself. The year was 1919. The book was known on the campus in those days as "the little book," with the stress on the word "little." It had been privately printed by the author.

I passed the course, graduated from the university, and forgot the book but not the professor. Some thirty-eight years later, the book bobbed up again in my life when Macmillan commissioned me to revise it for the college market and the general trade. Meantime, Professor Strunk had died.

*The Elements of Style*, when I re-examined it in 1957, seemed to me to contain rich deposits of gold. It was Will Strunk's *parvum opus*, his attempt to cut the vast tangle of English rhetoric down to size and write its rules and principles on the head of a pin. Will himself had hung the tag "little" on the book; he referred to it sardonically and with secret pride as "the *little* book," always giving the word "little" a special twist, as though he were putting a spin on a ball. In its original form, it was a forty-three-page summation of the case for cleanliness, accuracy, and brevity in the use of English. Today, fifty-two years later, its vigor is unimpaired, and for sheer pith I think it probably sets a record that is not likely to be broken. Even after I got through tampering with it, it was still a tiny thing, a barely tarnished gem. Seven rules of usage, eleven principles of composition, a few matters of form, and a list of words and expressions commonly misused—that was the sum and substance of Professor Strunk's work. Somewhat audaciously, and in an attempt to give my publisher his money's worth, I added a chapter called "An Approach to Style," setting forth my own prejudices, my notions of error, my articles of faith. This chapter (Chapter V) is addressed particularly to those who feel that English prose composition is not only a necessary skill but a sensible pursuit as well—a way to spend one's days. I think Professor Strunk would not object to that.

A second edition of the book was published in 1972. I have now completed a third revision. Chapter IV has been refurbished with words and expressions of a recent vintage; four rules of usage have been added to Chapter I. Fresh examples have been added to some of the rules and principles, amplification has reared its head in a few places in the text where I felt an assault could successfully be made on the bastions of its brevity, and in general the book has received a thorough overhaul—to correct errors, delete bewhiskered entries, and enliven the argument.

Professor Strunk was a positive man. His book contains rules of grammar phrased as direct orders. In the main I have not tried to soften his commands, or modify his pronouncements, or remove the special objects of his scorn. I have tried, instead, to preserve the flavor of his discontent while slightly enlarging the scope of the discussion. *The Elements of Style* does not pretend to survey the whole field. Rather it proposes to give in brief space the principal requirements of plain English style. It concentrates on fundamentals: the rules of usage and principles of composition most commonly violated.

The reader will soon discover that these rules and principles are in the form of sharp commands, Sergeant

Strunk snapping orders to his platoon. "Do not join independent clauses by a comma." (Rule 5.) "Do not break sentences in two." (Rule 6.) "Use the active voice." (Rule 14.) "Omit needless words." (Rule 17.) "Avoid a succession of loose sentences." (Rule 18.) "In summaries, keep to one tense." (Rule 21.) Each rule or principle is followed by a short hortatory essay, and usually the exhortation is followed by, or interlarded with, examples in parallel columns—the true vs. the false, the right vs. the wrong, the timid vs. the bold, the ragged vs. the trim. From every line there peers out at me the puckish face of my professor, his short hair parted neatly in the middle and combed down over his forehead, his eyes blinking incessantly behind steel-rimmed spectacles as though he had just emerged into strong light, his lips nibbling each other like nervous horses, his smile shuttling to and fro under a carefully edged mustache.

"Omit needless words!" cries the author on page 23, and into that imperative Will Strunk really put his heart and soul. In the days when I was sitting in his class, he omitted so many needless words, and omitted them so forcibly and with such eagerness and obvious relish, that he often seemed in the position of having shortchanged himself—a man left with nothing more to say yet with time to fill, a radio prophet who had outdistanced the clock. Will Strunk got out of this predicament by a simple trick: he uttered every sentence three times. When he delivered his oration on brevity to the class, he leaned forward over his desk, grasped his coat lapels in his hands, and, in a husky, conspiratorial voice, said, "Rule Seventeen. Omit needless words! Omit needless words! Omit needless words!"

He was a memorable man, friendly and funny. Under the remembered sting of his kindly lash, I have been trying to omit needless words since 1919, and although there are still many words that cry for omission and the huge task will never be accomplished, it is exciting to me to reread the masterly Strunkian elaboration of this noble theme. It goes:

Vigorous writing is concise. A sentence should contain no unnecessary words, a paragraph no unnecessary sentences, for the same reason that a drawing should have no unnecessary lines and a machine no unnecessary parts. This requires not that the writer make all his sentences short, or that he avoid all detail and treat his subjects only in outline, but that every word tell.

There you have a short, valuable essay on the nature and beauty of brevity—sixty-three words that could change the world. Having recovered from his adventure in prolixity (sixty-three words were a lot of words in the tight world of William Strunk Jr.), the professor proceeds to give a few quick lessons in pruning. The student learns to cut the deadwood from "this is a subject that," reducing it to "this subject," a saving of three words. He learns to trim "used for fuel purposes" down to "used for fuel." He learns that he is being a chatterbox when he says "the question as to whether" and that he should just say "whether"—a saving of four words out of a possible five.

The professor devotes a special paragraph to the vile expression *the fact that*, a phrase that causes him to quiver with revulsion. The expression, he says, should be "revised out of every sentence in which it occurs." But a shadow of gloom seems to hang over the page, and you feel that he knows how hopeless his cause is. I suppose I have written *the fact that* a thousand times in the heat of composition, revised it out maybe five hundred times in the cool aftermath. To be batting only .500 this late in the season, to fail half the time to connect with this fat pitch, saddens me, for it seems a betrayal of the man who showed me how to swing at it and made the swinging seem worth while.

I treasure *The Elements of Style* for its sharp advice, but I treasure it even more for the audacity and self-confidence of its author. Will knew where he stood. He was so sure of where he stood, and made his position so clear and so plausible, that his peculiar stance has continued to invigorate me—and, I am sure, thousands

a drafty time, erect, resolute, and assured. I still find
the Strunkian wisdom a comfort, the Strunkian humor
a delight, and the Strunkian attitude toward right-and-
wrong a blessing undisguised.

E. B. WHITE

observation," he wrote, "that the best writers sometimes disregard the rules of rhetoric. When they do so, however, the reader will usually find in the sentence some compensating merit, attained at the cost of the violation. Unless he is certain of doing as well, he will probably do best to follow the rules."

It is encouraging to see how perfectly a book, even a dusty rule book, perpetuates and extends the spirit of a man. Will Strunk loved the clear, the brief, the bold, and his book is clear, brief, bold. Boldness is perhaps its chief distinguishing mark. On page 27, explaining one of his parallels, he says, "The left-hand version gives the impression that the writer is undecided or timid; he seems unable or afraid to choose one form of expression and hold to it." And his Rule 11 was "Make definite assertions." That was Will all over. He scorned the vague, the tame, the colorless, the irresolute. He felt it was worse to be irresolute than to be wrong. I remember a day in class when he leaned far forward, in his characteristic pose—the pose of a man about to impart a secret—and croaked, "If you don't know how to pronounce a word, say it loud! If you don't know how to pronounce a word, say it loud!" This comical piece of advice struck me as sound at the time, and I still respect it. Why compound ignorance with inaudibility? Why run and hide?

All through *The Elements of Style* one finds evidences of the author's deep sympathy for the reader. Will felt that the reader was in serious trouble most of the time, a man floundering in a swamp, and that it was the duty of anyone attempting to write English to drain this swamp quickly and get his man up on dry ground, or at least throw him a rope. In revising the text, I have tried to hold steadily in mind this belief of his, this concern for the bewildered reader.

In the English classes of today, "the little book" is surrounded by longer, lower textbooks—books with permissive steering and automatic transitions. Perhaps the book has become something of a curiosity. To me, it still seems to maintain its original poise, standing, in

of other ex-students—during the years that have inter-
vened since our first encounter. He had a number of
like and dislikes that were almost as whimsical as the
choice of a necktie, yet he made them seem utterly convincing. He disliked the word *forceful* and advised us to
use *forcible* instead. He felt that the word *clever* was
greatly overused: "It is best restricted to ingenuity displayed in small matters." He despised the expression
*student body*, which he termed gruesome, and made a
special trip downtown to the *Alumni News* office one
day to protest the expression and suggest that *studentry*
be substituted—a coinage of his own, which he felt
was similar to *citizenry*. I am told that the *News* editor
was so charmed by the visit, if not by the word, that he
ordered the student body buried, never to rise again.
*Studentry* has taken its place. It's not much of an im-
provement, but it does sound less cadaverous, and it
made Will Strunk quite happy.

Some years ago, when the heir to the throne of England was a child, I noticed a headline in the *Times*
about Bonnie Prince Charlie: "CHARLES' TONSILS OUT."
Immediately Rule 1 leapt to mind.

> 1. Form the possessive singular of nouns by adding *'s*.
> Follow this rule whatever the final consonant. Thus write,
>> Charles's friend
>> Burns's poems
>> the witch's malice

Clearly, Will Strunk had foreseen, as far back as 1918,
the dangerous tonsillectomy of a prince, in which the
surgeon removes the tonsils and the *Times* copy desk
removes the final *s*. He started his book with it. I com-
mend Rule 1 to the *Times*, and I trust that Charles's
throat, not Charles' throat, is in fine shape today.

Style rules of this sort are, of course, somewhat a
matter of individual preference, and even the established rules of grammar are open to challenge. Professor Strunk, although one of the most inflexible and
choosy of men, was quick to acknowledge the fallacy of
inflexibility and the danger of doctrine. "It is an old

# The Elements of Style

# I
# *Elementary Rules of Usage*

**1. *Form the possessive singular of nouns by adding 's.***

Follow this rule whatever the final consonant. Thus write,

> Charles's friend
> Burns's poems
> the witch's malice

Exceptions are the possessives of ancient proper names in *-es* and *-is,* the possessive *Jesus',* and such forms as *for conscience' sake, for righteousness' sake.* But such forms as *Moses' Laws, Isis' temple* are commonly replaced by

> the laws of Moses
> the temple of Isis

The pronominal possessives *hers, its, theirs, yours,* and *ours* have no apostrophe. Indefinite pronouns, however, use the apostrophe to show possession.

> one's rights
> somebody else's umbrella

A common error is to write *it's* for *its,* or vice versa. The first is a contraction, meaning "it is." The second is a possessive.

> It's a wise dog that scratches its own fleas.

**2. In a series of three or more terms with a single conjunction, use a comma after each term except the last.**

Thus write,

> red, white, and blue
>
> gold, silver, or copper
>
> He opened the letter, read it, and made a note of its contents.

This comma is often referred to as the "serial" comma.

In the names of business firms the last comma is usually omitted. Follow the usage of the individual firm.

> Brown, Shipley and Co.
>
> Merrill Lynch, Pierce, Fenner & Smith Incorporated

**3. Enclose parenthetic expressions between commas.**

> The best way to see a country, unless you are pressed for time, is to travel on foot.

This rule is difficult to apply; it is frequently hard to decide whether a single word, such as *however*, or a brief phrase is or is not parenthetic. If the interruption to the flow of the sentence is but slight, the writer may safely omit the commas. But whether the interruption is slight or considerable, he must never omit one comma and leave the other. There is no defense for such punctuation as

> Marjorie's husband, Colonel Nelson paid us a visit yesterday.

or

> My brother you will be pleased to hear, is now in perfect health.

Dates usually contain parenthetic words or figures. Punctuate as follows:

My cousin Bob is a talented harpist. (*restrictive*)

Our oldest daughter, Mary, sings. (*nonrestrictive*)

When the main clause of a sentence is preceded by a phrase or a subordinate clause, use a comma to set off these elements.

Partly by hard fighting, partly by diplomatic skill, they enlarged their dominions to the east and rose to royal rank with the possession of Sicily.

### 4. *Place a comma before a conjunction introducing an independent clause.*

The early records of the city have disappeared, and the story of its first years can no longer be reconstructed.

The situation is perilous, but there is still one chance of escape.

Two-part sentences of which the second member is introduced by *as* (in the sense of "because"), *for, or, nor,* or *while* (in the sense of "and at the same time") likewise require a comma before the conjunction.

If a dependent clause, or an introductory phrase requiring to be set off by a comma, precedes the second independent clause, no comma is needed after the conjunction.

The situation is perilous, but if we are prepared to act promptly, there is still one chance of escape.

When the subject is the same for both clauses and is expressed only once, a comma is useful if the connective is *but*. When the connective is *and*, the comma should be omitted if the relation between the two statements is close or immediate.

I have heard his arguments, but am still unconvinced.

He has had several years' experience and is thoroughly competent.

### 5. *Do not join independent clauses by a comma.*

If two or more clauses grammatically complete and not joined by a conjunction are to form a single compound sentence, the proper mark of punctuation is a semicolon.

> Stevenson's romances are entertaining; they are full of exciting adventures.
>
> It is nearly half past five; we cannot reach town before dark.

It is, of course, equally correct to write each of these as two sentences, replacing the semicolons with periods.

> Stevenson's romances are entertaining. They are full of exciting adventures.
>
> It is nearly half past five. We cannot reach town before dark.

If a conjunction is inserted, the proper mark is a comma. (Rule 4.)

> Stevenson's romances are entertaining, for they are full of exciting adventures.
>
> It is nearly half past five, and we cannot reach town before dark.

A comparison of the three forms given above will show clearly the advantage of the first. It is, at least in the examples given, better than the second form because it suggests the close relationship between the two statements in a way that the second does not attempt, and better than the third because it is briefer and therefore more forcible. Indeed, this simple method of indicating relationship between statements is one of the most useful devices of composition. The relationship, as above, is commonly one of cause and consequence.

Note that if the second clause is preceded by an adverb, such as *accordingly, besides, then, therefore,* or *thus,* and not by a conjunction, the semicolon is still required.

> I had never been in the place before; besides, it was dark as a tomb.

An exception to the semicolon rule is worth noting here. A comma is preferable when the clauses are very short and alike in form, or when the tone of the sentence is easy and conversational.

> Man proposes, God disposes.

> The gates swung apart, the bridge fell, the portcullis was drawn up.

> I hardly knew him, he was so changed.

> Here today, gone tomorrow.

### 6. *Do not break sentences in two.*

In other words, do not use periods for commas.

> I met them on a Cunard liner many years ago. Coming home from Liverpool to New York.

> He was an interesting talker. A man who had traveled all over the world and lived in half a dozen countries.

In both these examples, the first period should be replaced by a comma and the following word begun with a small letter.

It is permissible to make an emphatic word or expression serve the purpose of a sentence and to punctuate it accordingly:

> Again and again he called out. No reply.

The writer must, however, be certain that the emphasis is warranted, lest his clipped sentence seem merely a blunder in syntax or in punctuation. Generally speaking, the place for broken sentences is in dialogue, when a character happens to speak in a clipped or fragmentary way.

Rules 3, 4, 5, and 6 cover the most important principles that govern punctuation. They should be so thoroughly mastered that their application becomes second nature.

### 7. *Use a colon after an independent clause to introduce a list of particulars, an appositive, an amplification, or an illustrative quotation.*

A colon tells the reader that what follows is closely related to the preceding clause. The colon has more effect than the comma, less power to separate than the semicolon, and more formality than the dash. It usually follows an independent clause and should not separate a verb from its complement or a preposition from its object. The examples in the left-hand column, below, are wrong; they should be rewritten as in the right-hand column.

| | |
|---|---|
| Your dedicated whittler requires: a knife, a piece of wood, and a back porch. | Your dedicated whittler requires three props: a knife, a piece of wood, and a back porch. |
| Understanding is that penetrating quality of knowledge that grows from: theory, practice, conviction, assertion, error, and humiliation. | Understanding is that penetrating quality of knowledge that grows from theory, practice, conviction, assertion, error, and humiliation. |

Join two independent clauses with a colon if the second interprets or amplifies the first.

But even so, there was a directness and dispatch about animal burial: there was no stopover in the undertaker's foul parlor, no wreath or spray.

A colon may introduce a quotation that supports or contributes to the preceding clause.

The squalor of the streets reminded him of a line from Oscar Wilde: "We are all in the gutter, but some of us are looking at the stars."

The colon also has certain functions of form: to follow the salutation of a formal letter, to separate hour from minute in a notation of time, and to separate the title of a work from its subtitle or a Bible chapter from a verse.

Dear Mr. Montague:

*Practical Calligraphy: An Introduction to Italic Script*

departs at 10:48 P.M.

Nehemiah 11:7

**8. *Use a dash to set off an abrupt break or interruption, and to announce a long appositive or summary.***

A dash is a mark of separation stronger than a comma, less formal than a colon, and more relaxed than parentheses.

> His first thought on getting out of bed—if he had any thought at all—was to get back in again.

> The rear axle began to make a noise—a grinding, chattering, teeth-gritting rasp.

> The increasing reluctance of the sun to rise, the extra nip in the breeze, the patter of shed leaves dropping—all the evidences of fall drifting into winter were clearer each day.

Use a dash only when a more common mark of punctuation seems inadequate.

| | |
|---|---|
| Her father's suspicions proved well-founded—it was not Edward she cared for —it was San Francisco. | Her father's suspicions proved well-founded. It was not Edward she cared for, it was San Francisco. |
| Violence—the kind you see on television—is not honestly violent—there lies its harm. | Violence, the kind you see on television, is not honestly violent. There lies its harm. |

**9. *The number of the subject determines the number of the verb.***

Words that intervene between subject and verb do not affect the number of the verb.

| | |
|---|---|
| The bittersweet flavor of youth—its trials, its joys, its adventures, its challenges—are not soon forgotten. | The bittersweet flavor of youth—its trials, its joys, its adventures, its challenges —is not soon forgotten. |

A common blunder is the use of a singular verb form in a relative clause following "one of . . ." or a similar expression when the relative is the subject.

| One of the ablest men who has attacked this problem | One of the ablest men who have attacked this problem |
| One of those people who is never ready on time | One of those people who are never ready on time |

Use a singular verb form after *each, either, everyone, everybody, neither, nobody, someone.*

Everybody thinks he has a sense of humor.

Although both clocks strike cheerfully, neither keeps good time.

With *none,* use the singular verb when the word means "no one" or "not one."

None of us are perfect.     None of us is perfect.

A plural verb is commonly used when *none* suggests more than one thing or person

None are so fallible as those who are sure they're right.

A compound subject formed of two or more nouns joined by *and* almost always requires a plural verb.

The walrus and the carpenter were walking close at hand.

But certain compounds, often clichés, are so inseparable they are considered a unit and so take a singular verb, as do compound subjects qualified by *each* or *every.*

The long and the short of it is . . .

Bread and butter was all she served.

Give and take is essential to a happy household.

Every window, picture, and mirror was smashed.

A singular subject remains singular even if other nouns are connected to it by *with, as well as, in addition to, except, together with,* and *no less than.*

His speech as well as his manner is objectionable.

A linking verb agrees with the number of its subject.

What is wanted is a few more pairs of hands.

The trouble with truth is its many varieties.

Some nouns that appear to be plural are usually construed as singular and given a singular verb.

Politics is an art, not a science.

The Republican Headquarters is on this side of the tracks.

But

The general's quarters are over the river.

In these cases the writer must simply learn the idioms. The contents of a book is singular. The contents of a jar may be either singular or plural, depending on what's in the jar—jam or marbles.

### 10. *Use the proper case of pronoun.*

The personal pronouns, as well as the pronoun *who*, change form as they function as subject or object.

Will Jane or he be hired, do you think?

The culprit, it turned out, was he.

We heavy eaters would rather walk than ride.

Who knocks?

Give this work to whoever looks idle.

In the last example, *whoever* is the subject of *looks idle;* the object of the preposition *to* is the entire clause *whoever looks idle.* When *who* introduces a subordinate clause, its case depends on its function in that clause.

| | |
|---|---|
| Virgil Soames is the candidate whom we think will win. | Virgil Soames is the candidate who we think will win. |
| Virgil Soames is the candidate who we hope to elect. | Virgil Soames is the candidate whom we hope to elect. |

A pronoun in a comparison is nominative if it is the subject of a stated or understood verb.

Sandy writes better than I. (Than I write.)

In general, avoid "understood" verbs by supplying them.

| | |
|---|---|
| I think Horace admires Jessica more than I. | I think Horace admires Jessica more than I do. |
| Polly loves cake more than me. | Polly loves cake more than she loves me. |

The objective case is correct in the following examples.

The ranger offered Shirley and him some advice on campsites.

They came to meet the Baldwins and us.

Let's talk it over between us, then, you and me.

Whom should I ask?

A group of us taxpayers protested.

*Us* in the last example is in apposition to taxpayers, the object of the preposition *of*. The wording, although grammatically defensible, is rarely apt. "A group of us protested as taxpayers" is better, if not exactly equivalent.

Use the simple personal pronoun as a subject.

| | |
|---|---|
| Blake and myself stayed home. | Blake and I stayed home. |
| Howard and yourself brought the lunch, I thought. | Howard and you brought the lunch, I thought. |

The possessive case of pronouns is used to show ownership. It has two forms: the adjectival modifier, *your* hat, and the noun form, a hat of *yours*.

The dog has buried one of your gloves and one of mine in the flower bed.

Gerunds usually require the possessive case.

Mother objected to our driving on the icy roads.

A present participle as a verbal, on the other hand, takes the objective case.

> They heard him singing in the shower.

The difference between a verbal participle and a gerund is not always obvious, but note what is really said in each of the following.

> Do you mind me asking a question?
> Do you mind my asking a question?

In the first sentence, the queried objection is to *me*, as opposed to other members of the group, putting one of the questions. In the second example, the issue is whether a question may be asked at all.

**11. A *participial phrase at the beginning of a sentence must refer to the grammatical subject*.**

> Walking slowly down the road, he saw a woman accompanied by two children.

The word *walking* refers to the subject of the sentence, not to the woman. If the writer wishes to make it refer to the woman, he must recast the sentence.

> He saw a woman, accompanied by two children, walking slowly down the road.

Participial phrases preceded by a conjunction or by a preposition, nouns in apposition, adjectives, and adjective phrases come under the same rule if they begin the sentence.

| | |
|---|---|
| On arriving in Chicago, his friends met him at the station. | On arriving in Chicago, he was met at the station by his friends. |
| A soldier of proved valor, they entrusted him with the defense of the city. | A soldier of proved valor, he was entrusted with the defense of the city. |
| Young and inexperienced, the task seemed easy to me. | Young and inexperienced, I thought the task easy. |

| | |
|---|---|
| Without a friend to counsel him, the temptation proved irresistible. | Without a friend to counsel him, he found the temptation irresistible. |

Sentences violating Rule 11 are often ludicrous:

Being in a dilapidated condition, I was able to buy the house very cheap.

Wondering irresolutely what to do next, the clock struck twelve.

As a mother of five, with another on the way, my ironing board is always up.

# II

# *Elementary Principles of Composition*

### 12. *Choose a suitable design and hold to it.*

A basic structural design underlies every kind of writing. The writer will in part follow this design, in part deviate from it, according to his skill, his needs, and the unexpected events that accompany the act of composition. Writing, to be effective, must follow closely the thoughts of the writer, but not necessarily in the order in which those thoughts occur. This calls for a scheme of procedure. In some cases the best design is no design, as with a love letter, which is simply an outpouring, or with a casual essay, which is a ramble. But in most cases planning must be a deliberate prelude to writing. The first principle of composition, therefore, is to foresee or determine the shape of what is to come and pursue that shape.

A sonnet is built on a fourteen-line frame, each line containing five feet. Hence, the sonneteer knows exactly where he is headed, although he may not know how to get there. Most forms of composition are less clearly defined, more flexible, but all have skeletons to which the writer will bring the flesh and the blood. The more clearly he perceives the shape, the better are his chances of success.

### 13. *Make the paragraph the unit of composition.*

The paragraph is a convenient unit; it serves all forms of literary work. As long as it holds together, a paragraph may be of any length—a single, short sentence or a passage of great duration.

If the subject on which you are writing is of slight extent, or if you intend to treat it briefly, there may be no need to divide it into topics. Thus, a brief description, a brief book review, a brief account of a single incident, a narrative merely outlining an action, the setting forth of a single idea—any one of these is best written in a single paragraph. After the paragraph has been written, examine it to see whether division will improve it.

Ordinarily, however, a subject requires division into topics, each of which should be dealt with in a paragraph. The object of treating each topic in a paragraph by itself is, of course, to aid the reader. The beginning of each paragraph is a signal to him that a new step in the development of the subject has been reached.

As a rule, single sentences should not be written or printed as paragraphs. An exception may be made of sentences of transition, indicating the relation between the parts of an exposition or argument.

In dialogue, each speech, even if only a single word, is usually a paragraph by itself; that is, a new paragraph begins with each change of speaker. The application of this rule when dialogue and narrative are combined is best learned from examples in well-edited works of fiction. Sometimes a writer, seeking to create an effect of rapid talk or for some other reason, will elect not to set off each speech in a separate paragraph and instead will run speeches together. The common practice, however, and the one that serves best in most instances, is to give each speech a paragraph of its own.

As a rule, begin each paragraph either with a sentence that suggests the topic or with a sentence that helps the transition. If a paragraph forms part of a larger composition, its relation to what precedes, or its function as a part of the whole, may need to be expressed. This can sometimes be done by a mere word or phrase (*again*; *therefore*; *for the same reason*) in the first sentence. Sometimes, however, it is expedient to get into the

topic slowly, by way of a sentence or two of introduction or transition.

In narration and description, the paragraph sometimes begins with a concise, comprehensive statement
serving to hold together the details that follow.

> The breeze served us admirably.

> The campaign opened with a series of reverses.

> The next ten or twelve pages were filled with a curious
> set of entries.

But when this device, or any device, is too often used,
it becomes a mannerism. More commonly the opening
sentence simply indicates by its subject the direction the
paragraph is to take.

> At length I thought I might return toward the stockade.

> He picked up the heavy lamp from the table and began
> to explore.

> Another flight of steps, and they emerged on the roof.

In animated narrative, the paragraphs are likely to be
short and without any semblance of a topic sentence,
the writer rushing headlong, event following event in
rapid succession. The break between such paragraphs
merely serves the purpose of a rhetorical pause, throwing into prominence some detail of the action.

In general, remember that paragraphing calls for a
good eye as well as a logical mind. Enormous blocks of
print look formidable to a reader. He has a certain re-
luctance to tackle them; he can lose his way in them.
Therefore, breaking long paragraphs in two, even if it is
not necessary to do so for sense, meaning, or logical development, is often a visual help. But remember, too,
that firing off many short paragraphs in quick succession
can be distracting. Paragraph breaks used only for show
read like the writing of commerce or of display advertising. Moderation and a sense of order should be the
main considerations in paragraphing.

**14.** *Use the active voice.*

The active voice is usually more direct and vigorous than the passive:

> I shall always remember my first visit to Boston.

This is much better than

> My first visit to Boston will always be remembered by me.

The latter sentence is less direct, less bold, and less concise. If the writer tries to make it more concise by omitting "by me,"

> My first visit to Boston will always be remembered,

it becomes indefinite: is it the writer or some person undisclosed or the world at large that will always remember this visit?

This rule does not, of course, mean that the writer should entirely discard the passive voice, which is frequently convenient and sometimes necessary.

> The dramatists of the Restoration are little esteemed today.

> Modern readers have little esteem for the dramatists of the Restoration.

The first would be the preferred form in a paragraph on the dramatists of the Restoration, the second in a paragraph on the tastes of modern readers. The need of making a particular word the subject of the sentence will often, as in these examples, determine which voice is to be used.

The habitual use of the active voice, however, makes for forcible writing. This is true not only in narrative concerned principally with action but in writing of any kind. Many a tame sentence of description or exposition can be made lively and emphatic by substituting a transitive in the active voice for some such perfunctory expression as *there is* or *could be heard.*

| | |
|---|---|
| There were a great number of dead leaves lying on the ground. | Dead leaves covered the ground. |
| At dawn the crowing of a rooster could be heard. | The cock's crow came with dawn. |
| The reason he left college was that his health became impaired. | Failing health compelled him to leave college. |
| It was not long before he was very sorry that he had said what he had. | He soon repented his words. |

Note, in the examples above, that when a sentence is made stronger, it usually becomes shorter. Thus, brevity is a by-product of vigor.

### 15. *Put statements in positive form.*

Make definite assertions. Avoid tame, colorless, hesitating, noncommittal language. Use the word *not* as a means of denial or in antithesis, never as a means of evasion.

| | |
|---|---|
| He was not very often on time. | He usually came late. |
| He did not think that studying Latin was a sensible way to use one's time. | He thought the study of Latin a waste of time. |
| *The Taming of the Shrew* is rather weak in spots. Shakespeare does not portray Katharine as a very admirable character, nor does Bianca remain long in memory as an important character in Shakespeare's works. | The women in *The Taming of the Shrew* are unattractive. Katharine is disagreeable, Bianca insignificant. |

The last example, before correction, is indefinite as well as negative. The corrected version, consequently, is simply a guess at the writer's intention.

All three examples show the weakness inherent in the word *not*. Consciously or unconsciously, the reader is

dissatisfied with being told only what is not; he wishes to be told what is. Hence, as a rule, it is better to express even a negative in positive form.

| | |
|---|---|
| not honest | dishonest |
| not important | trifling |
| did not remember | forgot |
| did not pay any attention to | ignored |
| did not have much confidence in | distrusted |

Placing negative and positive in opposition makes for a stronger structure.

Not charity, but simple justice.

Not that I loved Caesar less, but that I loved Rome more.

Ask not what your country can do for you—ask what you can do for your country.

Negative words other than *not* are usually strong.

Her loveliness I never knew/Until she smiled on me.

Statements qualified with unnecessary auxiliaries or conditionals sound irresolute.

| | |
|---|---|
| If you would let us know the time of your arrival, we would be happy to arrange your transportation from the airport. | If you will let us know the time of your arrival, we shall be happy to arrange your transportation from the airport. |
| The applicant can make a good impression by being neat and punctual. | The applicant will make a good impression if he is neat and punctual. |
| Keats may be ranked among those romantic poets who died young. | Keats was one of those romantic poets who died young. |

If your every sentence admits a doubt, your writing will lack authority. Save the auxiliaries *would, should, could, may, might,* and *can* for situations involving real uncertainty.

### 16. *Use definite, specific, concrete language.*

Prefer the specific to the general, the definite to the vague, the concrete to the abstract.

| | |
|---|---|
| A period of unfavorable weather set in. | It rained every day for a week. |
| He showed satisfaction as he took possession of his well-earned reward. | He grinned as he pocketed the coin. |

If those who have studied the art of writing are in accord on any one point, it is on this: the surest way to arouse and hold the attention of the reader is by being specific, definite, and concrete. The greatest writers— Homer, Dante, Shakespeare—are effective largely because they deal in particulars and report the details that matter. Their words call up pictures.

Jean Stafford, to cite a modern author, demonstrates in her short story "In the Zoo" how prose is made vivid by the use of words that evoke images and sensations:

> . . . Daisy and I in time found asylum in a small managerie down by the railroad tracks. It belonged to a gentle alcoholic ne'er-do-well, who did nothing all day long but drink bathtub gin in rickeys and play solitaire and smile to himself and talk to his animals. He had a little, stunted red vixen and a deodorized skunk, a parrot from Tahiti that spoke Parisian French, a woebegone coyote, and two capuchin monkeys, so serious and humanized, so small and sad and sweet, and so religious-looking with their tonsured heads that it was impossible not to think their gibberish was really an ordered language with a grammar that someday some philologist would understand.
>
> Gran knew about our visits to Mr. Murphy and she did not object, for it gave her keen pleasure to excoriate him when we came home. His vice was not a matter of guesswork; it was an established fact that he was half-seas over from dawn till midnight. "With the black Irish," said Gran, "the taste for drink is taken in with the mother's milk and is never mastered. Oh, I know all about those promises to join the temperance movement and not

to touch another drop. The way to Hell is paved with good intentions."

We were still little girls when we discovered Mr. Murphy, before the shattering disease of adolescence was to make our bones and brains ache even more painfully than before, and we loved him and we hoped to marry him when we grew up. We loved him, and we loved his monkeys to exactly the same degree and in exactly the same way; they were husbands and fathers and brothers, these little, ugly, dark, secret men who minded their own business and let us mind ours. If we stuck our fingers through the bars of the cage, the monkeys would sometimes take them in their tight, tiny hands and look into our faces with a tentative, somehow absent-minded sorrow, as if they terribly regretted that they could not place us but were glad to see us all the same. Mr. Murphy, playing a solitaire game of cards called "once in a blue moon" on a kitchen table in his back yard beside the pens, would occasionally look up and blink his beautiful blue eyes and say, "You're peaches to make over my wee friends. I love you for it." There was nothing demanding in his voice, and nothing sticky; on his lips the word "love" was jocose and forthright, it had no strings attached. We would sit on either side of him and watch him regiment his ranks of cards and stop to drink as deeply as if he were dying of thirst and wave to his animals and say to them, "Yes, lads, you're dandies."*

If the experiences of Walter Mitty, of Dick Diver, of Rabbit Angstrom have seemed for the moment real to countless readers, if in reading Faulkner we have almost the sense of inhabiting Yoknapatawpha County during the decline of the South, it is because the details used are definite, the terms concrete. It is not that every detail is given—that would be impossible, as well as to no purpose—but that all the significant details are given, and with such accuracy and vigor that the reader, in imagination, can project himself into the scene.

In exposition and in argument, the writer must like-

* A selection from "In the Zoo" from *Bad Characters* by Jean Stafford. Copyright © 1953, 1964 by Jean Stafford. This selection appeared originally in *The New Yorker*. Reprinted with the permission of Farrar, Straus & Giroux, Inc.

wise never lose his hold upon the concrete; and even when he is dealing with general principles, he must furnish particular instances of their application.

In his *Philosophy of Style,* Herbert Spencer gives two sentences to illustrate how the vague and general can be turned into the vivid and particular:

| | |
|---|---|
| In proportion as the manners, customs, and amusements of a nation are cruel and barbarous, the regulations of its penal code will be severe. | In proportion as men delight in battles, bullfights, and combats of gladiators, will they punish by hanging, burning, and the rack. |

To show what happens when strong writing is deprived of its vigor, George Orwell once took a passage from the Bible and drained it of its blood. On the left, below, is Orwell's translation; on the right, the verse from Ecclesiastes (King James Version).

| | |
|---|---|
| Objective consideration of contemporary phenomena compels the conclusion that success or failure in competitive activities exhibits no tendency to be commensurate with innate capacity, but that a considerable element of the unpredictable must inevitably be taken into account. | I returned, and saw under the sun, that the race is not to the swift, nor the battle to the strong, neither yet bread to the wise, nor yet riches to men of understanding, nor yet favor to men of skill; but time and chance happeneth to them all. |

## 17. *Omit needless words.*

Vigorous writing is concise. A sentence should contain no unnecessary words, a paragraph no unnecessary sentences, for the same reason that a drawing should have no unnecessary lines and a machine no unnecessary parts. This requires not that the writer make all his sentences short, or that he avoid all detail and treat his subjects only in outline, but that every word tell.

Many expressions in common use violate this principle.

| | |
|---|---|
| the question as to whether | whether (the question whether) |
| there is no doubt but that | no doubt (doubtless) |
| used for fuel purposes | used for fuel |
| he is a man who | he |
| in a hasty manner | hastily |
| this is a subject that | this subject |
| His story is a strange one. | His story is strange. |
| the reason why is that | because |

An expression that is especially debilitating is *the fact that*. It should be revised out of every sentence in which it occurs.

| | |
|---|---|
| owing to the fact that | since (because) |
| in spite of the fact that | though (although) |
| call your attention to the fact that | remind you (notify you) |
| I was unaware of the fact that | I was unaware that (did not know) |
| the fact that he had not succeeded | his failure |
| the fact that I had arrived | my arrival |

See also the words *case, character, nature* in Chapter IV.

*Who is, which was,* and the like are often superfluous.

| | |
|---|---|
| His brother, who is a member of the same firm | His brother, a member of the same firm |
| Trafalgar, which was Nelson's last battle | Trafalgar, Nelson's last battle |

As a positive statement is more concise than a negative one, and the active voice more concise than the passive, many of the examples given under Rules 14 and 15 illustrate this rule as well.

A common way to fall into wordiness is to present a

single complex idea, step by step, in a series of sentences that might to advantage be combined into one.

Macbeth was very ambitious. This led him to wish to become king of Scotland. The witches told him that this wish of his would come true. The king of Scotland at this time was Duncan. Encouraged by his wife, Macbeth murdered Duncan. He was thus enabled to succeed Duncan as king. (51 words)

Encouraged by his wife, Macbeth achieved his ambition and realized the prediction of the witches by murdering Duncan and becoming king of Scotland in his place. (26 words)

## 18. *Avoid a succession of loose sentences.*

This rule refers especially to loose sentences of a particular type: those consisting of two clauses, the second introduced by a conjunction or relative. A writer may err by making his sentences too compact and periodic. An occasional loose sentence prevents the style from becoming too formal and gives the reader a certain relief. Consequently, loose sentences are common in easy, unstudied writing. The danger is that there may be too many of them.

An unskilled writer will sometimes construct a whole paragraph of sentences of this kind, using as connectives *and*, *but*, and, less frequently, *who*, *which*, *when*, *where*, and *while*, these last in nonrestrictive senses. (See Rule 3.)

The third concert of the subscription series was given last evening, and a large audience was in attendance. Mr. Edward Appleton was the soloist, and the Boston Symphony Orchestra furnished the instrumental music. The former showed himself to be an artist of the first rank, while the latter proved itself fully deserving of its high reputation. The interest aroused by the series has been very gratifying to the Committee, and it is planned to give a similar series annually hereafter. The fourth concert will be given on Tuesday, May 10, when an equally attractive program will be presented.

Apart from its triteness and emptiness, the paragraph above is bad because of the structure of its sentences, with their mechanical symmetry and singsong. Compare these sentences from the chapter "What I Believe" in E. M. Forster's *Two Cheers for Democracy:*

> I believe in aristocracy, though—if that is the right word, and if a democrat may use it. Not an aristocracy of power, based upon rank and influence, but an aristocracy of the sensitive, the considerate and the plucky. Its members are to be found in all nations and classes, and all through the ages, and there is a secret understanding between them when they meet. They represent the true human tradition, the one permanent victory of our queer race over cruelty and chaos. Thousands of them perish in obscurity, a few are great names. They are sensitive for others as well as for themselves, they are considerate without being fussy, their pluck is not swankiness but the power to endure, and they can take a joke.*

If the writer finds that he has written a series of loose sentences, he should recast enough of them to remove the monotony, replacing them by simple sentences, by sentences of two clauses joined by a semicolon, by periodic sentences of two clauses, by sentences (loose or periodic) of three clauses—whichever best represent the real relations of the thought.

### 19. *Express coordinate ideas in similar form.*

This principle, that of parallel construction, requires that expressions similar in content and function be outwardly similar. The likeness of form enables the reader to recognize more readily the likeness of content and function. The familiar Beatitudes exemplify the virtue of parallel construction.

> Blessed are the poor in spirit: for theirs is the kingdom of heaven.
> Blessed are they that mourn: for they shall be comforted.
> Blessed are the meek: for they shall inherit the earth.

* From *Two Cheers for Democracy,* copyright, 1951, by E. M. Forster. Published by Harcourt, Brace and Company, Inc.

Blessed are they which do hunger and thirst after righteousness: for they shall be filled.

The unskillful writer often violates this principle, from a mistaken belief that he should constantly vary the form of his expressions. When repeating a statement to emphasize it, the writer may need to vary its form. But apart from this he should follow the principle of parallel construction.

| | |
|---|---|
| Formerly, science was taught by the textbook method, while now the laboratory method is employed. | Formerly, science was taught by the textbook method; now it is taught by the laboratory method. |

The left-hand version gives the impression that the writer is undecided or timid; he seems unable or afraid to choose one form of expression and hold to it. The right-hand version shows that the writer has at least made his choice and abided by it.

By this principle, an article or a preposition applying to all the members of a series must either be used only before the first term or else be repeated before each term.

| | |
|---|---|
| the French, the Italians, Spanish, and Portuguese | the French, the Italians, the Spanish, and the Portuguese |
| in spring, summer, or in winter | in spring, summer, or winter (in spring, in summer, or in winter) |

Some words require a particular preposition in certain idiomatic uses. When such words are joined in a compound construction, all the appropriate prepositions must be included, unless they are the same.

| | |
|---|---|
| His speech was marked by disagreement and scorn for his opponent's position. | His speech was marked by disagreement with and scorn for his opponent's position. |

Correlative expressions (*both, and; not, but; not only, but also; either, or; first, second, third;* and the like) should be followed by the same grammatical construction. Many violations of this rule can be corrected by rearranging the sentence.

| | |
|---|---|
| It was both a long ceremony and very tedious. | The ceremony was both long and tedious. |
| A time not for words but action. | A time not for words but for action. |
| Either you must grant his request or incur his ill will. | You must either grant his request or incur his ill will. |
| My objections are, first, the injustice of the measure; second, that it is unconstitutional. | My objections are, first, that the measure is unjust; second, that it is unconstitutional. |

It may be asked, what if a writer needs to express a rather large number of similar ideas—say, twenty? Must he write twenty consecutive sentences of the same pattern? On closer examination he will probably find that the difficulty is imaginary—that his twenty ideas can be classified in groups, and that he need apply the principle only within each group. Otherwise he had best avoid the difficulty by putting his statements in the form of a table.

### 20. *Keep related words together.*

The position of the words in a sentence is the principal means of showing their relationship. Confusion and ambiguity result when words are badly placed. The writer must, therefore, bring together the words and groups of words that are related in thought and keep apart those that are not so related.

| | |
|---|---|
| He noticed a large stain in the rug that was right in the center. | He noticed a large stain right in the center of the rug. |
| You can call your mother in London and tell her all about George's taking you out to dinner for just sixty cents. | For just sixty cents you can call your mother in London and tell her all about George's taking you out to dinner. |

| | |
|---|---|
| New York's first commercial human-sperm bank opened Friday with semen samples from 18 men frozen in a stainless steel tank. | New York's first commercial human-sperm bank opened Friday when semen samples were taken from 18 men. The samples were then frozen and stored in a stainless steel tank. |

In the left-hand version of the first example, the reader has no way of knowing whether the stain was in the center of the rug or the rug was in the center of the room. In the left-hand version of the second example, the reader may well wonder which cost sixty cents—the phone call or the dinner. In the left-hand version of the third example, the reader's heart goes out to those eighteen poor fellows frozen in a steel tank.

The subject of a sentence and the principal verb should not, as a rule, be separated by a phrase or clause that can be transferred to the beginning.

| | |
|---|---|
| Wordsworth, in the fifth book of *The Excursion*, gives a minute description of this church. | In the fifth book of *The Excursion*, Wordsworth gives a minute description of this church. |
| A dog, if you fail to discipline him, becomes a household pest. | Unless disciplined, a dog becomes a household pest. |

Interposing a phrase or a clause, as in the left-hand examples above, interrupts the flow of the main clause. This interruption, however, is not usually bothersome when the flow is checked only by a relative clause or by an expression in apposition. Sometimes, in periodic sentences, the interruption is a deliberate device for creating suspense. (See examples under Rule 22.)

The relative pronoun should come, in most instances, immediately after its antecedent.

| | |
|---|---|
| There was a stir in the audience that suggested disapproval. | A stir that suggested disapproval swept the audience. |
| He wrote three articles about his adventures in | He published three articles in *Harper's Magazine* |

| Spain, which were published in *Harper's Magazine*. | about his adventures in Spain. |
| --- | --- |
| This is a portrait of Benjamin Harrison, grandson of William Henry Harrison, who became President in 1889. | This is a portrait of Benjamin Harrison, who became President in 1889. He was the grandson of William Henry Harrison. |

If the antecedent consists of a group of words, the relative comes at the end of the group, unless this would cause ambiguity.

> The Superintendent of the Chicago Division, who

No ambiguity results from the above. But

> A proposal to amend the Sherman Act, which has been variously judged

leaves the reader wondering whether it is the proposal or the Act that has been variously judged. The relative clause must be moved forward, to read, "A proposal, which has been variously judged, to amend the Sherman Act. . . ." Similarly

| The grandson of William Henry Harrison, who | William Henry Harrison's grandson, Benjamin Harrison, who |
| --- | --- |

A noun in apposition may come between antecedent and relative, because in such a combination no real ambiguity can arise.

> The Duke of York, his brother, who was regarded with hostility by the Whigs

Modifiers should come, if possible, next to the word they modify. If several expressions modify the same word, they should be so arranged that no wrong relation is suggested.

| All the members were not present. | Not all the members were present. |
| --- | --- |
| He only found two mistakes. | He found only two mistakes. |

| | |
|---|---|
| The chairman said he hoped all members would give generously to the Fund at a meeting of the committee yesterday. | At a meeting of the committee yesterday, the chairman said he hoped all members would give generously to the Fund. |
| Major R. E. Joyce will give a lecture on Tuesday evening in Bailey Hall, to which the public is invited on "My Experiences in Mesopotamia" at eight P.M. | On Tuesday evening at eight, Major R. E. Joyce will give a lecture in Bailey Hall on "My Experiences in Mesopotamia." The public is invited. |

Note, in the last left-hand example, how swiftly meaning departs when words are wrongly juxtaposed.

### 21. *In summaries, keep to one tense.*

In summarizing the action of a drama, the writer should use the present tense. In summarizing a poem, story, or novel, he should also use the present, though he may use the past if it seems more natural to do so. If the summary is in the present tense, antecedent action should be expressed by the perfect; if in the past, by the past perfect.

> Chance prevents Friar John from delivering Friar Lawrence's letter to Romeo. Meanwhile, owing to her father's arbitrary change of the day set for her wedding, Juliet has been compelled to drink the potion on Tuesday night, with the result that Balthasar informs Romeo of her supposed death before Friar Lawrence learns of the nondelivery of the letter.

But whichever tense is used in the summary, a past tense in indirect discourse or in indirect question remains unchanged.

> The Friar confesses that it was he who married them.

Apart from the exceptions noted, whichever tense the writer chooses he should use throughout. Shifting from one tense to another gives the appearance of uncertainty and irresolution.

In presenting the statements or the thought of someone else, as in summarizing an essay or reporting a speech, the writer should not overwork such expressions as "he said," "he stated," "the speaker added," "the speaker then went on to say," "the author also thinks." He should indicate clearly at the outset, once for all, that what follows is summary, and then waste no words in repeating the notification.

In notebooks, in newspapers, in handbooks of literature, summaries of one kind or another may be indispensable, and for children in primary schools retelling a story in their own words is a useful exercise. But in the criticism or interpretation of literature the writer should be careful to avoid dropping into summary. He may find it necessary to devote one or two sentences to indicating the subject, or the opening situation, of the work he is discussing; he may cite numerous details to illustrate its qualities. But he should aim at writing an orderly discussion supported by evidence, not a summary with occasional comment. Similarly, if the scope of his discussion includes a number of works, he will as a rule do better not to take them up singly in chronological order but to aim from the beginning at establishing general conclusions.

### 22. Place the emphatic words of a sentence at the end.

The proper place in the sentence for the word or group of words that the writer desires to make most prominent is usually the end.

| | |
|---|---|
| Humanity has hardly advanced in fortitude since that time, though it has advanced in many other ways. | Since that time, humanity has advanced in many ways, but it has hardly advanced in fortitude. |
| This steel is principally used for making razors, because of its hardness. | Because of its hardness, this steel is used principally for making razors. |

The word or group of words entitled to this position of prominence is usually the logical predicate—that is, the *new* element in the sentence, as it is in the second example.

The effectiveness of the periodic sentence arises from the prominence it gives to the main statement.

> Four centuries ago, Christopher Columbus, one of the Italian mariners whom the decline of their own republics had put at the service of the world and of adventure, seeking for Spain a westward passage to the Indies to offset the achievement of Portuguese discoverers, lighted on America.

> With these hopes and in this belief I would urge you, laying aside all hindrance, thrusting away all private aims, to devote yourself unswervingly and unflinchingly to the vigorous and successful prosecution of this war.

The other prominent position in the sentence is the beginning. Any element in the sentence other than the subject becomes emphatic when placed first.

> Deceit or treachery he could never forgive.

> Vast and rude, fretted by the action of nearly three thousand years, the fragments of this architecture may often seem, at first sight, like works of nature.

> Home is the sailor.

A subject coming first in its sentence may be emphatic, but hardly by its position alone. In the sentence

> Great kings worshiped at his shrine

the emphasis upon *kings* arises largely from its meaning and from the context. To receive special emphasis, the subject of a sentence must take the position of the predicate.

> Through the middle of the valley flowed a winding stream.

The principle that the proper place for what is to be made most prominent is the end applies equally to the words of a sentence, to the sentences of a paragraph, and to the paragraphs of a composition.

# III

## *A Few Matters of Form*

**Colloquialisms.** If you use a colloquialism or a slang word or phrase, simply use it; do not draw attention to it by enclosing it in quotation marks. To do so is to put on airs, as though you were inviting the reader to join you in a select society of those who know better.

**Exclamations.** Do not attempt to emphasize simple statements by using a mark of exclamation.

It was a wonderful show!  It was a wonderful show.

The exclamation mark is to be reserved for use after true exclamations or commands.

What a wonderful show!

Halt!

**Headings.** If a manuscript is to be submitted for publication, leave plenty of space at the top of page 1. The editor will need this space for his penciled directions to the compositor. Place the heading, or title, at least a fourth of the way down the page. Leave a blank line, or its equivalent in space, after the heading. On succeeding pages, begin near the top, but not so near as to give a crowded appearance. Omit the period after a title or heading. A question mark or an exclamation point may be used if the heading calls for it.

**Hyphen.** When two or more words are combined to form a compound adjective, a hyphen is usually required. "He belonged to the leisure class and enjoyed leisure-class pursuits." "He entered his boat in the round-the-island race."

Do not use a hyphen between words that can better be written as one word: *water-fowl, waterfowl.* Your common sense will aid you in the decision, but a dictionary is more reliable. The steady evolution of the language seems to favor union: two words eventually become one, usually after a period of hyphenation.

| | | |
|---|---|---|
| bed chamber | bed-chamber | bedchamber |
| wild life | wild-life | wildlife |
| bell boy | bell-boy | bellboy |

The hyphen can play tricks on the unwary, as it did in Chattanooga when two newspapers merged—the *News* and the *Free Press.* Someone introduced a hyphen into the merger, and the paper became *The Chattanooga News-Free Press,* which sounds as though the paper were news-free, or devoid of news. Obviously, we ask too much of a hyphen when we ask it to cast its spell over words it does not adjoin.

*Margins.* Keep right-hand and left-hand margins roughly the same width. Exception: If a great deal of annotating or editing is anticipated, the left-hand margin should be roomy enough to accommodate this work.

*Numerals.* Do not spell out dates or other serial numbers. Write them in figures or in Roman notation, as may be appropriate.

| | |
|---|---|
| August 9, 1968 | Chapter XII |
| Rule 3 | 352d Infantry |

Exception: When they occur in dialogue, most dates and numbers are best spelled out.

"I arrived home on August ninth."
"In the year 1970, I turned twenty-one."
"I shall read Chapter Twelve."

*Parentheses.*   A sentence containing an expression in parentheses is punctuated outside the marks of parenthesis exactly as if the parenthetical expression were absent. The expression within the marks is punctuated as if it stood by itself, except that the final stop is omitted unless it is a question mark or an exclamation point.

> I went to his house yesterday (my third attempt to see him), but he had left town.

> He declares (and why should we doubt his good faith?) that he is now certain of success.

(When a wholly detached expression or sentence is parenthesized, the final stop comes before the last mark of parenthesis.)

*Quotations.*   Formal quotations cited as documentary evidence are introduced by a colon and enclosed in quotation marks.

> The United States Coast Pilot has this to say of the place: "Bracy Cove, 0.5 mile eastward of Bear Island, is exposed to southeast winds, has a rocky and uneven bottom, and is unfit for anchorage."

A quotation grammatically in apposition or the direct object of a verb is preceded by a comma and enclosed in quotation marks.

> I am reminded of the advice of my neighbor, "Never worry about your heart till it stops beating."

> Mark Twain says, "A classic is something that everybody wants to have read and nobody wants to read."

When a quotation is followed by an attributive phrase, the comma is enclosed within the quotation marks.

> "I can't attend," she said.

Typographical usage dictates that the comma be inside the marks, though logically it often seems not to belong there.

"The Clerks," "Luke Havergal," and "Richard Cory" are in Robinson's *Children of the Night.*

When quotations of an entire line, or more, of either verse or prose are to be distinguished typographically from text matter, as are the quotations in this book, begin on a fresh line and indent. Quotation marks should not be used unless they appear in the original, as in dialogue.

> Wordsworth's enthusiasm for the French Revolution was at first unbounded:
>> Bliss was it in that dawn to be alive,
>> But to be young was very heaven!

Quotations introduced by *that* are indirect discourse and not enclosed in quotation marks.

> Keats declares that beauty is truth, truth beauty.

Proverbial expressions and familiar phrases of literary origin require no quotation marks.

> These are the times that try men's souls.
>
> He lives far from the madding crowd.

**References.** In scholarly work requiring exact references, abbreviate titles that occur frequently, giving the full forms in an alphabetical list at the end. As a general practice, give the references in parentheses or in footnotes, not in the body of the sentence. Omit the words *act, scene, line, book, volume, page,* except when referring by only one of them. Punctuate as indicated below.

| | |
|---|---|
| in the second scene of the third act | in iii.ii (Still better, simply insert iii.ii in parentheses at the proper place in the sentence.) |

> After the killing of Polonius, Hamlet is placed under guard (iv.ii. 14).
>
> 2 Samuel i:17–27
>
> *Othello* ii.iii. 264–267, iii.iii. 155–161

**Syllabication.**    When a word must be divided at the end of a line, consult a dictionary to learn the syllables between which division should be made. The student will do well to examine the syllable division in a number of pages of any carefully printed book.

**Titles.**    For the titles of literary works, scholarly usage prefers italics with capitalized initials. The usage of editors and publishers varies, some using italics with capitalized initials, others using Roman with capitalized initials and with or without quotation marks. Use italics (indicated in manuscript by underscoring) except in writing for a periodical that follows a different practice. Omit initial *A* or *The* from titles when you place the possessive before them.

A *Tale of Two Cities*; Dickens's *Tale of Two Cities*.

# IV

## Words and Expressions Commonly Misused

MANY of the words and expressions here listed are not so much bad English as bad style, the commonplaces of careless writing. As is illustrated under *Feature*, the proper correction is likely to be not the replacement of one word or set of words by another but the replacement of vague generality by definite statement.

The shape of our language is not rigid; in questions of usage we have no lawgiver whose word is final. Students whose curiosity is aroused by the interpretations that follow, or whose doubts are raised, will wish to pursue their investigations further. Books useful in such pursuits are *Webster's New Collegiate Dictionary*, Revised Edition; *The Random House College Dictionary*; *The American Heritage Dictionary of the English Language*; *Webster's New International Dictionary of the English Language*, Second Edition; H. W. Fowler's *Dictionary of Modern English Usage*, Second Edition; *Watch Your Language*, by Theodore M. Bernstein; and Roy H. Copperud's *American Usage: The Consensus*.

**Aggravate. Irritate.**   The first means "to add to" an already troublesome or vexing matter or condition. The second means "to vex" or "to annoy" or "to chafe."

**All right.**   Idiomatic in familiar speech as a detached phrase in the sense "Agreed," or "Go ahead," or "O.K." Properly written as two words—*all right*.

**Allude.**   Do not confuse with *elude*. You *allude* to a book; you *elude* a pursuer. Note, too, that *allude* is not synonymous with *refer*. An allusion is an indirect mention, a reference is a specific one.

**Allusion.**   Easily confused with *illusion*. The first means "an indirect reference"; the second means "an unreal image" or "a false impression."

**Alternate. Alternative.**   The words are not always interchangeable as nouns or adjectives. The first means every other one in a series; the second, one of two possibilities. As the other one of a series of two, an *alternate* may stand for "a substitute," but an *alternative*, although used in a similar sense, connotes a matter of choice that is never present with *alternate*.

> As the flooded road left them no alternative, they took the alternate route.

**Among. Between.**   When more than two things or persons are involved, *among* is usually called for: "The money was divided among the four players." When, however, more than two are involved but each is considered individually, *between* is preferred: "an agreement between the six heirs."

**And/or.**   A device, or shortcut, that damages a sentence and often leads to confusion or ambiguity.

| | |
|---|---|
| First of all, would an honor system successfully cut down on the amount of stealing and/or cheating? | First of all, would an honor system reduce the incidence of stealing or cheating or both? |

**Anticipate.**   Use *expect* in the sense of simple expectation.

| | |
|---|---|
| I anticipated that she would look older. | I expected that she would look older. |
| My brother anticipated the upturn in the market. | My brother expected the upturn in the market. |

In the second example, the word *anticipated* is ambiguous. It could mean simply that the brother believed the upturn would occur, or it could mean that he acted in advance of the expected upturn—by buying stock, perhaps.

**Anybody.**  In the sense of "any person" not to be written as two words. *Any body* means "any corpse," or "any human form," or "any group." The rule holds equally for *everybody, nobody,* and *somebody.*

**Anyone.**  In the sense of "anybody," written as one word. *Any one* means "any single person" or "any single thing."

**As good or better than.**  Expressions of this type should be corrected by rearranging the sentences.

| | |
|---|---|
| My opinion is as good or better than his. | My opinion is as good as his, or better (if not better). |

**As to whether.**  *Whether* is sufficient.

**As yet.**  *Yet* nearly always is as good, if not better.

| | |
|---|---|
| No agreement has been reached as yet. | No agreement has yet been reached. |

The chief exception is at the beginning of a sentence, where *yet* means something different.

Yet (*or* despite everything) he has not succeeded.

As yet (*or* so far) he has not succeeded.

**Being.**  Not appropriate after *regard . . . as.*

| | |
|---|---|
| He is regarded as being the best dancer in the club. | He is regarded as the best dancer in the club. |

**But.**  Unnecessary after *doubt* and *help.*

| | |
|---|---|
| I have no doubt but that | I have no doubt that |
| He could not help but see that | He could not help seeing that |

The too-frequent use of *but* as a conjunction leads to the fault discussed under Rule 18. A loose sentence formed with *but* can usually be converted into a periodic sentence formed with *although*, as illustrated under Rule 4.

Particularly awkward is one *but* closely following another, thus making a contrast to a contrast, or a reservation to a reservation. This is easily corrected by rearrangement.

| | |
|---|---|
| America had vast resources, but she seemed almost wholly unprepared for war. But within a year she had created an army of four million men. | America seemed almost wholly unprepared for war, but she had vast resources. Within a year she had created an army of four million men. |

**Can.** Means "am (is, are) able." Not to be used as a substitute for *may*.

**Case.** Often unnecessary.

| | |
|---|---|
| In many cases, the rooms were poorly ventilated. | Many of the rooms were poorly ventilated. |
| It has rarely been the case that any mistake has been made. | Few mistakes have been made. |

**Certainly.** Used indiscriminately by some speakers, much as others use *very*, in an attempt to intensify any and every statement. A mannerism of this kind, bad in speech, is even worse in writing.

**Character.** Often simply redundant, used from a mere habit of wordiness.

| | |
|---|---|
| acts of a hostile character | hostile acts |

*Claim* (*verb*). With object-noun, means "lay claim to." May be used with a dependent clause if this sense is clearly intended: "He claimed that he was the sole heir." (But even here *claimed to be* would be better.) Not to be used as a substitute for *declare, maintain,* or *charge.*

| | |
|---|---|
| He claimed he knew how. | He declared he knew how. |

*Clever.* Note that the word means one thing when applied to men, another when applied to horses. A clever horse is a good-natured one, not an ingenious one.

*Compare.* To *compare to* is to point out or imply resemblances between objects regarded as essentially of a different order; to *compare with* is mainly to point out differences between objects regarded as essentially of the same order. Thus, life has been *compared to* a pilgrimage, *to* a drama, *to* a battle; Congress may be *compared with* the British Parliament. Paris has been *compared to* ancient Athens; it may be *compared with* modern London.

*Comprise.* Literally, "embrace": A zoo comprises mammals, reptiles, and birds (because it "embraces," or "includes," them). But animals do not comprise ("embrace") a zoo—they constitute a zoo.

*Consider.* Not followed by *as* when it means "believe to be."

| | |
|---|---|
| I consider him as competent. | I consider him competent. |

When *considered* means "examined" or "discussed," it is followed by *as:*

The lecturer considered Eisenhower first as soldier and second as administrator.

**Contact.** As a transitive verb, the word is vague and self-important. Do not *contact* anybody; get in touch with him, or look him up, or phone him, or find him, or meet him.

**Cope.** An intransitive verb used with *with*. In formal writing, one doesn't "cope," one "copes with" something or somebody.

| | |
|---|---|
| I knew she'd cope. (jocular) | I knew she would cope with the situation. |

**Currently.** In the sense of *now* with a verb in the present tense, *currently* is usually redundant; emphasis is better achieved through a more precise reference to time.

| | |
|---|---|
| We are currently reviewing your application. | We are at this moment reviewing your application. |

**Data.** Like *strata, phenomena,* and *media, data* is a plural and is best used with a plural verb. The word, however, is slowly gaining acceptance as a singular.

| | |
|---|---|
| The data is misleading. | These data are misleading. |

**Different than.** Here logic supports established usage: one thing differs *from* another, hence, *different from.* Or, *other than, unlike.*

**Disinterested.** Means "impartial." Do not confuse it with *uninterested,* which means "not interested in."

Let a disinterested person judge our dispute. (an impartial person)

This man is obviously uninterested in our dispute. (couldn't care less)

**Divided into.** Not to be misused for *composed of.* The line is sometimes difficult to draw; doubtless plays are divided into acts, but poems are composed of stanzas. An apple, halved, is divided into sections, but an apple is composed of seeds, flesh, and skin.

**Due to.** Loosely used for *through, because of,* or *owing to,* in adverbial phrases.

| | |
|---|---|
| He lost the first game due to carelessness. | He lost the first game because of carelessness. |

In correct use synonymous with *attributable to:* "The accident was due to bad weather"; "losses due to preventable fires."

**Each and every one.** Pitchman's jargon. Avoid, except in dialogue.

| | |
|---|---|
| It should be a lesson to each and every one of us. | It should be a lesson to every one of us (to us all). |

**Effect.** As a noun, means "result"; as a verb, means "to bring about," "to accomplish" (not to be confused with *affect,* which means "to influence").

As a noun, often loosely used in perfunctory writing about fashions, music, painting, and other arts: "an Oriental effect"; "effects in pale green"; "very delicate effects"; "subtle effects"; "a charming effect was produced." The writer who has a definite meaning to express will not take refuge in such vagueness.

**Enormity.** Use only in the sense "monstrous wickedness." Misleading, if not wrong, when used to express bigness.

**Enthuse.** An annoying verb growing out of the noun *enthusiasm.* Not recommended.

| | |
|---|---|
| She was enthused about her new car. | She was enthusiastic about her new car. |
| She enthused about her new car. | She talked enthusiastically (expressed enthusiasm) about her new car. |

**Etc.** Literally, "and other things"; sometimes loosely used to mean "and other persons." The phrase is equivalent to *and the rest, and so forth,* and hence is not to be used if one of these would be insufficient— that is, if the reader would be left in doubt as to any important particulars. Least open to objection when it represents the last terms of a list already given almost in full, or immaterial words at the end of a quotation.

At the end of a list introduced by *such as, for example,* or any similar expression, *etc.* is incorrect. In formal writing, *etc.* is a misfit. An item important enough to call for *etc.* is probably important enough to be named.

**Fact.**    Use this word only of matter capable of direct verification, not of matters of judgment. That a particular event happened on a given date, that lead melts at a certain temperature are facts. But such conclusions as that Napoleon was the greatest of modern generals or that the climate of California is delightful, however defensible they may be, are not properly called facts.

**Facility.**    Why must jails, hospitals, schools suddenly become "facilities"?

| | |
|---|---|
| Parents complained bitterly about the fire hazard in the wooden facility. | Parents complained bitterly about the fire hazard in the wooden schoolhouse. |
| He has been appointed warden of the new facility. | He has been appointed warden of the new prison. |

**Factor.**    A hackneyed word; the expressions of which it forms part can usually be replaced by something more direct and idiomatic.

| | |
|---|---|
| His superior training was the great factor in his winning the match. | He won the match by being better trained. |
| Air power is becoming an increasingly important factor in deciding battles. | Air power is playing a larger and larger part in deciding battles. |

**Farther. Further.**    The two words are commonly interchanged, but there is a distinction worth observing:

*farther* serves best as a distance word, *further* as a time or quantity word. You chase a ball *farther* than the other fellow; you pursue a subject *further*.

**Feature.** Another hackneyed word; like *factor*, it usually adds nothing to the sentence in which it occurs.

| | |
|---|---|
| A feature of the entertainment especially worthy of mention was the singing of Miss A. | (Better use the same number of words to tell what Miss A. sang and how she sang it.) |

As a verb, in the sense of "offer as a special attraction," to be avoided.

**Finalize.** A pompous, ambiguous verb. (See Chapter V, Reminder 21.)

**Fix.** Colloquial in America for *arrange, prepare, mend*. The usage is well established. But bear in mind that this verb is from *figere*: "to make firm," "to place definitely." These are the preferred meanings of the word.

**Flammable.** An oddity, chiefly useful in saving lives. The common word meaning "combustible" is *inflammable*. But some people are thrown off by the *in-* and think *inflammable* means "not combustible." For this reason, trucks carrying gasoline or explosives are now marked FLAMMABLE. Unless you are operating such a truck and hence are concerned with the safety of children and illiterates, use *inflammable*.

**Folk.** A collective noun, equivalent to *people*. Use the singular form only. *Folks*, in the sense of "parents," "family," "those present," is colloquial and too folksy for formal writing.

| | |
|---|---|
| Her folks arrived by the afternoon train. | Her father and mother arrived by the afternoon train. |

**Fortuitous.**  Limited to what happens by chance. Not to be used for *fortunate* or *lucky.*

**Get.**  The colloquial *have got* for *have* should not be used in writing. The preferable form of the participle is *got,* not *gotten.*

| | |
|---|---|
| He has not got any sense. | He has no sense. |
| They returned without having gotten any. | They returned without having got any. |

**Gratuitous.**  Means "unearned," or "unwarranted."

The insult seemed gratuitous. (undeserved)

**He is a man who.**  A common type of redundant expression; see Rule 17.

| | |
|---|---|
| He is a man who is very ambitious. | He is very ambitious. |
| Vermont is a state that attracts visitors because of its winter sports. | Vermont attracts visitors because of its winter sports. |

**Hopefully.**  This once-useful adverb meaning "with hope" has been distorted and is now widely used to mean "I hope" or "it is to be hoped." Such use is not merely wrong, it is silly. To say, "Hopefully I'll leave on the noon plane" is to talk nonsense. Do you mean you'll leave on the noon plane in a hopeful frame of mind? Or do you mean you hope you'll leave on the noon plane? Whichever you mean, you haven't said it clearly. Although the word in its new, free-floating capacity may be pleasurable and even useful to many, it offends the ear of many others, who do not like to see words dulled or eroded, particularly when the erosion leads to ambiguity, softness, or nonsense.

**However.**  Avoid starting a sentence with *however* when the meaning is "nevertheless." The word usually serves better when not in first position.

| The roads were almost impassable. However, we at last succeeded in reaching camp. | The roads were almost impassable. At last, however, we succeeded in reaching camp. |
|---|---|

When *however* comes first, it means "in whatever way" or "to whatever extent."

However you advise him, he will probably do as he thinks best.

However discouraging the prospect, he never lost heart.

**Illusion.** See *allusion.*

**Imply. Infer.** Not interchangeable. Something implied is something suggested or indicated, though not expressed. Something inferred is something deduced from evidence at hand.

Farming implies early rising.

Since he was a farmer, we inferred that he got up early.

**Importantly.** Avoid by rephrasing.

| More importantly, he paid for the damages. | What's more, he paid for the damages. |
|---|---|
| With the breeze freshening, he altered course to pass inside the island. More importantly, as things turned out, he tucked in a reef. | With the breeze freshening, he altered course to pass inside the island. More important, as things turned out, he tucked in a reef. |

**In regard to.** Often wrongly written *in regards to.* But *as regards* is correct, and means the same thing.

**In the last analysis.** A bankrupt expression.

**Inside of. Inside.** The *of* following *inside* is correct in the adverbial meaning "in less than." In other meanings *of* is unnecessary.

Inside of five minutes I'll be inside the bank.

*Insightful.* The word is a suspicious overstatement for "perceptive." If it is to be used at all, it should be used for instances of remarkably penetrating vision. Usually, it crops up merely to inflate the commonplace.

| | |
|---|---|
| That was an insightful remark you made. | That was a perceptive remark you made. |

*In terms of.* A piece of padding usually best omitted.

| | |
|---|---|
| The job was unattractive in terms of salary. | The salary made the job unattractive. |

*Interesting.* An unconvincing word; avoid it as a means of introduction. Instead of announcing that what you are about to tell is interesting, make it so.

| | |
|---|---|
| An interesting story is told of | (Tell the story without preamble.) |
| In connection with the forthcoming visit of Mr. B. to America, it is interesting to recall that he | Mr. B., who will soon visit America |

Also to be avoided in introduction is the word *funny*. Nothing becomes funny by being labeled so.

*Irregardless.* Should be *regardless*. The error results from failure to see the negative in *-less* and from a desire to get it in as a prefix, suggested by such words as *irregular, irresponsible*, and, perhaps especially, *irrespective*.

*-ize.* Do not coin verbs by adding this tempting suffix. Many good and useful verbs do end in *-ize*: *summarize, temporize, fraternize, harmonize, fertilize*. But there is a growing list of abominations: *containerize, customize, prioritize, finalize*, to name four. Be suspicious of *-ize*; let your ear and your eye guide you. Never tack *-ize* onto a noun to create a verb. Usually you will discover that a useful verb already exists. Why

say "moisturize" when there is the simple, unpretentious word *moisten?*

**Kind of.** Except in familiar style, not to be used as a substitute for *rather* or *something like.* Restrict it to its literal sense: "Amber is a kind of fossil resin"; "I dislike that kind of publicity." The same holds true of *sort of.*

**Lay.** A transitive verb. Except in slang ("Let it lay"), do not misuse it for the intransitive verb *lie.* The hen, or the play, *lays* an egg; the llama *lies* down. The playwright went home and *lay* down.

    lie; lay; lain; lying
    lay; laid; laid; laying

**Leave.** Not to be misused for *let.*

| | |
|---|---|
| Leave it stand the way it is | Let it stand the way it is. |
| Leave go of that rope! | Let go of that rope! |

**Less.** Should not be misused for *fewer.*

| | |
|---|---|
| He had less men than in the previous campaign. | He had fewer men than in the previous campaign. |

*Less* refers to quantity, *fewer* to number. "His troubles are less than mine" means "His troubles are not so great as mine." "His troubles are fewer than mine" means "His troubles are not so numerous as mine."

**Like.** Not to be used for the conjunction *as. Like* governs nouns and pronouns; before phrases and clauses the equivalent word is *as.*

| | |
|---|---|
| We spent the evening like in the old days. | We spent the evening as in the old days. |
| Chloë smells good, like a pretty girl should. | Chloë smells good, as a pretty girl should. |

The use of *like* for *as* has its defenders; they argue that any usage that achieves currency becomes valid automatically. This, they say, is the way the language is formed. It is and it isn't. An expression sometimes merely enjoys a vogue, much as an article of apparel does. *Like* has long been widely misused by the illiterate; lately it has been taken up by the knowing and the well-informed, who find it catchy, or liberating, and who use it as though they were slumming. If every word or device that achieved currency were immediately authenticated, simply on the ground of popularity, the language would be as chaotic as a ball game with no foul lines. For the student, perhaps the most useful thing to know about *like* is that most carefully edited publications regard its use before phrases and clauses as simple error.

**Line. Along these lines.** *Line* in the sense of "course of procedure, conduct, thought" is allowable, but has been so overworked, particularly in the phrase *along these lines,* that a writer who aims at freshness or originality had better discard it entirely.

| | |
|---|---|
| Mr. B. also spoke along the same lines. | Mr. B. also spoke to the same effect. |
| He is studying along the line of French literature. | He is studying French literature. |

**Literal. Literally.** Often incorrectly used in support of exaggeration or violent metaphor.

| | |
|---|---|
| a literal flood of abuse | a flood of abuse |
| literally dead with fatigue | almost dead with fatigue (dead tired) |

**Loan.** A noun. As a verb, prefer *lend.*

Lend me your ears.
the loan of your ears

*Meaningful.* A bankrupt adjective. Choose another, or rephrase.

| | |
|---|---|
| His was a meaningful contribution. | His contribution counted heavily. |
| We are instituting many meaningful changes in the curriculum. | We are improving the curriculum in many ways. |

*Memento.* Often incorrectly written *momento.*

*Most.* Not to be used for *almost* in formal composition.

| | |
|---|---|
| most everybody | almost everybody |
| most all the time | almost all the time |

*Nature.* Often simply redundant, used like *character.*

| | |
|---|---|
| acts of a hostile nature | hostile acts |

*Nature* should be avoided in such vague expressions as "a lover of nature," "poems about nature." Unless more specific statements follow, the reader cannot tell whether the poems have to do with natural scenery, rural life, the sunset, the untracked wilderness, or the habits of squirrels.

*Nauseous. Nauseated.* The first means "sickening to contemplate"; the second means "sick at the stomach." Do not, therefore, say "I feel nauseous," unless you are sure you have that effect on others.

*Nice.* A shaggy, all-purpose word, to be used sparingly in formal composition. "I had a nice time." "It was nice weather." "She was so nice to her mother." The meanings are indistinct. *Nice* is most useful in the sense of "precise" or "delicate": "a nice distinction."

*Nor.* Often used wrongly for *or* after negative expressions.

| | |
|---|---|
| He cannot eat nor sleep. | He cannot eat or sleep. |
| | He can neither eat nor sleep. |
| | He cannot eat nor can he sleep. |

**Noun used as verb.** Many nouns have lately been pressed into service as verbs. Not all are bad, but all are suspect.

| | |
|---|---|
| Be prepared for kisses when you gift your girl with this merry scent. | Be prepared for kisses when you give your girl this merry scent. |
| The candidate hosted a dinner for fifty of his workers. | The candidate gave a dinner for fifty of his workers. |
| The meeting was chaired by Mr. Oglethorp. | Mr. Oglethorp was chairman of the meeting. |
| He headquarters in Newark. | He has headquarters in Newark. |
| She debuted last fall. | She made her debut last fall. |

**Offputting. Ongoing.** Newfound adjectives, to be avoided because they are inexact and clumsy. *Ongoing* is a mix of "continuing" and "active" and is usually superfluous.

| | |
|---|---|
| She devoted all her spare time to the ongoing program for aid to the elderly. | She devoted all her spare time to the program for aid to the elderly. |

*Offputting* might mean "objectionable," "disconcerting," "distasteful." Select instead a word whose meaning is clear. As a simple test, transform the participles to verbs. It is possible to *upset* something. But to *offput?* To *ongo?*

**One.** In the sense of "a person," not to be followed by *his.*

| One must watch his step. | One must watch one's step. (You must watch your step.) |

**One of the most.**   Avoid this feeble formula. "One of the most exciting developments of modern science is . . ."; "Switzerland is one of the most beautiful countries of Europe." There is nothing wrong with the grammar; the formula is simply threadbare.

**-oriented.**   A clumsy, pretentious device, much in vogue. Find a better way of indicating orientation or alignment or direction.

| His was a manufacturing-oriented company. | His was a company chiefly concerned with manufacturing. |
| Many of the skits are situation-oriented. | Many of the skits rely on situation. |

**Partially.**   Not always interchangeable with *partly*. Best used in the sense of "to a certain degree," when speaking of a condition or state: "I'm partially resigned to it." *Partly* carries the idea of a part as distinct from the whole—usually a physical object.

| The log was partially submerged. | The log was partly submerged. |
| He was partially in and partially out. | He was partly in and partly out. |
| | He was part in, part out. |

**Participle for verbal noun.**

| There was little prospect of the Senate accepting even this compromise. | There was little prospect of the Senate's accepting even this compromise. |

In the left-hand column, *accepting* is a present participle; in the right-hand column, it is a verbal noun (gerund). The construction shown in the left-hand column is occasionally found, and has its defenders.

Yet it is easy to see that the second sentence has to do not with a prospect of the Senate but with a prospect of accepting.

Any sentence in which the use of the possessive is awkward or impossible should of course be recast.

| | |
|---|---|
| In the event of a reconsideration of the whole matter's becoming necessary | If it should become necessary to reconsider the whole matter |
| There was great dissatisfaction with the decision of the arbitrators being favorable to the company. | There was great dissatisfaction with the arbitrators' decision in favor of the company. |

**People.** A word with many meanings. (*The American Heritage Dictionary* gives ten.) *The people* is a political term, not to be confused with *the public*. From the people comes political support or opposition; from the public comes artistic appreciation or commercial patronage.

The word *people* is best not used with words of number, in place of *persons*. If of "six people" five went away, how many people would be left? Answer: one people.

**Personalize.** A pretentious word, often carrying bad advice. Do not *personalize* your prose; simply make it good and keep it clean. See Chapter V, Reminder 1.

| | |
|---|---|
| a highly personalized affair | a highly personal affair |
| Personalize your stationery. | Get up a letterhead. |

**Personally.** Often unnecessary.

| | |
|---|---|
| Personally, I thought it was a good book. | I thought it a good book. |

**Possess.** Often used because to the writer it sounds more impressive than *have* or *own*. Such usage is not incorrect but is to be guarded against.

| He possessed great courage. | He had great courage (was very brave). |
| He was the fortunate possessor of | He was lucky enough to own |

**Presently.** Has two meanings: "in a short while" and "currently." Because of this ambiguity it is best restricted to the first meaning: "He'll be here presently" ("soon," or "in a short time").

**Prestigious.** Often an adjective of last resort. It's in the dictionary, but that doesn't mean you have to use it.

**Refer.** See *allude*.

**Regretful.** Sometimes carelessly used for *regrettable*: "The mixup was due to a regretful breakdown in communications."

**Relate.** Not to be used intransitively to suggest rapport.

| I relate well to Janet. | Janet and I see things the same way.<br>Janet and I have a lot in common. |

**Respective. Respectively.** These words may usually be omitted with advantage.

| Works of fiction are listed under the names of their respective authors. | Works of fiction are listed under the names of their authors. |
| The mile run and the two-mile run were won by Jones and Cummings respectively. | The mile run was won by Jones, the two-mile run by Cummings. |

**Secondly, thirdly, etc.** Unless you are prepared to begin with *firstly* and defend it (which will be difficult), do not prettify numbers with *-ly*. Modern usage prefers *second, third,* and so on.

**Shall. Will.** In formal writing, the future tense requires *shall* for the first person, *will* for the second and third. The formula to express the speaker's belief regarding his future action or state is *I shall; I will* expresses his determination or his consent. A swimmer in distress cries, "I shall drown; no one will save me!" A suicide puts it the other way: "I will drown; no one shall save me!" In relaxed speech, however, the words *shall* and *will* are seldom used precisely; our ear guides us or fails to guide us, as the case may be, and we are quite likely to drown when we want to survive and survive when we want to drown.

**So.** Avoid, in writing, the use of *so* as an intensifier: "so good"; "so warm"; "so delightful."

**Sort of.** See *kind of*.

**Split infinitive.** There is precedent from the fourteenth century down for interposing an adverb between *to* and the infinitive it governs, but the construction should be avoided unless the writer wishes to place unusual stress on the adverb.

| | |
|---|---|
| to diligently inquire | to inquire diligently |

For another side to the split infinitive, see Chapter V, Reminder 14.

**State.** Not to be used as a mere substitute for *say, remark*. Restrict it to the sense of "express fully or clearly": "He refused to state his objections."

**Student body.** Nine times out of ten a needless and awkward expression, meaning no more than the simple word *students*.

| | |
|---|---|
| a member of the student body | a student |
| popular with the student body | liked by the students |

**Than.** Any sentence with *than* (to express comparison) should be examined to make sure no essential words are missing.

| | |
|---|---|
| I'm probably closer to my mother than my father. (Ambiguous.) | I'm probably closer to my mother than to my father. |
| | I'm probably closer to my mother than my father is. |
| It looked more like a cormorant than a heron. | It looked more like a cormorant than like a heron. |

**Thanking you in advance.** This sounds as if the writer meant, "It will not be worth my while to write to you again." In making your request, write, "Will you please," or "I shall be obliged." Then, later, if you feel moved to do so, or if the circumstances call for it, write a letter of acknowledgment.

**That. Which.** *That* is the defining, or restrictive pronoun, *which* the nondefining, or nonrestrictive. See Rule 3.

The lawn mower that is broken is in the garage. (Tells which one)

The lawn mower, which is broken, is in the garage. (Adds a fact about the only mower in question)

The use of *which* for *that* is common in written and spoken language ("Let us now go even unto Bethlehem, and see this thing which is come to pass.") Occasionally *which* seems preferable to *that*, as in the sentence from the Bible. But it would be a convenience to all if these two pronouns were used with precision. The careful writer, watchful for small conveniences, goes *which*-hunting, removes the defining *whiches*, and by so doing improves his work.

**The foreseeable future.** A cliché, and a fuzzy one. How much of the future is foreseeable? Ten minutes? Ten years? Any of it? By whom is it foreseeable? Seers? Experts? Everybody?

**The truth is. . . . The fact is. . . .** A bad beginning for a sentence. If you feel you are possessed of the truth, or of the fact, simply state it. Do not give it advance billing.

**They.** Not to be used when the antecedent is a distributive expression such as *each, each one, everybody, every one, many a man.* Use the singular pronoun.

| | |
|---|---|
| Every one of us knows they are fallible. | Every one of us knows he is fallible. |
| Everyone in the community, whether they are a member of the Association or not, is invited to attend. | Everyone in the community, whether he is a member of the Association or not, is invited to attend. |

A similar fault is the use of the plural pronoun with the antecedent *anybody, anyone, somebody, someone,* the intention being either to avoid the awkward "he or she" or to avoid committing oneself to one or the other. Some bashful speakers even say, "A friend of mine told me that they. . . ."

The use of *he* as pronoun for nouns embracing both genders is a simple, practical convention rooted in the beginnings of the English language. *He* has lost all suggestion of maleness in these circumstances. The word was unquestionably biased to begin with (the dominant male), but after hundreds of years it has become seemingly indispensible. It has no pejorative connotation; it is never incorrect. Substituting *he or she* in its place is the logical thing to do if it works. But it often doesn't work, if only because repetition makes it sound boring or silly. Consider the following unexceptional sentences from *The Summing Up*, by W. Somerset Maugham:

Another cause of obscurity is that the writer is himself not quite sure of his meaning. He has a vague impression of what he wants to say, but has not, either from lack of mental power or from laziness, exactly formulated it in his mind, and it is natural enough that he should not find a precise expression for a confused idea.

Rewritten to affirm equality of the sexes, the same statement verges on nonsense:

> Another cause of obscurity is that the writer is herself or himself not quite sure of her or his meaning. He or she has a vague impression of what he or she wants to say, but has not, either from lack of mental power or from laziness, exactly formulated it in her or his mind, and it is natural enough that he or she should not find a precise expression for a confused idea.

No one need fear to use *he* if common sense supports it. The furor recently raised about *he* would be more impressive if there were a handy substitute for the word. Unfortunately, there isn't—or, at least, no one has come up with one yet. If you think *she* is a handy substitute for *he*, try it and see what happens. Alternatively, put all controversial nouns in the plural and avoid the choice of sex altogether, and you may find your prose sounding general and diffuse as a result.

**This.** The pronoun *this*, referring to the complete sense of a preceding sentence or clause, can't always carry the load and so may produce an imprecise statement.

| | |
|---|---|
| Visiting dignitaries watched yesterday as ground was broken for the new high-energy physics laboratory with a blowout safety wall. This is the first visible evidence of the university's plans for modernization and expansion. | Visiting dignitaries watched yesterday as ground was broken for the new high-energy physics laboratory with a blowout safety wall. The ceremony afforded the first visible evidence of the university's plans for modernization and expansion. |

In the left-hand example above, *this* does not immediately make clear what the first visible evidence is.

**Thrust.** This showy noun, suggestive of power, hinting of sex, is the darling of executives, politicos, and speech-writers. Use it sparingly. Save it for specific application.

| | |
|---|---|
| Our reorganization plan has a tremendous thrust. | The piston has a five-inch thrust. |
| The thrust of his letter was that he was working more hours than he'd bargained for. | The point he made in his letter was that he was working more hours than he'd bargained for. |

**Tortuous. Torturous.**   A winding road is *tortuous*, a painful ordeal is *torturous*. Both words carry the idea of "twist," the twist having been a form of torture.

**Transpire.**   Not to be used in the sense of "happen," "come to pass." Many writers so use it (usually when groping toward imagined elegance), but their usage finds little support in the Latin "breathe across or through." It is correct, however, in the sense of "become known." "Eventually, the grim account of his villainy transpired" (literally, "leaked through or out").

**Try.**   Takes the infinitive: "try to mend it," not "try *and* mend it." Students of the language will argue that *try and* has won through and become idiom. Indeed it has, and it is relaxed and acceptable. But *try to* is precise, and when you are writing formal prose, try and write *try to*.

**Type.**   Not a synonym for *kind of*. The examples below are common vulgarisms.

| | |
|---|---|
| that type employee | that kind of employee |
| I dislike that type publicity. | I dislike that kind of publicity. |
| small, home-type hotels | small, homelike hotels |
| a new type plane | a plane of a new design (new kind) |

**Unique.**   Means "without like or equal." Hence, there can be no degrees of uniqueness.

| | |
|---|---|
| It was the most unique egg beater on the market. | It was a unique egg beater. |

| | |
|---|---|
| The balancing act was very unique. | The balancing act was unique. |
| Of all the spiders, the one that lives in a bubble under water is the most unique. | Among spiders, the one that lives in a bubble under water is unique. |

**Utilize.** Prefer *use*.

| | |
|---|---|
| I utilized the facilities. | I used the toilet. |
| She utilized the dishwasher. | She used the dishwasher. |

**Verbal.** Sometimes means "word for word" and in this sense may refer to something expressed in writing. *Oral* (from Latin *ōs,* "mouth") limits the meaning to what is transmitted by speech. *Oral agreement* is more precise than *verbal agreement.*

**Very.** Use this word sparingly. Where emphasis is necessary, use words strong in themselves.

**While.** Avoid the indiscriminate use of this word for *and, but,* and *although.* Many writers use it frequently as a substitute for *and* or *but,* either from a mere desire to vary the connective or from doubt about which of the two connectives is the more appropriate. In this use it is best replaced by a semicolon.

| | |
|---|---|
| The office and salesrooms are on the ground floor, while the rest of the building is used for manufacturing. | The office and salesrooms are on the ground floor; the rest of the building is used for manufacturing. |

Its use as a virtual equivalent of *although* is allowable in sentences where this leads to no ambiguity or absurdity.

> While I admire his energy, I wish it were employed in a better cause.

This is entirely correct, as is shown by the paraphrase

> I admire his energy; at the same time, I wish it were employed in a better cause.

Compare:

> While the temperature reaches 90 or 95 degrees in the daytime, the nights are often chilly.

The paraphrase shows why the use of *while* is incorrect:

> The temperature reaches 90 or 95 degrees in the daytime; at the same time the nights are often chilly.

In general, the writer will do well to use *while* only with strict literalness, in the sense of "during the time that."

**-wise.**  Not to be used indiscriminately as a pseudosuffix: *taxwise, pricewise, marriagewise, prosewise, saltwater taffywise.* Chiefly useful when it means "in the manner of": *clockwise.* There is not a noun in the language to which *-wise* cannot be added if the spirit moves one to add it. The sober writer will abstain from the use of this wild additive.

**Worth while.**  Overworked as a term of vague approval and (with *not*) of disapproval. Strictly applicable only to actions: "Is it worth while to telegraph?"

| | |
|---|---|
| His books are not worth while. | His books are not worth reading (are not worth one's while to read; do not repay reading). |

The adjective *worthwhile* (one word) is acceptable but emaciated. Use a stronger word.

| | |
|---|---|
| a worthwhile project | a promising (useful, valuable, exciting) project |

**Would.**  Commonly used to express habitual or repeated action. ("He would get up early and prepare his own breakfast before he went to work.") But when the idea of habit or repetition is expressed, in such phrases as *once a year, every day, each Sunday,* the past tense, without *would,* is usually sufficient, and, from its brevity, more emphatic.

| Once a year he would visit the old mansion. | Once a year he visited the old mansion. |

In narrative writing, always indicate the transition from the general to the particular—that is, from sentences that merely state a general habit to those that express the action of a specific day or period. Failure to indicate the change will cause confusion.

> Townsend would get up early and prepare his own breakfast. If the day was cold, he filled the stove and had a warm fire burning before he left the house. On his way out to the garage, he noticed that there were footprints in the new-fallen snow on the porch.

The reader is lost, having received no signal that Townsend has changed from a mere man of habit to a man who has seen a particular thing on a particular day.

> Townsend would get up early and prepare his own breakfast. If the day was cold, he filled the stove and had a warm fire burning before he left the house. One morning in January, on his way out to the garage, he noticed footprints in the new-fallen snow on the porch.

# V

## An Approach to Style

### (With a List of Reminders)

Up to this point, the book has been concerned with what is correct, or acceptable, in the use of English. In this final chapter, we approach style in its broader meaning: style in the sense of what is distinguished and distinguishing. Here we leave solid ground. Who can confidently say what ignites a certain combination of words, causing them to explode in the mind? Who knows why certain notes in music are capable of stirring the listener deeply, though the same notes slightly rearranged are impotent? These are high mysteries, and this chapter is a mystery story, thinly disguised. There is no satisfactory explanation of style, no infallible guide to good writing, no assurance that a person who thinks clearly will be able to write clearly, no key that unlocks the door, no inflexible rule by which the young writer may shape his course. He will often find himself steering by stars that are disturbingly in motion.

The preceding chapters contain instructions drawn from established English usage; this one contains advice drawn from a writer's experience of writing. Since the book is a rule book, these cautionary remarks, these subtly dangerous hints, are presented in the form of rules, but they are, in essence, mere gentle reminders: they state what most of us know and at times forget.

Style is an increment in writing. When we speak of Fitzgerald's style, we don't mean his command of the relative pronoun, we mean the sound his words make on paper. Every writer, by the way he uses the language, reveals something of his spirit, his habits, his capacities, his bias. This is inevitable as well as enjoyable. All writing is communication; creative writing is communication through revelation—it is the Self escaping into the open. No writer long remains incognito.

If the student doubts that style is something of a mystery, let him try rewriting a familiar sentence and see what happens. Any much-quoted sentence will do. Suppose we take "These are the times that try men's souls." Here we have eight short, easy words, forming a simple declarative sentence. The sentence contains no flashy ingredient such as "Damn the torpedoes!" and the words, as you see, are ordinary. Yet in that arrangement they have shown great durability; the sentence is almost into its third century. Now compare a few variations:

> Times like these try men's souls.
> How trying it is to live in these times!
> These are trying times for men's souls.
> Soulwise, these are trying times.

It seems unlikely that Thomas Paine could have made his sentiment stick if he had couched it in any of these forms. But why not? No fault of grammar can be detected in them, and in every case the meaning is clear. Each version is correct, and each, for some reason that we can't readily put our finger on, is marked for oblivion. We could, of course, talk about "rhythm" and "cadence," but the talk would be vague and unconvincing. We could declare *soulwise* to be a silly word, inappropriate to the occasion; but even that won't do—it does not answer the main question. Are we even sure *soulwise* is silly? If *otherwise* is a serviceable word, what's the matter with *soulwise*?

Here is another sentence, this one by a later Tom. It is not a famous sentence, although its author (Thomas Wolfe) is well known. "Quick are the mouths of earth, and quick the teeth that fed upon this loveliness." The sentence would not take a prize for clarity, and rhetorically it is at the opposite pole from "These are the times." Try it in a different form, without the inversions:

> The mouths of earth are quick, and the teeth that fed upon this loveliness are quick, too.

The author's meaning is still intact, but not his overpowering emotion. What was poetical and sensuous has become prosy and wooden; instead of the secret sounds of beauty, we are left with the simple crunch of mastication. (Whether Mr. Wolfe was guilty of overwriting is, of course, another question—one that is not pertinent here.)

With some writers, style not only reveals the spirit of the man but reveals his identity, as surely as would his fingerprints. Here, following, are two brief passages from the works of two American novelists. The subject in each case is languor. In both, the words used are ordinary, and there is nothing eccentric about the construction.

> He did not still feel weak, he was merely luxuriating in that supremely gutful lassitude of convalescence in which time, hurry, doing, did not exist, the accumulating seconds and minutes and hours to which in its well state the body is slave both waking and sleeping, now reversed and time now the lip-server and mendicant to the body's pleasure instead of the body thrall to time's headlong course.

> Manuel drank his brandy. He felt sleepy himself. It was too hot to go out into the town. Besides there was nothing to do. He wanted to see Zurito. He would go to sleep while he waited.

Anyone acquainted with Faulkner and Hemingway will have recognized them in these passages and perceived which was which. How different are their languors!

Or take two American poets, stopping at evening. One stops by woods, the other by laughing flesh.

> My little horse must think it queer
> To stop without a farmhouse near

Between the woods and frozen lake
The darkest evening of the year.*

I have perceived that to be with those I like is enough,
To stop in company with the rest at evening is enough,
To be surrounded by beautiful, curious, breathing,
  laughing flesh is enough . . .

Because of the characteristic styles, there is little question about identity here, and if the situations were reversed, with Whitman stopping by woods and Frost by laughing flesh (not one of his regularly scheduled stops), the reader would still know who was who.

Young writers often suppose that style is a garnish for the meat of prose, a sauce by which a dull dish is made palatable. Style has no such separate entity; it is nondetachable, unfilterable. The beginner should approach style warily, realizing that it is himself he is approaching, no other; and he should begin by turning resolutely away from all devices that are popularly believed to indicate style—all mannerisms, tricks, adornments. The approach to style is by way of plainness, simplicity, orderliness, sincerity.

Writing is, for most, laborious and slow. The mind travels faster than the pen; consequently, writing becomes a question of learning to make occasional wing shots, bringing down the bird of thought as it flashes by. A writer is a gunner, sometimes waiting in his blind for something to come in, sometimes roaming the countryside hoping to scare something up. Like other gunners, he must cultivate patience; he may have to work many covers to bring down one partridge. Here, following, are some suggestions and cautionary hints that may help the beginner find his way to a satisfactory style.

* From "Stopping by Woods on a Snowy Evening" from *The Poetry of Robert Frost,* edited by Edward Connery Latham. Copyright 1923, © 1969 by Holt, Rinehart, and Winston, Inc. Copyright 1951 by Robert Frost. Reprinted by permission of Holt, Rinehart, and Winston, Inc., and Jonathan Cape Ltd.

### 1. *Place yourself in the background.*

Write in a way that draws the reader's attention to the sense and substance of the writing, rather than to the mood and temper of the author. If the writing is solid and good, the mood and temper of the writer will eventually be revealed, and not at the expense of the work. Therefore, the first piece of advice is this: to achieve style, begin by affecting none—that is, place yourself in the background. A careful and honest writer does not need to worry about style. As he becomes proficient in the use of the language, his style will emerge, because he himself will emerge, and when this happens he will find it increasingly easy to break through the barriers that separate him from other minds, other hearts—which is, of course, the purpose of writing, as well as its principal reward. Fortunately, the act of composition, or creation, disciplines the mind; writing is one way to go about thinking, and the practice and habit of writing not only drain the mind but supply it, too.

### 2. *Write in a way that comes naturally.*

Write in a way that comes easily and naturally to you, using words and phrases that come readily to hand. But do not assume that because you have acted naturally your product is without flaw.

The use of language begins with imitation. The infant imitates the sounds made by its parents; the child imitates first the spoken language, then the stuff of books. The imitative life continues long after the writer is on his own in the language, for it is almost impossible to avoid imitating what one admires. Never imitate consciously, but do not worry about being an imitator; take pains instead to admire what is good. Then when you write in a way that comes naturally, you will echo the halloos that bear repeating.

### 3. *Work from a suitable design.*

Before beginning to compose something, gauge the nature and extent of the enterprise and work from a

suitable design. (See Chapter II, Rule 12.) Design in-
forms even the simplest structure, whether of brick and
steel or of prose. You raise a pup tent from one sort of
vision, a cathedral from another. This does not mean
that you must sit with a blueprint always in front of
you, merely that you had best anticipate what you are
getting into. To compose a laundry list, a writer can
work directly from the pile of soiled garments, ticking
them off one by one. But to write a biography the writer
will need at least a rough scheme; he cannot plunge in
blindly and start ticking off fact after fact about his
man, lest he miss the forest for the trees and there be
no end to his labors.

Sometimes, of course, impulse and emotion are more
compelling than design. A deeply troubled person, com-
posing a letter appealing for mercy or for love, had best
not attempt to organize his emotions; his prose will
have a better chance if he leaves his emotions in dis-
array—which he'll probably have to do anyway, since
one's feelings do not usually lend themselves to rearrangement. But even the kind of writing that is essentially adventurous and impetuous will on examination be found to have a secret plan: Columbus didn't
just sail, he sailed west, and the New World took shape
from this simple and, we now think, sensible design.

### 4. *Write with nouns and verbs.*

Write with nouns and verbs, not with adjectives and
adverbs. The adjective hasn't been built that can pull a
weak or inaccurate noun out of a tight place. This is not
to disparage adjectives and adverbs; they are indispensable parts of speech. Occasionally they surprise us with
their power, as in

> Up the airy mountain,
>  Down the rushy glen,
> We daren't go a-hunting
>  For fear of little men . . .

The nouns *mountain* and *glen* are accurate enough, but
had the mountain not become airy, the glen rushy, Wil-

liam Allingham might never have got off the ground with his poem. In general, however, it is nouns and verbs, not their assistants, that give to good writing its toughness and color.

### 5. *Revise and rewrite.*

Revising is part of writing. Few writers are so expert that they can produce what they are after on the first try. Quite often the writer will discover, on examining the completed work, that there are serious flaws in the arrangement of the material, calling for transpositions. When this is the case, he can save himself much labor and time by using scissors on his manuscript, cutting it to pieces and fitting the pieces together in a better order. If the work merely needs shortening, a pencil is the most useful tool; but if it needs rearranging, or stirring up, scissors should be brought into play. Do not be afraid to seize whatever you have written and cut it to ribbons; it can always be restored to its original condition in the morning, if that course seems best. Remember, it is no sign of weakness or defeat that your manuscript ends up in need of major surgery. This is a common occurrence in all writing, and among the best writers.

### 6. *Do not overwrite.*

Rich, ornate prose is hard to digest, generally unwholesome, and sometimes nauseating. If the sickly-sweet word, the overblown phrase are a writer's natural form of expression, as is sometimes the case, he will have to compensate for it by a show of vigor, and by writing something as meritorious as the Song of Songs, which is Solomon's.

### 7. *Do not overstate.*

When you overstate, the reader will be instantly on guard, and everything that has preceded your overstatement as well as everything that follows it will be suspect in his mind because he has lost confidence in your judgment or your poise. Overstatement is one of the common faults. A single overstatement, wherever or however it occurs, diminishes the whole, and a single carefree superlative has the power to destroy, for the reader, the object of the writer's enthusiasm.

## 8. Avoid the use of qualifiers.

*Rather, very, little, pretty*—these are the leeches that infest the pond of prose, sucking the blood of words. The constant use of the adjective *little* (except to indicate size) is particularly debilitating; we should all try to do a little better, we should all be very watchful of this rule, for it is a rather important one and we are pretty sure to violate it now and then.

## 9. Do not affect a breezy manner.

The volume of writing is enormous, these days, and much of it has a sort of windiness about it, almost as though the author were in a state of euphoria. "Spontaneous me," sang Whitman, and, in his innocence, let loose the hordes of uninspired scribblers who would one day confuse spontaneity with genius.

The breezy style is often the work of an egocentric, the person who imagines that everything that pops into his head is of general interest and that uninhibited prose creates high spirits and carries the day. Open any alumni magazine, turn to the class notes, and you are quite likely to encounter old Spontaneous Me at work —an aging collegian who writes something like this:

> Well, chums, here I am again with my bagful of dirt about your disorderly classmates, after spending a helluva weekend in N'Yawk trying to view the Columbia game from behind two bumbershoots and a glazed cornea. And speaking of news, howzabout tossing a few chirce nuggets my way?

This is an extreme example, but the same wind blows, at lesser velocities, across vast expanses of journalistic prose. The author in this case has managed in two sentences to commit most of the unpardonable sins: he obviously has nothing to say, he is showing off and directing the attention of the reader to himself, he is using slang with neither provocation nor ingenuity, he adopts a patronizing air by throwing in the word *chirce*, he is tasteless, humorless (though full of fun), dull, and empty. He has not done his work. Compare his opening remarks with the following—a plunge directly into the news:

> Clyde Crawford, who stroked the varsity shell in 1928, is swinging an oar again after a lapse of forty years. Clyde resigned last spring as executive sales manager of the Indiana Flotex Company and is now a gondolier in Venice.

This, although conventional, is compact, informative, unpretentious. The writer has dug up an item of news and presented it in a straightforward manner. What the first writer tried to accomplish by cutting rhetorical capers and by breeziness, the second writer managed to achieve by good reporting, by keeping a tight rein on his material, and by staying out of the act.

### 10. *Use orthodox spelling.*

In ordinary composition, use orthodox spelling. Do not write *nite* for *night, thru* for *through, pleez* for *please,* unless you plan to introduce a complete system of simplified spelling and are prepared to take the consequences.

In the original edition of *The Elements of Style,* there was a chapter on spelling. In it, the author had this to say:

> The spelling of English words is not fixed and invariable, nor does it depend on any other authority than general agreement. At the present day there is practically unanimous agreement as to the spelling of most words. . . . At any given moment, however, a relatively small number of words may be spelled in more than one way. Gradually, as a rule, one of these forms comes to be generally preferred, and the less customary form comes to look obsolete and is discarded. From time to time new forms, mostly simplifications, are introduced by innovators, and either win their place or die of neglect.

The practical objection to unaccepted and oversimplified spellings is the disfavor with which they are received by the reader. They distract his attention and exhaust his patience. He reads the form *though* automatically, without thought of its needless complexity; he reads the abbreviation *tho* and mentally supplies the missing letters, at the cost of a fraction of his attention. The writer has defeated his own purpose.

The language manages somehow to keep pace with events. A word that has taken hold in our century is *thruway;* it was born of necessity and is apparently here to stay. In combination with *way, thru* is more serviceable than *through;* it is a high-speed word for readers who are going sixty. *Throughway* would be too long to fit on a road sign, too slow to serve the speeding eye. It is conceivable that because of our thruways, *through* will eventually become *thru*—after many more thousands of miles of travel.

## 11. *Do not explain too much.*

It is seldom advisable to tell all. Be sparing, for instance, in the use of adverbs after "he said," "she replied," and the like: "he said consolingly"; "she replied grumblingly." Let the conversation itself disclose the speaker's manner or condition. Dialogue heavily weighted with adverbs after the attributive verb is cluttery and annoying. Inexperienced writers not only overwork their adverbs but load their attributives with explantory verbs: "he consoled," "she congratulated." They do this, apparently, in the belief that the word *said* is always in need of support, or because they have been told to do it by experts in the art of bad writing.

## 12. *Do not construct awkward adverbs.*

Adverbs are easy to build. Take an adjective or a participle, add *-ly,* and behold! you have an adverb. But you'd probably be better off without it. Do not write *tangledly.* The word itself is a tangle. Do not even write *tiredly.* Nobody says *tangledly* and not many people say *tiredly.* Words that are not used orally are seldom the ones to put on paper.

| | |
|---|---|
| He climbed tiredly to bed. | He climbed wearily to bed. |
| The lamp cord lay tangledly beneath his chair. | The lamp cord lay in tangles beneath his chair. |

Do not dress words up by adding *ly* to them, as though putting a hat on a horse.

| | |
|---|---|
| overly | over |
| muchly | much |
| thusly | thus |

### 13. *Make sure the reader knows who is speaking.*

Dialogue is a total loss unless you indicate who the speaker is. In long dialogue passages containing no attributives, the reader may become lost and be compelled to go back and reread in order to puzzle the thing out. Obscurity is an imposition on the reader, to say nothing of its damage to the work.

In dialogue, make sure that your attributives do not awkwardly interrupt a spoken sentence. Place them where the break would come naturally in speech—that is, where the speaker would pause for emphasis, or take a breath. The best test for locating an attributive is to speak the sentence aloud.

| | |
|---|---|
| "Now, my boy, we shall see," he said, "how well you have learned your lesson." | "Now, my boy," he said, "we shall see how well you have learned your lesson." |
| "What's more, they would never," he added, "consent to the plan." | "What's more," he added, "they would never consent to the plan." |

### 14. *Avoid fancy words.*

Avoid the elaborate, the pretentious, the coy, and the cute. Do not be tempted by a twenty-dollar word when there is a ten-center handy, ready and able. Anglo-Saxon is a livelier tongue than Latin, so use Anglo-Saxon words. In this, as in so many matters pertaining to style, one's ear must be one's guide: *gut* is a lustier noun than *intestine*, but the two words are not interchangeable, because *gut* is often inappropriate, being too coarse for the context. Never call a stomach a tummy without good reason.

If you admire fancy words, if every sky is *beauteous*, every blonde *curvaceous*, if you are tickled by *discombobulate*, you will have a bad time with Reminder 14. What is wrong, you ask, with *beauteous?* No one knows, for sure. There is nothing wrong, really, with any word—all are good, but some are better than others. A matter of ear, a matter of reading the books that sharpen the ear.

The line between the fancy and the plain, between the atrocious and the felicitous, is sometimes alarmingly fine. The opening phrase of the Gettysburg address is close to the line, at least by our standards today, and Mr. Lincoln, knowingly or unknowingly, was flirting with disaster when he wrote "Four score and seven years ago." The President could have got into his sentence with plain "Eighty-seven"—a saving of two words and less of a strain on the listeners' powers of multiplication. But Lincoln's ear must have told him to go ahead with four score and seven. By doing so, he achieved cadence while skirting the edge of fanciness. Suppose he had blundered over the line and written, "In the year of our Lord seventeen hundred and seventy-six." His speech would have sustained a heavy blow. Or suppose he had settled for "Eighty-seven." In that case he would have got into his introductory sentence too quickly; the timing would have been bad.

The question of ear is vital. Only the writer whose ear is reliable is in a position to use bad grammar deliberately; only he knows for sure when a colloquialism is better than formal phrasing; only he is able to sustain his work at the level of good taste. So cock your ear. Years ago, students were warned not to end a sentence with a preposition; time, of course, has softened that rigid decree. Not only is the preposition acceptable at the end, sometimes it is more effective in that spot than anywhere else. "A claw hammer, not an ax, was the tool he murdered her with." This is preferable to "A claw hammer, not an ax, was the tool with which he murdered her." Why? Because it sounds more violent, more like murder. A matter of ear.

And would you write "The worst tennis player around here is I" or "The worst tennis player around here is me"? The first is good grammar, the second is good judgment—although the *me* might not do in all contexts.

The split infinitive is another trick of rhetoric in which the ear must be quicker than the handbook. Some infinitives seem to improve on being split, just as a stick of round stovewood does. "I cannot bring myself to really like the fellow." The sentence is relaxed, the meaning is clear, the violation is harmless and scarcely perceptible. Put the other way, the sentence becomes stiff, needlessly formal. A matter of ear.

There are times when the ear not only guides us through difficult situations but also saves us from minor or major embarrassments of prose. The ear, for example, must decide when to omit *that* from a sentence, when to retain it. "He knew he could do it" is preferable to "He knew that he could do it"—simpler and just as clear. But in many cases the *that* is needed. "He felt that his big nose, which was sunburned, made him look ridiculous." Omit the *that* and you have "He felt his big nose. . . ."

### 15. *Do not use dialect unless your ear is good.*

Do not attempt to use dialect unless you are a devoted student of the tongue you hope to reproduce. If you use dialect, be consistent. The reader will become impatient or confused if he finds two or more versions of the same word or expression. In dialect it is necessary to spell phonetically, or at least ingeniously, to capture unusual inflections. Take, for example, the word *once*. It often appears in dialect writing as *oncet*, but *oncet* looks as though it should be pronounced "onset."

A better spelling would be *wunst*. But if you write it *oncet* once, write it that way throughout. The best dialect writers, by and large, are economical of their talents, they use the minimum, not the maximum, of deviation from the norm, thus sparing the reader as well as convincing him.

## 16. *Be clear.*

Clarity is not the prize in writing, nor is it always the principal mark of a good style. There are occasions when obscurity serves a literary yearning, if not a literary purpose, and there are writers whose mien is more overcast than clear. But since writing is communication, clarity can only be a virtue. And although there is no substitute for merit in writing, clarity comes closest to being one. Even to a writer who is being intentionally obscure or wild of tongue we can say, "Be obscure clearly! Be wild of tongue in a way we can understand!" Even to writers of market letters, telling us (but not telling us) which securities are promising, we can say, "Be cagey plainly! Be elliptical in a straightforward fashion!"

Clarity, clarity, clarity. When you become hopelessly mired in a sentence, it is best to start fresh; do not try to fight your way through against the terrible odds of syntax. Usually what is wrong is that the construction has become too involved at some point; the sentence needs to be broken apart and replaced by two or more shorter sentences.

Muddiness is not merely a disturber of prose, it is also a destroyer of life, of hope: death on the highway caused by a badly worded road sign, heartbreak among lovers caused by a misplaced phrase in a well-intentioned letter, anguish of a traveler expecting to be met at a railroad station and not being met because of a slipshod telegram. Usually we think only of the ludicrous aspect of ambiguity; we enjoy it when the *Times* tells us that Nelson Rockefeller is "chairman of the Museum of Modern Art, which he entered in a fireman's raincoat during a recent fire, and founded the

Museum of Primitive Art." This we all love. But think of the tragedies that are rooted in ambiguity; think of that side, and be clear! When you say something, make sure you have said it. The chances of your having said it are only fair.

### 17. *Do not inject opinion.*

Unless there is a good reason for its being there, do not inject opinion into a piece of writing. We all have opinions about almost everything, and the temptation to toss them in is great. To air one's views gratuitously, however, is to imply that the demand for them is brisk, which may not be the case, and which, in any event, may not be relevant to the discussion. Opinions scattered indiscriminately about leave the mark of egotism on a work. Similarly, to air one's views at an improper time may be in bad taste. If you have received a letter inviting you to speak at the dedication of a new cat hospital, and you hate cats, your reply, declining the invitation, does not necessarily have to cover the full range of your emotions. You must make it clear that you will not attend, but you do not have to let fly at cats. The writer of the letter asked a civil question; attack cats, then, only if you can do so with good humor, good taste, and in such a way that your answer will be courteous as well as responsive. Since you are out of sympathy with cats, you may quite properly give this as a reason for not appearing at the dedicatory ceremonies of a cat hospital. But bear in mind that your opinion of cats was not sought, only your services as a speaker. Try to keep things straight.

### 18. *Use figures of speech sparingly.*

The simile is a common device and a useful one, but similes coming in rapid fire, one right on top of another, are more distracting than illuminating. The reader needs time to catch his breath; he can't be expected to compare everything with something else, and no relief in sight.

When you use metaphor, do not mix it up. That is, don't start by calling something a swordfish and end by calling it an hourglass.

### 19. *Do not take shortcuts at the cost of clarity.*

Do not use initials for the names of organizations or movements unless you are certain the initials will be readily understood. Write things out. Not everyone knows that SALT means Strategic Arms Limitation Talks, and even if everyone did, there are babies being born every minute who will someday encounter the name for the first time. They deserve to see the words, not simply the initials. A good rule is to start your article by writing out names in full, and then, later, when the reader has got his bearings, to shorten them.

Many shortcuts are self-defeating; they waste the reader's time instead of conserving it. There are all sorts of rhetorical stratagems and devices that attract writers who hope to be pithy, but most of them are simply bothersome. The longest way round is usually the shortest way home, and the one truly reliable shortcut in writing is to choose words that are strong and sure-footed to carry the reader on his way.

### 20. *Avoid foreign languages.*

The writer will occasionally find it convenient or necessary to borrow from other languages. Some writers, however, from sheer exuberance or a desire to show off, sprinkle their work liberally with foreign expressions, with no regard for the reader's comfort. It is a bad habit. Write in English.

### 21. *Prefer the standard to the offbeat.*

The young writer will be drawn at every turn toward eccentricities in language. He will hear the beat of new vocabularies, the exciting rhythms of special segments of his society, each speaking a language of its own. All of us come under the spell of these unsettling drums; the problem for the beginner is to listen to them, learn the words, feel the vibrations, and not be carried away.

Youth invariably speaks to youth in a tongue of his own devising: he renovates the language with a wild vigor, as he would a basement apartment. By the time this paragraph sees print, *uptight, ripoff, rap, dude, vibes, copout,* and *funky* will be the words of yesteryear, and we will be fielding more recent ones that have come bouncing into our speech—some of them into our dictionary as well. A new word is always up for survival. Many do survive. Others grow stale and disappear. Most are, at least in their infancy, more appropriate to conversation than to composition.

Today, the language of advertising enjoys an enormous circulation. With its deliberate infractions of grammatical rules and its crossbreeding of the parts of speech, it profoundly influences the tongues and pens of children and adults. Your new kitchen range is so revolutionary it *obsoletes* all other ranges. Your counter top is beautiful because it is *accessorized* with gold-plated faucets. Your cigarette tastes good *like* a cigarette should. And, *like the man says,* you will want to try one. You will also, in all probability, want to try writing that way, using that language. You do so at your peril, for it is the language of mutilation.

Advertisers are quite understandably interested in what they call "attention getting." The man photographed must have lost an eye or grown a pink beard, or he must have three arms or be sitting wrong-end-to on a horse. This technique is proper in its place, which is the world of selling, but the young writer had best not adopt the device of mutilation in ordinary composition, whose purpose is to engage, not paralyze, the reader's senses. Buy the gold-plated faucets if you will, but do not accessorize your prose. To use the language well, do not begin by hacking it to bits; accept the whole body of it, cherish its classic form, its variety, and its richness.

Another segment of society that has constructed a language of its own is business. The businessman says that ink erasers are *in short supply,* that he has *updated*

the next shipment of these erasers, and that he will
*finalize* his recommendations at the next meeting of the
board. He is speaking a language that is familiar to him
and dear to him. Its portentous nouns and verbs invest
ordinary events with high adventure; the executive
walks among ink erasers, caparisoned like a knight. We
should tolerate him—every man of spirit wants to ride a
white horse. The only question is whether his vocabu-
lary is helpful to ordinary prose. Usually, the same ideas
can be expressed less formidably, if one makes the effort.
A good many of the special words of business seem designed more to express the user's dreams than to express
his precise meaning. Not all such words, of course, can
be dismissed summarily; indeed, no word in the language can be dismissed offhand by anyone who has a
healthy curiosity. *Update* isn't a bad word; in the right
setting it is useful. In the wrong setting, though, it is
destructive, and the trouble with adopting coinages too
quickly is that they will bedevil one by insinuating
themselves where they do not belong. This may sound
like rhetorical snobbery, or plain stuffiness; but the
writer will discover, in the course of his work, that the
setting of a word is just as restrictive as the setting of a
jewel. The general rule here is to prefer the standard.
*Finalize*, for instance, is not standard; it is special, and
it is a peculiarly fuzzy and silly word. Does it mean
"terminate," or does it mean "put into final form"?
One can't be sure, really, what it means, and one gets
the impression that the person using it doesn't know,
either, and doesn't want to know.

The special vocabularies of the law, of the military,
of government are familiar to most of us. Even the
world of criticism has a modest pouch of private words
(*luminous, taut*), whose only virtue is that they are ex-
ceptionally nimble and can escape from the garden of
meaning over the wall. Of these Critical words, Wolcott
Gibbs once wrote, ". . . they are detached from the
language and inflated like little balloons." The young
writer should learn to spot them—words that at first
glance seem freighted with delicious meaning but

that soon burst in air, leaving nothing but a memory of bright sound.

The language is perpetually in flux: it is a living stream, shifting, changing, receiving new strength from a thousand tributaries, losing old forms in the backwaters of time. To suggest that a young writer not swim in the main stream of this turbulence would be foolish indeed, and such is not the intent of these cautionary remarks. The intent is to suggest that in choosing between the formal and the informal, the regular and the offbeat, the general and the special, the orthodox and the heretical, the beginner err on the side of conservatism, on the side of established usage. No idiom is taboo, no accent forbidden; there is simply a better chance of doing well if the writer holds a steady course, enters the stream of English quietly, and does not thrash about.

"But," the student may ask, "what if it comes natural to me to experiment rather than conform? What if I am a pioneer, or even a genius?" Answer: then be one. But do not forget that what may seem like pioneering may be merely evasion, or laziness—the disinclination to submit to discipline. Writing good standard English is no cinch, and before you have managed it you will have encountered enough rough country to satisfy even the most adventurous spirit.

Style takes its final shape more from attitudes of mind than from principles of composition, for, as an elderly practitioner once remarked, "Writing is an act of faith, not a trick of grammar." This moral observation would have no place in a rule book were it not that style *is* the writer, and therefore what a man is, rather than what he knows, will at last determine his style. If one is to write, one must believe—in the truth and worth of the scrawl, in the ability of the reader to receive and decode the message. No one can write decently who is distrustful of the reader's intelligence, or whose attitude is patronizing.

Many references have been made in this book to "the

reader"—he has been much in the news. It is now necessary to warn the writer that his concern for the reader must be pure: he must sympathize with the reader's plight (most readers are in trouble about half the time) but never seek to know his wants. The whole duty of a writer is to please and satisfy himself, and the true writer always plays to an audience of one. Let him start sniffing the air, or glancing at the Trend Machine, and he is as good as dead, although he may make a nice living.

Full of his beliefs, sustained and elevated by the power of his purpose, armed with the rules of grammar, the writer is ready for exposure. At this point, he may well pattern himself on the fully exposed cow of Robert Louis Stevenson's rhyme. This friendly and commendable animal, you may recall, was "blown by all the winds that pass/And wet with all the showers." And so must the young writer be. In our modern idiom, we would say that he must get wet all over. Mr. Stevenson, working in a plainer style, said it with felicity, and suddenly one cow, out of so many, received the gift of immortality. Like the steadfast writer, she is at home in the wind and the rain; and, thanks to one moment of felicity, she will live on and on and on.

# *Index*

ESPECIALLY FOR

..................................................................................................................

FROM

..................................................................................................................

DATE

..................................................................................................................

# DAILY WISDOM
# FOR WOMEN
## —— 2022 ——
## DEVOTIONAL COLLECTION

BARBOUR
PUBLISHING

*Those who trust in the L*ORD *are like Mount Zion.*
*It cannot be shaken; it remains forever.*
*Jerusalem—the mountains surround her.*
*And the L*ORD *surrounds His people,*
*both now and forever.*
PSALM 125:1-2 HCSB

No matter what happens in your life, you can rely on God to surround you with His outstretched arm, His heart drenched in love, His hands dripping with grace. When you trip up, when you're too weak to stand, when you're lower than low, God is ready to catch you, prop you up, and lift you up.

No matter where you go or what you do, God's help and provision, His strength and power will always be with you. For although you may change, God will not (James 1:17). He's your anchor in the storm (Hebrews 6:18-19); your firm foundation (Isaiah 28:16); and the One who'll never leave or forsake you (Hebrews 13:5).

When all hope seems lost, when everything around you appears to be falling apart, you need not be shaken. For you've got a God you can trust to always be there, looking out for you, protecting you, providing for you, all day every day.

To help you grow your trust and hope in God, we offer you 365 scripture-based readings written by eight women just like you. Each day's devotion corresponds to a particular day's reading based on Barbour's Read through the Bible in a Year plan found at the back of this book. We pray that as you read each day's devotion, your trust and confidence in God will help you become unshakable.

## ALL THINGS NEW

*In the beginning God created the heavens and*
*the earth. The earth was formless and empty,*
*and darkness covered the deep waters. And the Spirit*
*of God was hovering over the surface of the waters.*
GENESIS 1:1-2 NLT*

D on't you wish you could have peeked over the veil during creation week? God took nothing. . .and created everything. Wow! The earth, in its initial stage, was formless and empty—totally dark. Deep waters covered it all. But here's the really cool part: the Spirit of God hovered over the surface of the waters.

Pause to think about that for a moment. When the Creator created, the Spirit hovered over what He was spinning into creation. The same thing is true today. When He re-created you (when you were born again), the Spirit of God played a key role. And when you create (whether a work of art, a plan, or a cake) the Spirit of God hovers over that too.

When you realize the Holy Spirit is ever-present in your life, everything changes! There's no need to be shaken when God Himself shows up. And though you may feel formless and empty at times, just as the earth was in its initial stages, the incoming Spirit brings life where there was no life and hope where there was no hope.

What are you creating today? Expect the Holy Spirit to show up and show off.

*Lord, I'm so grateful for Your Spirit. Thank You for*
*hovering over the things You're creating through me. Amen.*

*A Read through the Bible in a Year plan that follows each devotion can be found at the back of this book.

## BRING HIM YOUR GIFTS

*They entered the house and saw the child with his
mother, Mary, and they bowed down and worshiped him.
Then they opened their treasure chests and gave
him gifts of gold, frankincense, and myrrh.*

MATTHEW 2:11 NLT

I magine for a moment that you were there alongside the wise men as they carried in their gifts of gold, frankincense, and myrrh. If given the opportunity, what gifts would you bring the baby Jesus? You might think, *I have nothing of value to offer Him*, but that's simply not in line with what the Word of God says about you. You are created in the image of an awesome, holy, creative God, and He has placed countless gifts inside of you. Your very life is a gift, in service to Him.

Romans 11:29 (NLT) puts it this way: "For God's gift and his call can never be withdrawn." Maybe you read that and think, *I have yet to discover the gifts He's placed inside of me.* That's okay. There's plenty of time to discover and develop them. Just know that when you do, He means them to be offered back to Him as a praise offering. Perhaps today will give you opportunity to do that.

*Lord, thank You for the gifts You've placed inside of me.
Help me to discover them, hone them, and use them
for Your good and glory, I pray. Amen.*

## A SHIELD AROUND ME

*But you, O LORD, are a shield around me; you are my glory,*
*the one who holds my head high. I cried out to the LORD,*
*and he answered me from his holy mountain.*
PSALM 3:3-4 NLT

I magine an enemy was headed right toward you with the obvious intent to bring harm. Then, all of a sudden, your loved ones—friends, family members, fellow believers—swept in around you in a giant circle, pressing you to the center and completely guarding and shielding you from the oncoming attacker. Whew. How comforting it would be to realize they cared enough to provide a barrier so that you weren't vulnerable to the intended attack.

God cares about you too. In fact, if you took all the compassion in the hearts of your loved ones and multiplied it by infinity, it still wouldn't come close to how much the Lord adores you. And because of this deep, abiding adoration, He is determined to guard and protect you, to shield you from harm. Because of His great love, you can lift your head high, even when the enemy taunts you.

Today's verse should bring as much comfort as having a physical barrier between yourself and your enemies. The Author of all is your protector. You have nothing to fear.

*Lord, I'm so grateful for Your protection. You're surrounding me,*
*even now, forming a shield from those who would*
*seek to harm me. Thank You, Jesus! Amen.*

## HOLY ANTICIPATION

*He waited seven more days and again sent out the dove*
*from the ark. When the dove returned to him in the evening,*
*there in its beak was a freshly plucked olive leaf! Then Noah*
*knew that the water had receded from the earth.*
GENESIS 8:10-11 NIV

As a child, you probably had a sense of expectation in the days leading up to Christmas. You couldn't wait to find a particular gift under the tree. On Christmas morning you raced to the tree. . . and were not disappointed. There it was, that shiny new bike you'd been hoping for.

Years later you may have found yourself awaiting the birth of a child. The anticipation was almost more than you could stand as the days ticked by. Then, on the day of your child's birth, all your hopes and dreams came true.

Not many of us are good at waiting. But when you wait with a sense of eager anticipation for what's coming, there can be joy in the journey because you know that what's waiting for you is good, not bad.

God has amazing things in store for you. Sure, there might be some shaking in the waiting. And yes, you might not always get what you want when you want it. But you serve a loving heavenly Father who gives good gifts to His kids. So, hang in there. God's got great things ahead for you.

*Lord, thank You for the sense of expectation*
*I have as I wait in and on You. Amen.*

## LET IT SHINE

*"You are the light of the world.*
*A town built on a hill cannot be hidden."*
MATTHEW 5:14 NIV

B iblical towns were often built on a hill so that they were visible from a distance (and so that their occupants could keep a lookout on the goings-on below). Of course, those cities were well-protected by the walls that surrounded them.

Isn't it interesting, then, that Jesus tells His disciples they're like a city set on a hill. They're in full view—of the world and even the enemy. But He's placed them (and us) in a prominent position with the promise that He would be our guard. Although there are no physical walls to defend us when we let His light shine, we have Jesus' spiritual protection.

It's not always easy being a city on a hill. There are days when you may wish you could hide behind fortress walls and dim that light. The burden of being a good witness can be a lot to bear at times. But Jesus has set you on a hill, high and lifted up, so that your light can impact all who see you. You don't have to be shaken because of this vulnerability since He's right there, shining through you. He simply asks that you not hide your light.

What are you doing to shine His light today?

*Lord, I won't be shaken, no matter how visible my*
*witness is to others. I'll keep shining for You. Amen.*

## SEPARATING LIGHT
## FROM DARKNESS

*Away from me, all you who do evil,*
*for the LORD has heard my weeping.*
PSALM 6:8 NIV

Old Testament stories make one thing very clear—God intended for His people to separate themselves from the other tribes and to remain set apart. This was for their protection but also to guard their hearts against the infiltration of evil and/or ungodly customs.

This world is in a mess. As some would say "a hot mess." What used to be called evil is now good and what used to be held as irrefutable and good is now despised and rejected. It's almost as if the world has flipped upside-down.

Though thousands of years have passed, God hasn't changed His mind. When it comes to His kids, He still wants them to remain unchanged by the world. Untainted. He wants very clear lines to be drawn between dark and light, good and evil. No, He's not asking you to live in a bunker or to give up your friends, (though there might be a few you could let go of, if they're pulling you away from Him). He simply wants you to remain true to what you know to be true—His Word.

Be in the world but not of the world. It wasn't easy for the Israelites, and it's not easy for you, but with His help it is possible.

*Lord, I refuse to compromise. I will live*
*in the light all of my days. Amen.*

# A GENERATIONAL COVENANT

*And I will establish My covenant between Me and you
and your descendants after you throughout their generations
for an everlasting, solemn pledge, to be a God to
you and to your posterity after you.*

GENESIS 17:7 AMPC

In today's scripture, God promises that He will establish a covenant with Abraham, one that will include future generations. How wonderful would that be?

Sure, you hope and pray your children will carry on your legacy of faith. And when those grandchildren come along, you also pray they will continue what you've started. But your desire to see that come to pass starts with you. It's critical that you covenant with God—right here, right now—and don't ever step away from your faith. Your children are watching.

You certainly don't carry all of the weight, of course. God is the One making an oath with you, and He's trustworthy. He promises to be a "God to you and to your posterity after you." What He's started in you, He can continue through those future generations.

Long after you are gone from this earth, there will be those (relatives or loved ones) you've influenced for the better. What a precious legacy!

*Lord, start with me. I want my faith to be strong, and I
want to stand in agreement with You so that my future
generations (or those I love) will continue to blossom
and grow in You years and years from now. Amen.*

## AIM FOR THE BLACK DOT

*But seek (aim at and strive after) first of all His kingdom and
His righteousness (His way of doing and being right), and then
all these things taken together will be given you besides.*

MATTHEW 6:33 AMPC

Have you ever played darts? Aiming that tiny dart at the black dot in the middle of the board is the easy part. Getting it to land where you've *aimed* it is something else altogether.

Here's the truth: you won't hit anything you don't aim at. If you're hoping to lose weight, you need to give yourself goals (little black dots). If your goal is to pay off credit cards, make a plan and aim for it.

The Bible says we're to seek (aim at and strive after) God's kingdom and His way of doing and being right. Maybe you read that and think, *Well, that goal seems a little lofty!* Again, it's like aiming a dart at the black dot on the board. If you strive after the kingdom of Christ, you're aiming yourself at something wonderful.

The point is, you have to make a decision to seek His kingdom. It's not something that just happens. You have to strive after it. Make it a goal. Keep after it. When you do, everything else in life will come into alignment, and you can truly be unshakable.

*Lord, today I'll aim for the black dot. Amen.*

## PRAISE HIM AT THE ONSET

*I will praise You, O Lord, with my whole heart;*
*I will show forth (recount and tell aloud) all Your*
*marvelous works and wonderful deeds!*
PSALM 9:1 AMPC

You're facing a challenge. It's a big one. You're feeling a little overwhelmed, not knowing how things will go. Will God answer your prayers the way you hope or will you end up disappointed?

Then you're reminded of this scripture from Psalm 9:1—that you should praise the Lord with your whole heart and recount His wonderful deeds. So, you go there. You lift your voice and begin to proclaim all the many ways He's come through for you in the past. Doing so bolsters your courage for what you're facing and also serves as a testimony to others around you. And suddenly, in the middle of your praise, you begin to trust again. No matter how your situation evolves, you decide, you won't give up.

Praise is a wonderful tool, and it's just as powerful when you're setting off on your journey as it is after God has answered your prayer. Don't wait until you've got your miracle in hand to begin to praise Him. There's no time like the present to start!

*Lord, I won't wait. Today, even as I'm feeling a little*
*unsettled and confused about where my journey is taking me,*
*I choose to praise You! I lift Your name and praise You*
*for all You've already done in my life. Amen.*

## EXCITING OPPORTUNITIES AHEAD

*"The thing has come from the LORD; we cannot speak to you bad or good. Behold, Rebekah is before you; take her and go, and let her be the wife of your master's son, as the LORD has spoken."*
GENESIS 24:50-51 ESV

I t was a day like any other for Rebekah, daughter of Bethuel. She headed to the spring, jar perched on her shoulder. After filling the jar with water, a stranger approached her and said, "Please give me a sip from your jug." She responded with the words, "Drink, sir," and then gave him the jug. She then offered to water his camels, who were kneeling by the wall. Little did she know her words would serve as a sign to this man that she was the chosen one, meant to marry his master's son, Isaac.

The servant presented Rebekah's family with all the treasures Abraham had sent with him, and Rebekah (without hesitation) agreed to return with this stranger to his home country to marry Isaac.

That's a lot for a young woman to agree to—marrying a stranger from a foreign land! But when God's hand is on a situation, sometimes it's so obvious you just can't say no. You step out in faith, knowing there are exciting opportunities ahead.

What opportunities is the Lord giving you today? Are you ready to take a bold step of faith like Rebekah did?

*Lord, I'm ready! I'll take that first step toward the opportunities You're giving me. Amen.*

# FROM SICKBED TO
# SERVANT'S HEART

*And when Jesus entered Peter's house, he saw his*
*mother-in-law lying sick with a fever. He touched her hand,*
*and the fever left her, and she rose and began to serve him.*
MATTHEW 8:14-15 ESV

Peter's mother-in-law was terribly ill on the day that Jesus came by for a visit. If you've ever been down for the count with the flu or other feverish bug, you can imagine how she was feeling— definitely not up to a houseguest.

Oh, but this guest was different from all the others. He walked in, reached to touch her hand, and the fever immediately left her. (Can you imagine?) She jumped up out of bed and did what any hostess would do—began to serve Him.

Maybe you've been through a season of illness or pain and have wished Jesus would sweep in and touch you like that. You've prayed for instantaneous healing, but it didn't come in such a sweeping, awe-inspiring way.

Don't give up. Don't let the wait shake your faith. Just remember that one gentle touch from the Savior was enough to change absolutely everything. Keep your focus on Him until that moment comes.

*I won't give up, Lord. I'm ready to rise from this sickbed*
*and do great things for You. Touch me, I pray. Amen.*

## NEVER FORGOTTEN

*Arise, O Lord; O God, lift up your hand;*
*forget not the afflicted.*
PSALM 10:12 ESV

H ave you ever wondered why some people are healed and others aren't? It's not unusual for believers to ask gut-honest questions of the Lord like "Why is my child struggling with a disability when other children seem to have no cares in the world?" or "Why was my friend's mother healed from cancer when mine wasn't?" These questions often come from a place of deep pain, but the Lord is tough enough to handle them.

When we're at a loss to understand the whys and wherefores of God, we can only choose to trust. But today's verse clues us in on another important truth: we can (and should) keep on asking, even when things don't seem to be happening the way we expected. Asking is an act of faith. It's your way of saying, "Lord, I don't get it, but I know You do." And you never know when He will choose to move on your behalf. Or perhaps He will whisper, "It's okay. I've got a bigger plan."

What tough questions would you like to ask the Lord today? It's okay. Go ahead. Ask. He can take it.

*Lord, I don't always understand, but I will never stop asking. I'll never stop praying. I'll never stop believing. And I'll never stop trusting that You love me (and mine), no matter what. Amen.*

# GOD IS IN THIS PLACE

*When Jacob awoke from his sleep, he thought, "Surely the Lord is in this place, and I was not aware of it." He was afraid and said, "How awesome is this place! This is none other than the house of God; this is the gate of heaven."*
GENESIS 28:16-17 NIV

While journeying back to his grandfather's homeland, Jacob grew weary and laid down under the stars to sleep. An amazing dream followed. He saw a great stairway reaching up to the heavens. God's angels were going up and down the stairway. In the dream, the Lord stood right beside Jacob. He said, "Your descendants will be like the dust of the earth, and you will spread out to the west and to the east, to the north and to the south. All peoples on earth will be blessed through you and your offspring" (Genesis 28:14 NIV).

Jacob awoke from the dream, overcome by the promise he'd received in his sleep. Instead of simply moving on, he paused to acknowledge the place where the dream had taken place. He called the place Bethel.

Do you stop to acknowledge God when He speaks into your life? Can you think back to your "Bethel" moments? When and where did God speak to your heart and give you the courage to go on? Today, thank Him for His many Bethel encounters.

*Thank You, Lord, for my Bethel encounters! May I never forget those times when You've spoken to my heart. Amen.*

## BE ON YOUR WAY

*"When you knock on a door, be courteous in your greeting.*
*If they welcome you, be gentle in your conversation.*
*If they don't welcome you, quietly withdraw. Don't make a*
*scene. Shrug your shoulders and be on your way. You can*
*be sure that on Judgment Day they'll be mighty sorry—*
*but it's no concern of yours now."*
MATTHEW 10:12-15 MSG

Have you ever approached someone with kindness and compassion in your tone, and her response was anything but? It's hard, isn't it? If you're a softie, you probably replay the conversation in your mind, over and over, wondering what you could've said or done differently. You agonize over the misunderstanding. You pour out your heart to God. "Why doesn't she get me? What am I doing wrong?"

It's even tougher when people completely dismiss you or push you aside. Their dismissal can leave you shaken. They don't care to connect with you. . .at all. Ouch!

Jesus knew His followers weren't intended to be BFFs with everyone. No doubt that's why He added the line, "Shrug your shoulders and be on your way."

Jesus wants you to do your best to live at peace with everyone, but when you're not swept into the clique, don't fret. Brush the dust from your feet (and the cares from your heart) and move on. Without guilt. Without remorse. Without a second thought about what you could've done differently.

*Lord, show me how and when I need to brush the dust from my feet*
*and move on. Heal my heart from any broken places, I pray. Amen.*

# PRAISE FOR ANSWERED PRAYERS

*I've thrown myself headlong into your arms—*
*I'm celebrating your rescue. I'm singing at the top*
*of my lungs, I'm so full of answered prayers.*
PSALM 13:5-6 MSG

You know that wonderful feeling you get after eating a good meal? If you're from the south, you might push your chair back from the table and say, "I'm full as a tick!" There's a contentment you can't really put into words when you're full and satisfied.

The same is true of your walk with the Lord. When He rushes in to save you, when He fills you up with answered prayers, you can't help but push your chair back from the proverbial table and say, "Thank You, Lord!"

So, here's a question to ponder: How much time do you spend praising God after the fact? Are you like the leper in the story found in the Gospel of Luke 17:11-19? Are you one of the few who actually returns to thank Him for the prayers He answers? When your child is healed or a financial miracle takes place, do you gravitate back to the Savior to offer praise and thanksgiving? Or do you just let the craziness of life press you into that next important thing?

Today, make a mental list of the prayers God has recently answered for you. Begin to praise Him. For that praise will keep your knees from knocking when times are tough.

*Lord, You've done so many wonderful things and have answered*
*prayer after prayer. How can I help but praise You? Amen.*

# A NAME CHANGE

*"Your name will no longer be Jacob," the man told him.*
*"From now on you will be called Israel, because you have*
*fought with God and with men and have won."*
GENESIS 32:28 NLT

Have you ever wished for a do-over? Maybe you messed up in a major way and just wanted to go into hiding. Or perhaps the family you grew up in wasn't the best and you wanted to change your name and claim a completely different family.

God is in the name-changing business! There are multiple instances of name changes in both Old and New Testament stories. Perhaps God uses this tactic because we humans need convincing that we're not the same person we used to be. We need a tangible reminder of what He has saved us from and what He's saved us to.

Think about your life. Perhaps you have spoken words over your past, words like shame, bitterness, unforgiveness, guilt. Today, God longs to eradicate those names and give you a brand new one: forgiven! That's what happens when you have an encounter with the true and living God—everything changes!

*Lord, thank You for encountering my life with Your Spirit. I'm*
*not who I used to be, and I'm so grateful for that. I praise You for*
*giving me a new name, one that is written down in glory! Amen.*

# LOVE FOR THE
# LEAST OF THESE

*"I tell you the truth, of all who have ever lived, none*
*is greater than John the Baptist. Yet even the least person*
*in the Kingdom of Heaven is greater than he is!"*
MATTHEW 11:11 NLT

Today is Martin Luther King Jr. Day, the perfect time to examine this special verse from the eleventh chapter of the Gospel of Matthew. Jesus told His followers that John the Baptist (a true prophet) was the greatest of all the prophets who had ever lived. But then Jesus went on to say that, in spite of his earthly greatness, John was far less than the least person in heaven.

What did He mean?

When we get to heaven, we'll see people of every race, creed, and color. We won't look at them as "greater" or "lesser" in any way. We'll be one blood-bought tribe, singing the praises of our Savior forever. And, while John was great on earth, he'll be just one of the gang in heaven. We won't view him (or others like him) as any greater than the woman who begged for food on the side of the road.

Perhaps Jesus wanted His disciples to catch a glimpse of this truth: it's time to stop judging people by earthly standards. We're all one in Him—forgiven children of God.

*Lord, I get it! I'm not to elevate some and demean others.*
*We're one body, unified in You. Amen.*

## NIGHTTIME INSTRUCTION

*I will bless the LORD who guides me; even at night my
heart instructs me. I know the LORD is always with me.
I will not be shaken, for he is right beside me.*
PSALM 16:7-8 NLT

Ah, finally! You're all tucked in, the lights are off, and you're free to just relax. There, in that peaceful, quiet place, the Lord begins to whisper to your heart. He tickles your ear with His still, small voice and gives insight about the problems you're facing. Or perhaps He speaks to you through a dream, giving you ideas about how to handle a situation you're walking through.

Why do you suppose God often speaks in the night like this? You didn't deliberately set out to encounter Him in this way, after all! But, when your mind is finally free from the cares of the day, you're able to hear His voice. You aren't distracted by money worries or relationship squabbles or the roar of the television. You're finally free to just be. And the Lord sees this as the perfect time to give you instructions for the tasks ahead.

"I will not be shaken, for he is right beside me." This is true, you know. . .even when you sleep. So, whatever you're wrestling with during the daylight hours, sleep in peace, knowing God is still on the job, even when your eyes are closed.

*Lord, thank You for speaking to me in the night. Even then, my
heart instructs me as I hear Your still, small voice. Amen.*

## THE ENEMY'S TACTICS

*One day he went into the house to attend to his duties. . . .*
*She caught him by his cloak and said, "Come to bed with*
*me!" But he left his cloak in her hand and ran.*
GENESIS 39:11-12 NIV

The enemy is sly! He comes after you in such tricky ways that you don't always recognize his tactics. That's why it's so important to keep your guard up!

Maybe you've been there. You were trekking along just fine. Then, from out of the blue, you were hit with a false accusation or relationship struggle. You spent the first few minutes reeling, because it didn't make sense. Then, as the dust cleared, you began to see it for what it truly was. . .an attack.

When the enemy comes after you, you can (a) turn and run or (b) look him in the face and call him on his game. But remember, "No weapon forged against you will prevail, and you will refute every tongue that accuses you" (Isaiah 54:17 NIV).

The enemy can try all he likes, but you're God's anointed and covered by Him. Best of all, He'll fight your battles for you. So, don't panic when false accusations come. Don't let the attacks shake you or bring you down. God's going to rush to your defense. All you need to do is quiet your heart and trust Him.

*I trust You, Lord, even when everything inside of me is shaking*
*in anger. I'll look to You, my Defender! Amen.*

## GATHER, DON'T SCATTER

*"Whoever is not with me is against me,*
*and whoever does not gather with me scatters."*
MATTHEW 12:30 NIV

Remember playing Red Rover when you were a kid? You would link arms with several of your friends, then someone from the opposing team would race your way and try to break the chain of tightly linked arms.

That's how you must look at your witness. You're standing alongside the greats of the faith—Old and New Testament men and women who loved and served the Lord. So, you have to make sure your testimony (the way you live) lines up with the Word of God and with the testimonies of those who've walked before you.

Jesus says you're either a gatherer or a scatterer: your actions will either draw people to the Lord (gather) or send them running (scatter). So, which is it? When you look back over the way you've been living, would you say, in all honesty, that you're gathering souls for the kingdom, just as God calls you to do? Make the heart of the Lord happy by living a life that draws others to Him.

---

*Lord, I don't always get it right. Sometimes my example is flawed.*
*My actions are reactionary or based on whatever emotions I'm*
*feeling in the moment. But I want to set a good example so that*
*I can draw others to You. Help me, I pray. Amen.*

## DEEP WATERS

*He reached down from on high and took hold of me;*
*he drew me out of deep waters.*
PSALM 18:16 NIV

Have you ever been in a really dark place? Maybe you lost a spouse or a child and drifted into a deep depression, one you couldn't seem to pull yourself out of. Or maybe you were badly hurt by someone you trusted and sank to the depths after the fact.

Life has a way of tugging us downward. And sometimes, in spite of our best efforts, we have a hard time digging our way out. That's why it's so comforting to read today's verse. What we cannot do, God can.

Don't you just love the imagery here? God takes His hand, reaches down, and grabs hold of you when you're in the depths. He doesn't leave you there. He offers a way out. Then (no matter how hard you kick or scream) He "draws" you out.

There's something special about that word *draws*, isn't there? God doesn't yank you out. He doesn't holler and say, "Get out of there!" He gently, lovingly eases you out of the pit and sets your feet on solid ground. And when you're standing on the Rock (Jesus), you won't be shaken!

*Oh Lord, I'm so grateful for the many times You extended a hand my way. When I couldn't lift myself, You were right there, drawing me out. It's Your name I praise. Amen.*

## A FAMILY REUNION

*And Joseph said to his brothers, I am Joseph! Is my father
still alive? And his brothers could not reply, for they were
distressingly disturbed and dismayed at [the startling realization
that they were in] his presence. And Joseph said to his brothers,
Come near to me, I pray you. And they did so. And he said, I am
Joseph your brother, whom you sold into Egypt!*
GENESIS 45:3-4 AMPC

The story of Joseph is remarkable on many levels. He was an
avowed dreamer, one who claimed (based on his dreams) that
his brothers would one day bow down to him. They didn't take very
kindly to his bragging and tossed him into a pit, then sold him into
slavery.

After many years in Egypt, God elevated Joseph and put him in
a position of authority. In a random twist to the story, his hungry
brothers showed up, looking for food, but they didn't recognize him.
The brother they'd forsaken now had power to help them live or
allow them to perish (Genesis 42:5-7).

Joseph realized his childhood dream had come true. He drew
near to his brothers and welcomed them.

Maybe you're in a troubling situation with family members. It
has left you badly shaken. Let Joseph's story bring you hope. God
will honor the lost years if you keep on trusting and believing.

*Lord, there are hard situations in my family.
But I trust You. I won't give up. Amen.*

# A MUSTARD SEED OF FAITH

*The kingdom of heaven is like a grain of mustard seed,*
*which a man took and sowed in his field. Of all the seeds*
*it is the smallest, but when it has grown it is the largest of the*
*garden herbs and becomes a tree, so that the birds of*
*the air come and find shelter in its branches.*
MATTHEW 13:31-32 AMPC

Have you ever planted seeds in the ground? It's awe-inspiring to watch that teensy-tiny little seed blossom into a lovely plant. The process is remarkable, if you pause to think about it.

Jesus shared the story about the mustard seed to remind His followers that the burden of proof isn't on them. You don't have to have massive amounts of faith to witness a miracle in your life. You just need a teensy-tiny bit of faith in the One who's capable. If it were up to you (and aren't you glad it's not?), you could never grow your faith to the necessary proportions. But the weight is on God's shoulders, not yours. He's the miracle worker. He's the seed blossomer. He's the One who can take your impossible situation and (with a smidgeon of faith from you) completely turn it around.

What are you facing today? Take your mustard seed and plant it deep, then watch God intervene. He longs to grow your faith as He steps in to take control.

*Lord, thank You for growing my faith. I'll plant my little mustard*
*seed today and watch You perform on my behalf. Amen.*

## OUR TRUST IS IN HIM

*Now I know that the Lord saves His anointed; He will answer him from His holy heaven with the saving strength of His right hand. Some trust in and boast of chariots and some of horses, but we will trust in and boast of the name of the Lord our God.*

PSALM 20:6-7 AMPC

If someone were to ask you, "What do you put your trust in?" how would you respond? Some put their trust in their bank balance. Others put their trust in people. Still others put their trust in the stock market or in their jobs. Some trust in politicians or political parties.

God wants to remind you today that your trust needs to be in Him. If it's in anything earthly (or temporary), you'll be disappointed time and time again. But when you put your trust in the Lord, you will never face disappointment. He will answer you from heaven when you call. (Will your favorite politician do that?) He will reach down with His hand and save you. (Will your boss do that?) He has His grip on your circumstance. (Does your bank account have that?)

No one can do what God can do. No one (or no *thing*) can protect, guard, and secure you as the Lord can. So, shift your focus from the temporary to the eternal. Look to God, your Author and Salvation. He alone can save you.

*Lord, today I choose to place every situation I'm facing into Your capable hands. Do what only You can do, Father. Amen.*

## GOD MEANT IT FOR GOOD

*"As for you, you meant evil against me, but God meant it for good, to bring it about that many people should be kept alive, as they are today."*
GENESIS 50:20 ESV

"God can use it for good."

How many times have you heard those words? Maybe some well-meaning person spoke them after you lost your job. Or perhaps you read them in the Bible after the death of your spouse.

There are some situations so intense, so painful, that you doubt God can use them for good in your life. How can He take something so devastating and not only turn it around but bring good from it? It seems impossible when you're badly shaken.

It's time to take inventory. Grab a pen and paper. Begin to list the big crises you faced in your younger years—the things you felt sure you couldn't survive. Now, in a column to the right, list the good that has come out of those once-impossible situations.

There's an old saying that hindsight is 20/20. It's true. Looking back on what the Lord has done, could you conclude that He's truly in the business of turning things around? If so, then He can certainly take what you're walking through now and use it for good in your life. That's a promise!

*Lord, Your plan is to bring good from what I'm going through. So I'll speak words of faith over my situation, no matter how bleak things look in the natural. Amen.*

## LET IT NOT BE IN VAIN

*"This people honors me with their lips, but their heart
is far from me; in vain do they worship me, teaching
as doctrines the commandments of men."*

MATTHEW 15:8-9 ESV

**"D**o as I say, not as I do." Maybe you've heard those words. Perhaps you've even spoken them. It's one thing to espouse Christian beliefs, another thing to live them out in a way that proves your faith is unshakable. When your actions don't line up with the message coming from your lips, others will see you as being hypocritical. So, it's important to walk in alignment with the Word of God so your testimony isn't hampered.

No doubt you've met a few hypocrites in your day. The televangelist who screams at people to send in their hard-earned money but then ends up in a sex scandal. The friend who lectures others about their faith-walk then gossips behind their backs. The child who claims to love Jesus but cheats on a test.

It's not easy to walk the straight and narrow, but you've got to give it your best shot. And don't worry! Jesus is right there to help you get back on course if you veer to the right or left. Just do your best to honor Him with Your life, and you'll be an amazing testimony to all who're watching.

*Lord, I'm doing my best! Help me be a shining example
of what it means to follow after You. Amen.*

## SATISFIED

*The afflicted shall eat and be satisfied; those who seek him shall praise the LORD! May your hearts live forever!*
PSALM 22:26 ESV

Have you ever heard the expression "When you get to the end of your rope, tie a knot in it and hang on!"? Sometimes that's all you can do. But when you're hanging from that knot, it's good to know better days are coming so you won't be shaken or become too frayed. You have that assurance in today's scripture: "The afflicted shall eat and be satisfied."

Maybe you've had a terrible case of the flu. You went for a few days without food because your stomach just couldn't handle it. When you're in the middle of the pain, the notion of eating seems farfetched. But with the promise of eating and being satisfied, Jesus is giving you a hopeful message: "This won't last forever. Someday you're going to bounce back and life will seem normal again."

What do you do in the meantime? That answer is found in the second half of the verse: "Those who seek him shall praise the Lord!" Even if you're in a valley at the moment, go ahead and praise Him. Don't wait until you're seated at the banquet table to thank Him for the food. Praise Him now, ahead of your miracle.

*Lord, I won't wait. I'll praise You now. I know better days are coming. Life will go on. I will eat and be satisfied. Until then, my heart cries out a joyous, "Praise You, Father!" Amen.*

## A BOLD MOVE

*Then GOD said to Moses, "Go and speak to Pharaoh king of Egypt so that he will release the Israelites from his land." Moses answered GOD, "Look—the Israelites won't even listen to me. How do you expect Pharaoh to? And besides, I stutter."*

EXODUS 6:10-12 MSG

E xcuses, excuses. We're always loaded with excuses. "I can't do this because (fill in the blank)." "I can't do that because (list another excuse)." We let fear rob us of relationships, job opportunities, college educations, and even ministry moments. Fear grips our hearts. Our knees knock, our voice quivers, and we back down before we even start.

But why? Why do we freeze up? Why does our boldness go out of the window when given opportunities (or challenges from God)? He has promised to give us boldness in the moment, and we have to take those risks, scary as they might be.

Moses had his Pharaoh. David had his Goliath. You have your challenges. But you are up to the task. Ask the Lord for supernatural boldness to approach the things (or people) you need to approach. Don't back down. Stand up. . .and stand tall. When you do, God can use you to change not just your own life but (as in the case of Moses) countless others, as well.

*Lord, I'm facing some scary things. I don't have the courage on my own to do what needs to be done. But You have promised to fill me with boldness, and I'm counting on that, Father! Amen.*

# A DIVINE ENCOUNTER

*While he was going on like this, babbling, a light-radiant
cloud enveloped them, and sounding from deep in the
cloud a voice: "This is my Son, marked by my love,
focus of my delight. Listen to him."*

MATTHEW 17:5 MSG

Jesus led Peter, James, and John up a high mountain. When they got there, His entire appearance suddenly changed right in front of them. Sunlight beamed from His glowing face. Even His clothes were lit up!

Soon Moses and Elijah joined Jesus. They entered into a conversation with Him while the disciples looked on.

Then Peter gets a (very human) idea. He says, "Master, this is a great moment! What would you think if I built three memorials here on the mountain—one for you, one for Moses, one for Elijah?" (Matthew 17:4 MSG).

Before Jesus could respond, a bright light enveloped them and God spoke: "This is my Son, marked by love, focus of my delight. Listen to Him."

Whoa. No doubt you would've fallen to your face. That's what the disciples did. But when they opened their eyes, Moses and Elijah were gone. Only Jesus remained.

Isn't that the way it is? No matter who you want to build a shrine to—even those people you really admire—in the end it's only Jesus who is worthy of your love and praise. Stay focused on Him—unshaken and strong—and He will transform your heart!

*Lord, I'll keep my focus on You. I will give honor to no other! Amen.*

## HEADED IN THE RIGHT DIRECTION

*GOD is fair and just; He corrects the misdirected,
sends them in the right direction.*
PSALM 25:8 MSG

Maybe you've examined a situation you're going through and exclaimed, "It's just not fair!" Why does your child have to be the one with autism? Why is your mother the one with cancer? Why did your husband lose his job when your friends are all living in fancy houses and driving new cars?

Here's a difficult truth: no one ever said life was going to be fair. If it were, then why did Jesus Christ (who never committed a sin) have to die for you, a sinner? That's certainly not fair! But He made the choice to accept the "unfairness," to not let it deter Him. And you can have that same attitude: "I won't give up, even if this is wholly unfair."

Today, look at some of the areas of your life you've been grumbling about. What feels the most unfair? Your finances, aloneness, or health? Acknowledge it before God. Write it down. Then lift that paper up and say, "Jesus, this doesn't seem fair to me, but I won't let that come between us. I will keep on loving, serving, and praising You because I know I can trust You. You will work all out for good, Lord!"

*Yes, Lord! I can trust You! And You will work all things
out for good, even those things that seem totally unfair.
Because of that, I praise You. Amen.*

# THE BLOOD OF THE LAMB

*"When I see the blood I will pass over you."*
EXODUS 12:13 MSG

The story of what God did on the night of Passover has stood the test of time. Parents still tell their children about the night God passed over the homes of the Israelites and spared the lives of their first-born after seeing the blood on the doorpost. It's a compelling tale that points to an even greater one—the story of a King who gave His life on the "doorpost" of the cross so that God's vengeance would pass over you.

You are forgiven. You are set free! The blood of Jesus is not just your ticket to heaven, but the very essence of everything you are as a believer. It's your victory, when you feel like you're failing. It's your power, when you feel weak. The blood of Jesus is the gateway from the troubles of this life to the joys of the next.

Have you accepted Jesus into your heart? Have you allowed Him to cover your sins in that crimson flood? If not, then today is your day. Simply pray this prayer: "Father, I come to You a sinner, completely stained. I accept Your Son Jesus as my Savior and accept His cleansing work on Calvary as a covering for my sins. Thank You for the blood of the Lamb, Lord!" Amen.

*Oh, the blood of Jesus! How I praise You for that sacrifice, Father! It has changed everything! Amen.*

## STILL STANDING

*Fear not; stand still (firm, confident, undismayed)
and see the salvation of the Lord which He will work for
you today. For the Egyptians you have seen today you shall
never see again. The Lord will fight for you, and you
shall hold your peace and remain at rest.*
EXODUS 14:13-14 AMPC

*F*our times Moses reminds the people that God had brought them out of slavery by the strength of His hand (Exodus 13:3, 9, 14, 16). Why? Because he wants God's people to remember this fact and share it with their children.

Yet soon after God's miraculous plagues, His leading them by a cloud by day and a fire by night, as well as His foolproof escape plan, the people began to doubt as they stood between Pharaoh's army and the Red Sea. So Moses tells them to not fear but stand firm. The Israelites would never again see the Egyptian warriors plaguing them today. Not long after Moses' pronouncement, the Egyptians were swallowed up by the sea as God's people walked through on dry land.

Just as God was with those Israelites then, He's with you now. Their promises are yours. Thus, no matter how dire your circumstances, you can say with the psalmist, "I am certain that I will see the LORD's goodness in the land of the living" (Psalm 27:13 HCSB).

*Lord, thank You for freeing me, giving me the faith to
trust You, and giving me the confidence to stand
still as You work miracles in my life.*

## MULTIDIMENSIONAL

*The Lord is my Strength and my [impenetrable] Shield;*
*my heart trusts in, relies on, and confidently leans on Him.*
PSALM 28:7 AMPC

W ho is God to you?
    David, the singer and writer of Psalm 28, calls God his Rock. He asks Him to listen to his prayer and pleas. He voices and outlines his troubles, concerns, and fears. And before God does anything in his situation, David blesses Him just for listening to his prayer.

God was not just David's Strength but his Shield. A shield that no weapon could bend, dent, or destroy. God was not just someone but *the* Someone that David knew his heart could trust in, rely on, and lean on with confidence. Knowing this God was in his life, David was helped mentally, physically, emotionally, and spiritually. This knowledge, this confidence and surety, this certainty of God made David's heart sing to Him in joyful praise!

Toward the end of his psalm (Psalm 28:8), David calls God His Strength and Stronghold, his source of power and security. Yet David also knows God isn't just his defender but a gentle Leader who will nourish, shepherd, and carry His people forever (Psalm 28:9). David knew God was multidimensional—whoever David needed and claimed Him to be—in the moment.

Who is God to you today?

*God, You are my all in all, what I need in every situation. Be with me today, my Shield, Stronghold, Strength, and Shepherd.*

## THE POSSIBILITIES

*"It is easier for a camel to go through the eye of a needle than
for a rich person to enter the Kingdom of God! . . . Humanly
speaking, it is impossible. But with God everything is possible."*
MATTHEW 19:24, 26 NLT

Your God is a doer of the impossible.

At Mount Horeb, God's people were thirsty. So Moses cried out to God. And God told him to hit the rock with his staff. Moses did, and water flowed out (Exodus 17:1-6).

When an enemy army came out to fight the Israelites, Moses stood on the top of a hill. When he lifted "the rod of God" (Exodus 17:9) in his hands, the Israelites prevailed. When he lowered it, the enemy prevailed.

Woman of the Way, the Word reminds you that your God can do anything. No matter what your circumstances, there is no need for alarm, fright, despair, or hopelessness. For the One who can part the seas, calm the storms, and make a whale vomit can pull you out of harm's way, lift you from the pit, and shut the mouths of lions. All you need to do is trust, hope, pray, and believe. Your God will do the rest.

*Thank You, Lord, for giving me the hope and strength
I need to trust in You—the Doer of the impossible. Amen.*

## THE LIGHTNESS OF JOY

*He gets angry once in a while, but across a lifetime
there is only love. The nights of crying your eyes out give
way to days of laughter. . . . You changed wild lament
into whirling dance; you ripped off my black mourning
band and decked me with wildflowers.*

PSALM 30:5, 11 MSG

Because you have God in your life, any sorrows you may suffer are transient, temporary. But the joy you have in God, in Jesus, in the Spirit are persistent, eternal. And all you can do is laugh! For you know that your tears will fade. They will quickly dry up in the light of the morning. You'll find yourself willingly and easily praising God for bringing you out of the darkness of troubles and sorrow and back into the peace and lightness of joy.

How wonderful that after you pray to God, relating all your worries and woes, He turns things around for you. He changes your funeral dirge into a song and dance of celebration. He tears off your black mourning band and showers you with flowers. Next thing you know, you're bursting into songs of thanksgiving and praise of Him.

If you find yourself in the depths of sorrow and despair, go to the One who can pull you up out of the darkness and into the joy of the morning light.

*Lord, as I pray, take away my sorrows of the night
and lead me with the joy of Your morning light. Amen.*

# ANGEL AHEAD

*"Now get yourselves ready. I'm sending my Angel ahead
of you to guard you in your travels, to lead you to the place
that I've prepared. Pay close attention to him. Obey him.
Don't go against him. He won't put up with your
rebellions because he's acting on my authority."*
EXODUS 23:20-21 MSG

When you are walking God's way, treading upon the path He has laid out before you, you have nothing to fear. For God has sent His Angel ahead of you. And that Angel is going to guard you. He's going to make sure nothing outside of God's good will happens to you.

That very same Angel that has gone ahead of you is going to lead you safely as well. His mission is to help you get to the place God has already prepared for you. The only thing you must do is stay on God's path and listen to and obey what the Angel instructs you to do.

Amazingly enough, God not only sends His Angel ahead of you, He also sends His terror on ahead. Hornets will put to flight all those who might stand against you (Exodus 23:27-28).

The point is, when you are walking in God's will and way, you need not be worried about what lies ahead. God has a plan for your life. He's got you covered.

*I thank You, Lord, for taking care of me as I walk in the path
and abide by the plan You have put before me. Amen.*

## THE FAITH ADVANTAGE

*"If you embrace this kingdom life and don't doubt God, you'll not only do minor feats like I did to the fig tree, but also triumph over huge obstacles. This mountain, for instance, you'll tell, 'Go jump in the lake,' and it will jump. Absolutely everything, ranging from small to large, as you make it a part of your believing prayer, gets included as you lay hold of God."*
MATTHEW 21:21-22 MSG

J esus admitted that in this life you will have problems (John 16:33). Who doesn't? Even those who have money and treasures to fill twenty vacation homes have troubles. But those who are believers have an advantage over all the rest: their faith.

Jesus made sure His followers understood that as long as they had faith, as long as they didn't doubt the strength, the love, and the power of the God who created the universe, the visible and the invisible, they would overcome any obstacles that stood in their way—no matter how huge they appeared!

Some people see their obstacles as something they will never be able to overcome. Their doubts make them stop short, reconsider, then turn and run (Exodus 13:30-33). They see their obstacles as bigger than their own God!

Yet you're different. You know nothing—no barrier, problem, trouble, or burden—is bigger than your God. You have the faith advantage.

*I'm praying my believing prayer, Lord. Help me triumph over any obstacles that come my way, for nothing is bigger or more powerful than You!*

# GREAT GOODNESS

*How great is Your goodness that You have stored up for
those who fear You and. . .for those who take refuge in You.
You hide them in the protection of Your presence; You conceal
them in a shelter from the schemes of men. . . . Love the LORD,
all His faithful ones. . . . Be strong and courageous,
all you who put your hope in the LORD.*
PSALM 31:19-20, 23-24 HCSB

When you're up against it, where do you turn? When you see no way out, where do you go? When you are like a city under siege, who do you cry to?

No matter how far down you are, there's One waiting to grasp your hand, to pour blessings upon you, to provide you shelter. And that one person is God.

When you trust in God, He'll do anything to rescue you, protect you, and provide for you. The schemes others work against you will come to nothing. When you feel you've lost sight of His Light, when you cry out to Him, pleading to Him for help and mercy, He'll hear you. He'll move into action. He'll part the seas, stop the sun, and still the waves.

And what does God ask in return? That you love, obey, trust in, and follow Him. So, woman, be strong. Be brave. And put all your trust and hope in God. He will never fail you.

*I love You, Lord. Be my refuge,
my strength, my hope and heart. Amen.*

## YOUR HIDING PLACE

*Let everyone who is faithful pray to You at a time that You may
be found. When great floodwaters come, they will not reach him.
You are my hiding place; You protect me from trouble. . . .
I will instruct you and show you the way to go;
with My eye on you, I will give counsel.*
PSALM 32:6-8 HCSB

There are times when God calls His people to seek Him. He stirs
something within their hearts, reaching past their pain, and
touches their spirits. He wants them to respond to Him. To pray to
Him. For He is eager to answer, to help, to heal.

Throughout His Word, God makes it clear that all He wants is
the best for us. Yet all too often, we begin believing *we* know what's
best. So we step out in the direction that seems to be easiest, safest,
most prosperous.

Then, when troubles come, we realize our mistakes and missteps.
We begin to have misgivings, thinking that because we took our own
road, God may not answer us.

No matter where you are, what path you've taken, go to God.
Pray to Him. Let Him know what's happening in your life. Know that
He will hide you, protect you from trouble, and deliver you for the
darkness. Then allow Him teach you the *right* way to go.

*Lord, it's You I trust. Surround me with
Your faithful love as I come to You. Amen.*

## PERSONAL PRESENCE

*There I will meet with the Israelites, and the Tent of Meeting
shall be sanctified by My glory [the Shekinah, God's visible
presence]. . . . I will dwell among the Israelites and be their God.
And they shall know [from personal experience] that I am the
Lord their God, Who brought them forth out of the land of Egypt
that I might dwell among them.*
EXODUS 29:43, 45-46 AMPC

With God in our lives, we can be unshakable believers. Yet to maintain and replenish that unwavering confidence in our Lord God, we need to spend time in God's presence.

In the days of the Exodus, God made His presence known visibly. His people could see Him as the Shekinah, the visible presence in the Tent of Meeting. He has also appeared "before them by day in a pillar of cloud to lead them along the way and by night in a pillar of fire to give them light, that they might travel by day and by night" (Exodus 13:21 AMPC). God actually dwelt amid His people so that they could know Him from personal experience.

Today God's presence is within His people. Thus, to "see" Him or spend time with Him, all it takes is some quiet. Some silence. Some prayer. Some peace.

Find time each day to meet with your Lord, to personally experience His presence. And He will bring You forth.

*I come before You, Lord, seeking Your face. Make Your
presence known to me. Let's get personal. Amen.*

## NEVER SHAKEN

*The LORD's plans stand firm forever; his intentions can never be shaken. . . . The LORD watches over those who fear him, those who rely on his unfailing love. He rescues them. . . . He is our help and our shield. In him our hearts rejoice, for we trust in his holy name. Let your unfailing love surround us, LORD, for our hope is in you alone.*
PSALM 33:11, 18-22 NLT

G od has had a plan for you since the very beginning of time. Even before the world was founded, He chose you for a particular task, purpose, insight, reason (Ephesians 1:4-5). Along with creating you, God prepared you to do certain good works (Ephesians 2:10). In God's plan, you have a mission to perform.

Add God's mission for you to the fact that God's plans will never waver, that His "intentions can never be shaken," and you can be sure God will not only help you play it but protect, rescue, help, and shield you as you do so. Knowing you can always rely on God's unfailing love, that it surrounds you as a thick and high wall surrounds a city, what more is there to do but rejoice! For neither you nor God's plan for you will ever be shaken.

*Knowing Your plans for me can never be shaken nor Your great love for me ever be taken, I stand amazed, rejoicing in Your presence, my Lord, Help, and Shield! Amen.*

## NEEDING MORE

*Show me now Your way, that I may know You [progressively become more deeply and intimately acquainted with You, perceiving and recognizing and understanding more strongly and clearly] and that I may find favor in Your sight. . . . And the Lord said, My Presence shall go with you, and I will give you rest.*
EXODUS 33:13-14 AMPC

God had said He would send an angel to go before Moses and His people (Exodus 33:2, 12-16). But Moses told God that His sending an angel was not enough. Moses wanted more, so he asked for more. He asked for God's very presence to go with them, and God obliged.

Perhaps you too feel you need more. You want to know God better, to recognize Him, to understand His ways and means, to find out what He has in store for you and what His plans are.

Many of your questions can be answered by God's Word. Others can be addressed specifically to God in personal prayer.

Yet there is one thing that God wants you to be sure of, to take as fact. Just as with Moses, God's presence *is* walking with You. And He *will* give you all you need along the Way—including His rest.

*I want to know You more dearly and see You more clearly, Lord. Reveal Yourself to me. Walk with me and give me rest. Amen.*

## SEEKING GOD

*I sought the Lord, and he answered me and delivered me from all my fears. . . . The angel of the Lord encamps around those who fear him. . . . Those who seek the Lord lack no good thing. . . . Seek peace and pursue it. . . . The Lord is near to the brokenhearted and saves the crushed in spirit.*
PSALM 34:4, 7, 10, 14, 18 ESV

Anything you need can be found by applying to God. For He is the One listening, the One who will answer your cries and turn your fears into faith. When your courage is faltering, God will *thunk* down a wall of protection, surrounding you, keeping you from harm.

You see, God is looking to meet the eyes of those seeking His. And once that connection is made, there is nothing He will not do to bless you.

Your task is to simply do good things. To look for peace, embrace it. And on those days where your heart breaks, when you feel as if your spirit has been pounded down to the ground, He will be so close to you that You will feel His breath warm your neck. Feeling His presence so close, your spirit will immediately be lifted and embraced by His.

*You are my all in all, Lord. As I seek You, as I turn away from evil, as I look for Your peace, Lord, be ever so close to me.*

## JOY SHARE

*" 'Master, you gave me five talents. Look, I've earned five more talents.' "His master said to him, 'Well done, good and faithful slave! You were faithful over a few things; I will put you in charge of many things. Share your master's joy!' "*
MATTHEW 25:20-21 HCSB

God has given everyone at least one talent, something that each person is good at and the performance of which fits in with her circumstances. All He asks in return is that she *use* that talent. For as she does, He increases them. Jesus expresses this spiritual law with these words: "To everyone who has will more be given, and he will have an abundance. But from the one who has not, even what he has will be taken away" (Matthew 25:29 ESV).

In Jesus' eyes, this talentizing process is an ongoing one. For no matter how old you are, as you continue to use one talent, you'll be given more and more to use for the benefit of His unshakable kingdom.

Take some time to list all the talents God has given you. Consider which you are using or may have buried. Ask God for help in finding what you may be overlooking and discerning which new talents He has added. Then find a way to use them and, as you do so, share His joy!

*Thank You, Lord, for the talents with which You've gifted me. Help me to use them for Your glory. Amen.*

## SPREADING THE LOVE

*"Come, you who are blessed by my Father, inherit the Kingdom*
*prepared for you from the creation of the world. For I was*
*hungry, and you fed me. I was thirsty, and you gave me a drink.*
*I was a stranger, and you invited me into your home. I was*
*naked, and you gave me clothing. I was sick, and you cared*
*for me. I was in prison, and you visited me."*
MATTHEW 25:34-36 NLT

W ant to help God build up His unshakable kingdom? If your
answer is yes, you can do so by simply spreading His love
to others.

Eons ago, before the material world was made, God prepared
a kingdom for His followers, a wonderful and eternal paradise for
whoever believed in Him and followed His laws of love. Later His
Son Jesus made clear exactly what the Father wants from each of
His children: *to treat all people as if they were the sons and daughters*
*of God!*

That means that if you see a fellow female who's hungry, thirsty,
new in town, naked, ill, or in prison, you are to imagine she's Jesus—
and then feed her, give her water, welcome her, clothe her, take care
of her, and visit her. In other words, love her as you do yourself.

Today and every day, spread the love. And watch God's kingdom
grow.

*On this Valentine's Day, Lord, help me not look for what*
*I may get but for what I can give—in love. Amen.*

## GO WITH THE GLOW

*The Israelites set out whenever the cloud was taken up from
the tabernacle throughout all the stages of their journey. If the
cloud was not taken up, they did not set out until the day it was
taken up. For the cloud of the LORD was over the tabernacle by
day, and there was a fire inside the cloud by night, visible to the
entire house of Israel throughout all the stages of their journey.*
EXODUS 40:36-38 HCSB

When you are not sure where to go, when to go, or how long
to rest, look to the only guide you will ever need: God. That's
what the Israelites did.

The cloud was the token of God's presence. His people could
see it in the daytime hours, hovering over the tabernacle. At night,
the Israelites could see the fire aglow within the cloud. And these
symbols, these embodiments of God's presence could be seen by
everyone! The entire house of Israel. . .every. . .single. . .step. . .
and. . .stage. . .of. . .its. . .journey.

You too have a token of God's presence. You have the Holy Spirit
who teaches you how to follow the ways of Jesus. It's that burning
presence deep within you. Where and when it leads, you are to go.
Where and when it doesn't go, you are to rest.

*What a relief, Lord, knowing all I have to do is follow
the glow of the Spirit, and all will be well. Amen!*

## FOREVER FAITHFUL

*Your mercy and loving-kindness, O Lord, extend to
the skies, and Your faithfulness to the clouds.
Your righteousness is like the mountains of God.*
PSALM 36:5-6 AMPC

In this life, you have a choice. You can either go the way of the wicked, those to whom hearts sin whispers, making them blind to their own misdeeds. Or you can go the way of God's faithful love, allowing His mercy and loving-kindness to lead you in your journey.

Those who do evil have no fear of God. In fact, they think they're getting away with something, that God cannot see what they do. The words coming out of their mouths are full of lies, breeding trouble. At some point, says the psalmist, the evil ones will fall and be unable to rise again.

On the other hand, those who fear the awesome power of God yet follow Him, His light, and His love will always be helped up when they fall. God will rescue them, lift them above the fray, and bless them with His peace. They will find God's love is endless, His power unsurpassed, His protection unshakable.

When you feel as if the wicked are having their way, remember *they* can be shaken—whether they realize it or not. But you, woman of God, will never be moved!

*Lord, thank You for reminding me of Your love, light,
and power. You, my God and joy, are forever faithful!*

## CASCADING LIGHT

*How exquisite your love, O God! How eager we are to run under your wings, to eat our fill at the banquet you spread. . . . You're a fountain of cascading light, and you open our eyes to light. Keep on loving your friends; do your work in welcoming hearts. Don't let the bullies kick me around, the moral midgets slap me down. Send the upstarts sprawling flat on their faces.*

Psalm 36:7-11 msg

When you feel as if bullying bigwigs have their foot upon your neck, you have a place to go, a God to run to, One who will welcome you with open wings. This is not a manmade God. This is the God who made man, the Lord of light and love.

God is always there for you, waiting in the wings, waiting for you to look up, look over, look around for Him. He is the One holding the light for you so that you can find your way amid the darkness. He tells you which path to take, which decision to make. His love and light are never ending.

Need a break from the world's woes and evils? Run to God. Shelter under His wings. Make Him your ultimate refuge. He will keep you close, safe, and whole.

*Lord, I eagerly come to You, looking for shelter, help, light, and love. Be my refuge. Amen.*

## EYES ON GOD

*Delight yourself also in the Lord, and He will give you the
desires and secret petitions of your heart. Commit your way to
the Lord [roll and repose each care of your load on Him];
trust (lean on, rely on, and be confident) also in Him
and He will bring it to pass.*

PSALM 37:4-5 AMPC

God doesn't want you to waste your time and energy worrying about the wicked people around you, those who will soon be mowed over. God doesn't want you so focused on the shenanigans of ne'er-do-wells that you miss where He's working and where He's wanting your attention. Instead, He wants your eyes on Him.

Make it a point each day to move your focus away from all things but God. Spend your days and nights leaning on Him, relying on His Word, confident He will bring His promises to pass. Then you will have time and energy to do good, to hang out with the Lord of lords. Then, with your eyes on Him alone, He will fulfill all your desires.

In this moment, commit your way to God. Give Him every little and large concern that's on your mind. Trust Him to work things out. And you'll find yourself walking in and led by His warm, glowing, protective light.

*I come before You, Lord, leaving all my cares at Your feet,
trusting You to work all things out. In this moment I commit to
focusing on and delighting in You. Amen.*

## LEAN BACK

*Be still and rest in the Lord; wait for Him and patiently lean yourself upon Him; fret not yourself because of him who prospers in his way, because of the man who brings wicked devices to pass. Cease from anger and forsake wrath; fret not yourself—it tends only to evildoing. For evildoers shall be cut off, but those who wait and hope and look for the Lord. . .shall inherit the earth.*
PSALM 37:7-9 AMPC

When someone wants to pick a fight, it's hard to stand still, to not get angry. All those instincts that prompt you to strike back at the one who has struck you are just what God wants you to ignore. Getting angry and fighting back only makes things worse.

Instead of lifting a hand to harm the one who has harmed you, you're to lean back against God, to be still, to rest in the One who wants you to be a woman of peace, not turmoil. Why? Because it's peaceful women of strength, character, and faith who'll inherit the earth.

Remember, God will take care of the evildoers. He'll cut them off at the knees. Meanwhile, *your* steps and plans will be directed by the Lord. Walk in time with Him and you'll never lose your way.

*Thank You, Lord, for being my Guard, Guide, Refuge, and Stronghold. Help me to leave the wicked in Your hands so that I can keep my peace and joy in You. Amen.*

## "NOTHING TO FEAR HERE"

*The guards at the tomb were scared to death.*
*They were so frightened, they couldn't move. The angel*
*spoke to the women: "There is nothing to fear here."*
MATTHEW 28:4-5 MSG

The morning after Jesus' death on the cross, two women—Mary Magdalene and the other Mary—head to Jesus' tomb to keep vigil there. Suddenly, as the earth shakes, an angel of God descends from heaven. He rolls the rock away from the tomb entrance, then sits there on top of the boulder. The men guarding the tomb were so afraid they froze.

The angel begins speaking to the women, saying, "Don't be afraid. Don't be alarmed. All is well. I know you're looking for Jesus. He's not here but was raised, just as He said He would be."

Once he'd calmed down the Marys, the angel told them to tell the other believers that Jesus was alive and would meet up with them in Galilee. So the women ran off, filled with joy. When they met Jesus along the way, He too told them not to be afraid but to go and tell the others to meet Him in Galilee.

The message Jesus gave the Marys is the same message He gives you. Don't allow anything to shake you up. Don't fear anything or anyone. Simply do as Jesus has told you to do, with joy in every step.

*Lord Jesus, help me to look for You in all things,*
*to stay calm, and go Your Way in joy. Amen.*

## CONTINUAL CARE

*Immediately the [Holy] Spirit [from within] drove Him out
into the wilderness (desert), and He stayed in the wilderness
(desert) forty days, being tempted [all the while] by Satan;
and He was with the wild beasts, and the angels ministered
to Him [continually]. . . . Jesus said to them,
Come after Me and be My disciples.*
MARK 1:12-13, 17 AMPC

From the very beginning, God wanted us to be like Jesus, to follow His example, walk in His Way. And although that may be a huge challenge, remember the tasks God gives you are also the tasks for which He equips you (Hebrews 13:21). In other words, in all the challenges you face, you have a God who makes sure you have resources on which to rely.

After Jesus was baptized and the Holy Spirit lit on Him like a dove, that same Spirit drove Him into the wilderness where He was surrounded by wild beasts. There He stayed for over a month, all the while being teased and tempted by Satan. Talk about a challenge!

Yet Jesus remained unshaken. For not only was God the Spirit with Him, but God the Father had sent angels to take care of Him *continually*!

The next time you feel you're out in the wilderness among the beasts, surrounded by a myriad of temptations, don't crumble. Instead, take courage. For God has already equipped you with the Spirit and His caretaking angels.

*Thank You, Lord, for equipping me
with a calling as well as comforters! Amen.*

# A DESERTED PLACE

*In the morning, long before daylight, He got up and went out to
a deserted place, and there He prayed. And Simon [Peter] and
those who were with him followed Him [pursuing Him eagerly
and hunting Him out], and they found Him and said to Him,
Everybody is looking for You.*
MARK 1:35-37 AMPC

J esus, while passing by the Sea of Galilee, had met some men and
called them to follow Him. From there He traveled to Capernaum,
taught in the local synagogue, and rebuked a spirit from a man
attending the service.

Next Jesus went to Simon Peter's house. There He learned
Simon's mother-in-law was sick in bed with a fever. Immediately
Jesus approached her, took her hand, and raised her up. The fever
left, and she began to serve her son-in-law's guests. After sunset,
droves of townspeople with afflictions, diseases, and demons came
to Jesus, and He cured them.

The next morning, way before sunrise, Jesus got up, went out
alone, found a desolate spot, and began to pray. Yet even there His
seeking disciples found Him and called Him, back into their world.

Woman of the Way, even Jesus took a break. Even Jesus knew
the only way to be empowered and reenergized was to spend time
away and alone with God, in His world.

---

*Lord, here I am. Alone with You once more. May I find
peace and rejuvenation here in Your presence so that
I can continue the work You've called me to do.*

## GREAT PATIENCE AND FAITH

*I waited patiently for the LORD; he inclined to me and heard my cry. He drew me up from the pit of destruction, out of the miry bog, and set my feet upon a rock, making my steps secure. He put a new song in my mouth, a song of praise to our God.*

PSALM 40:1-3 ESV

God is always there to help you—even on those days when you're lower than low, when it takes all your strength to cry out to God. But there's some effort needed on your part to make this arrangement with God work.

When you need help, you may need to wait for God to move. And you must do so with great patience and faith. Patience to not give up but to persistently seek God's help. And faith that God has heard your cry and will move, according to His timing.

Know that God *will* pluck you from the miry bog in which your feet are stuck. Be certain He *will* plant you down upon a rock, making sure you've got your balance back. And remain confident that when you've had a chance to catch your breath, God *will* put a new song of praise in your mouth, a heavenly tune filled with love and thanksgiving.

*I'm keeping my eyes focused on You as I wait upon You, Lord. For I'm certain You'll see and hear my cries and lift me out of the pit and up to You. Amen.*

# A READY BOAT

*Jesus went off with his disciples to the sea to get away.*
*But a huge crowd from Galilee trailed after them. . . .*
*He told his disciples to get a boat ready so he*
*wouldn't be trampled by the crowd.*
MARK 3:7-9 MSG

J esus was having one of those days. A day when no matter where He went, He faced a myriad of people.

He tried to get away by going for a boat ride. But the crowds continued to follow Him. They'd heard all about how He'd healed many—spiritually, emotionally, mentally, physically. Some wanted to witness His work. Others wanted to receive their own healing.

Thus, amid this swarm of people, Jesus made sure His disciples would always have a little boat ready for Him, a safe haven where He could take refuge when the pressure was too great.

What safe haven do you have standing by? Where is your refuge, the place you can escape to when you need some space?

Jesus understands you will, from time to time, need a retreat. So why not ask Him what the perfect place would be for you, a place that would always be standing by, at the ready?

*Lord Jesus, help me find my own readied boat, a place where*
*I can run to when I need some breathing room. Help me find a*
*refuge where I can recharge and be renewed by You. Amen.*

## A BEAUTIFUL RECOMPENSE

*Oh, the joys of those who are kind to the poor! The LORD*
*rescues them when they are in trouble. The LORD protects*
*them and keeps them alive. He gives them prosperity in the*
*land and rescues them from their enemies. The LORD nurses*
*them when they are sick and restores them to health.*
PSALM 41:1-3 NLT

I n this world there are many people who are poor in spirit, health, and wisdom. Yet they are not without hope, for God encourages His believers to help those who cannot help themselves.

In fact, God promises to *bless* the believer who looks upon such people with a tender heart, with compassion, knowing that what others suffer could have been her lot as well. When such a child of God extends a hand to help others, showing her mercy and love, God will pay her back in kind.

When you endeavor to help others, you can be sure God will endeavor to help you, whether that means getting you out of trouble, protecting you, nourishing you, prospering you, rescuing you, nursing you, or restoring you. God promises you such a recompense in this world—and the next!

Blessed are you who has compassion for and moves to help those less fortunate. For as you bless others, God will bless you.

*Lord, open my eyes and heart to the people around me. Show*
*me today who I can bless. In Jesus' name I pray, amen.*

# A MIGHTY GOD

*When Jesus woke up, he rebuked the wind and said to the*
*waves, "Silence! Be still!" Suddenly the wind stopped,*
*and there was a great calm. Then he asked them,*
*"Why are you afraid? Do you still have no faith?"*
MARK 4:39-40 NLT

Jesus had spent a long day preaching to the crowds, then explaining His teachings to His disciples. When evening set in, He suggested they leave the crowd and go by boat across the sea.

While Jesus slept in the stern, His head resting on a cushion, a storm came up. The wind howled and the waves grew, breaking over the boat and filling it with water. Panicked, the disciples came to Jesus, waking Him up, and asking, "Don't you care that we're in such danger?"

Woman, Jesus knows that in this life you will have storms. In fact, He tells you to *expect* them (John 16:33). All He asks is that you not fear. For Jesus is already in your boat, riding the waves with you. Simply appeal to Him, and He will calm the storm with His words, "Silence! Be still!"

Remember: "Mightier than the violent raging of the seas, mightier than the breakers on the shore—the LORD above is mightier than these!" (Psalm 93:4 NLT). Never fear. God's got this.

*Help me, Lord, to remember You have power and might over*
*all things—and are riding the waves of the storms with me.*
*With You in my boat, I need never be afraid! Amen.*

## TAPPING INTO POWER

*She. . .touched his robe. For she thought to herself,*
*"If I can just touch his robe, I will be healed."*
*Immediately the bleeding stopped. . . . Jesus realized*
*at once that healing power had gone out from him.*
MARK 5:27-30 NLT

A nameless woman with an issue of blood had gone to so many doctors, trying to be healed of her internal hemorrhaging. She'd spent everything she'd had for a cure, but instead of getting better, she grew worse. Then she heard about Jesus.

One in a crowd of many, the woman came up behind Jesus. As she reached out to touch Him, she thought, "If I can just touch his robe, I will be healed." That silent prayer of faith enabled her to tap into the power of a living God. And she became whole once more.

Knowing His power had been released, Jesus stopped. He asked who'd touched Him. Trembling, the woman came before Him, fell at His feet, and confessed it had been she. His verbal response was as potent as His physical release of power as He put words to her experience, saying, "Daughter, your faith has made you well" (Mark 5:34 NLT).

When you need help, take up your mantle of trust, extend your hand, and make a connection with Jesus. And you too will be able to tap into His power.

*I reach out to You in this moment, Jesus, my faith in hand. Amen.*

# FORWARD IN FAITH

*While He was still speaking, there came some from the ruler's
house, who said [to Jairus], Your daughter has died. Why
bother and distress the Teacher any further? Overhearing but
ignoring what they said, Jesus said to the ruler of the synagogue,
Do not be seized with alarm and struck with fear;
only keep on believing.*
MARK 5:35-36 AMPC

J airus, a leader of a local synagogue, approached Jesus, then fell at
His feet. He begged Jesus to come lay His hands on his daughter
so that she would live. Jesus began following Jairus to his house. But
soon this mission was interrupted by a woman with an issue of blood.

While Jesus was dealing with the hemorrhaging woman, some
people came from Jairus's house, telling him, "Your daughter has
died. Why bother and distress the Teacher any further?" But Jesus
had overheard their words. And He ignored them, simply telling
Jairus to not fear but keep on believing. Jairus did. And his daughter
was healed.

Woman of God, Jesus calls you to a life full of trust in Him—
regardless of your current circumstances. He steers you away from
fear and forward in faith. For there your miracle, reward, and peace
await.

*There are times, Lord, when fear seems to overcome my faith.
Help me turn that around. Help me steer away from fear and
move forward in faith. In the name of Jesus, I pray. Amen.*

## RESPITE

*The Lord said to Moses, "Speak to the Israelites and say to them:
'These are my appointed festivals, the appointed festivals of
the Lord, which you are to proclaim as sacred assemblies. There
are six days when you may work, but the seventh day is a day
of sabbath rest, a day of sacred assembly. You are not to do any
work; wherever you live, it is a sabbath to the Lord.'"*

LEVITICUS 23:1-3 NIV

Through Moses, the Lord gave His people a solid foundation on which they can live a balanced life. This structure permits you six days in which to work, but declares that on the seventh day, you should rest for your well-being. It is a respite from everyday life and gives you a chance to slow things down from earthly activity.

In this fast-paced world, it is important to take some time for yourself and to give thanks to God for His many blessings. How wonderful that you can hit PAUSE on the remote control of your life and enjoy some quiet time with Him. Through God's grace, you have the foundation for a well-lived, balanced life. Empowered through God's perfect structure, you can be the best you can be.

*Dear Lord, help me structure my life based on your unshakable
foundation created just for me. Thank You for considering my every
need, both spiritual and physical, and for this day of rest. Amen.*

## STORM CHASER

*They all saw him and were terrified. Immediately he spoke
to them and said, "Take courage! It is I. Don't be afraid."
Then he climbed into the boat with them, and the wind
died down. They were completely amazed.*

MARK 6:50-51 NIV

If you have ever been caught driving in torrential weather, you
know the fear a storm can evoke. No longer in control, you feel
helpless. Mark says the disciples were "terrified" and that amid their
fright, Jesus boarded their boat and immediately quelled the storm.

In the boat of your life, Jesus is always with you. He's there to
chase away the storms you encounter upon your voyage. Jesus will
never abandon you, even in the fieriest of days. Simply ask Him to
stay with you, trusting He will help you navigate your way through
those tough times.

God says, "Follow my decrees and be careful to obey my laws,
and you will live safely in the land" (Leviticus 25:18 NIV). He promises
your safety, so you can rest assured He will always have your back.

The next time you find yourself in turbulent waters, remember
you're not alone. God will lead you through safely, as promised.
Simply trust in His guidance, even if He takes you through a channel
you would not have chosen. Remember, God's GPS is so much more
trustworthy than yours!

*Dear Lord, I put my faith in You. Lead me through the storms in
my life and help me stay afloat while in turbulent waters.*

## FEARLESS

*"If you follow my decrees and are careful to obey my commands. . .
I will grant peace in the land, and you will lie down and no one
will make you afraid. I will remove wild beasts from the land,
and the sword will not pass through your country."*
LEVITICUS 26:3, 6 NIV

D id you ever wake up in the middle of the night, filled with fear
for an unknown reason? Perhaps you had a nightmare. Maybe
you heard a noise. Whatever the reason, the fear was real in the
darkness of night.

In Leviticus 26, God reminds you that He will keep you safe and
will grant you peace in exchange for your faithfulness to Him and
your observance of His commandments. In Leviticus 2:26 (NIV), He
states, "I am the Lord." What a wonderful assurance of His sovereignty
and His ability to protect you!

God offers the same assurance to you. You can lie down and
trust that you will have peace and protection from all fears. Believe.
Have faith in God. It is such a small ask on your part for security
and tranquility in your life!

*Dear Lord, help me to adhere to Your observances and
commandments. Help me to do what is right in Your eyes
and to be able to enjoy Your peace and Your assurance so
that I will be unafraid. Help me to face each day in peace.*

## SHAKEN NOT STIRRED

*God is our refuge and strength, an ever-present help in trouble.
Therefore we will not fear, though the earth give way and the
mountains fall into the heart of the sea, though its waters roar
and foam and the mountains quake with their surging.*
PSALM 46:1-3 NIV

Remember the old James Bond films? The title character always took his martinis "shaken, not stirred." This is a perfect description of God's promise in this psalm. Though things around you may quake and mountains may tremble, you are always safe in His loving arms.

God is your refuge from any storm and your strength when times get tough. So while you can be shaken physically, you *cannot* be stirred spiritually. For you are held tight by God. And in His presence, there is no need to fear.

Need a little more proof? Psalm 46:7 reminds you that God, the One who holds the ultimate power in this world and the next, is the mighty fortress who is always surrounding you and always with you.

Today, recognize who God is. Then do as God, through the psalmist, suggests: "Let be and be still, and know (recognize and understand) that I am God" (Psalm 46:10 AMPC). And you'll find yourself unshaken and abiding in His everlasting peace.

*Dear God, as the world trembles and quakes around me,
help me to not be afraid. Remind me that You are my strength,
and I can always take refuge in Your great love.*

## MOMENTARILY TONGUE-TIED

*Then a cloud appeared and covered them, and a voice came
from the cloud: "This is my Son, whom I love. Listen to him!"*
MARK 9:7 NIV

During the Transfiguration, Elijah and Moses appeared on the
mountaintop with Jesus. When His clothes became "dazzling
white," Peter, James, and John were momentarily dumbstruck. Very
confused and astonished at this incredible sight, Peter, not really
sure what to say, offered to build three shelters for Elijah, Moses,
and Jesus. Then, suddenly, a voice from above made it all clear. God
spoke, saying, "This is my Son, whom I love. Listen to him!" And
suddenly, the three men saw no one but Jesus.

Jesus talks to all believers, including you, although sometimes
it may be hard to hear Him. Although His voice may sometimes get
lost in the clutter of life, He is most definitely there, waiting for you
to turn your mind to Him.

Listen for Jesus' words in your heart. Dive into the Gospels in
which you can see His words and their intent. Allow them to guide
your actions. Pray for direction, knowing that with Jesus the Word
in your heart, you will find peace of mind and clarity of thought.

*Dear God, I thank You for the gift of Your perfect Son.
Help me to listen to Him and to follow His Word and teachings.
For then I will find direction, wisdom, peace, and clarity.*

## AT YOUR SERVICE

*Sitting down, Jesus called the Twelve and said, "Anyone who wants to be first must be the very last, and the servant of all."*
MARK 9:35 NIV

A t first glance, the verse above might not make much sense. How can the last be first? If you run a race and come in last, you don't win, right? Or do you?

There was a runner in a cross-country competition who got injured mid-race. She collapsed, unable to get up. Many competitors ran past her, not giving her a second glance. However, one girl did not hesitate to stop to help her rival up. Putting her arms around her, she practically carried the injured girl toward the finish line. But her selflessness didn't stop there.

When she finally arrived at the finish line, the rescuer positioned herself in such a way that the injured girl would cross the line just before her. Though they were the last ones to cross, this heroine was the clear winner of the race. She was last. But she finished first.

When Jesus spoke the words of today's verse, He was preparing His disciples for a time when He would no longer be among them. He clearly urged them to serve others and in this way be first in the eyes of the Lord. If you follow His wisdom, you will always come out the winner.

*Dear God, help me to selflessly serve others and, in so doing, be first in Your eyes.*

## IMPOSSIBLE IS POSSIBLE

*The disciples were even more amazed,
and said to each other, "Who then can be saved?"
Jesus looked at them and said, "With man this is impossible,
but not with God; all things are possible with God."*
MARK 10:26-27 NIV

This passage from Mark is one of the most uplifting and powerful messages in the scriptures. It is a reassurance from Jesus that with His Father in your corner, nothing is impossible. These simple words pack a powerful punch. What is there to worry about if God is there for you to make all things possible?

In the struggles of everyday life, it's easy to get overwhelmed. But if you carry this idea—that with God *all* things are possible—within you and trust in God with all your heart, He will get you through even the toughest of times.

Sometimes, when you are in the bleakest of situations, it is difficult to see the light at the end of the tunnel. But God *is* that light. He *is* there. When the fog of doubt is lifted, you can see plainly that He's been there to guide you all along. Remember, God didn't say "*some* things are possible," He said "all."

*Dear God, help me trust in You completely. Remind me
each day that with You, I can face anything and everything.
For with You,* all *things* are *possible.*

## POWER OF FAITH

*"What do you want me to do for you?" Jesus asked him.*
*The blind man said, "Rabbi, I want to see."*
*"Go," said Jesus, "your faith has healed you." Immediately*
*he received his sight and followed Jesus along the road.*
MARK 10:51-52 NIV

Do you remember the 1930's children's book *The Little Engine That Could*? This American folktale, as related by Watty Piper, was meant to teach children optimism and belief in themselves. It was about a little train engine tasked with pulling a long train of stranded freight cars over a steep mountain. Larger engines declined to try, but this little engine took on the seemingly impossible task. What separated this little guy from the rest? He had faith. He believed. His mantra, "I think I can," resonated throughout his journey.

In the verses above, the blind man was healed by his faith in Jesus. Not by medicine, not by treatments, not by specialists. He was healed only because He believed in *God's Son who could do anything*.

Faith in God can help you get through any weighty issue. Nothing is too heavy for God to handle if you truly believe He can.

*Dear God, some days the load seems so heavy,*
*the burdens so great, the afflictions insurmountable.*
*Please help me to keep my faith strong, to know that*
*You will help me with any and all challenges if I simply*
*trust in You, convinced that You can do anything.*

## MORNING BLESSING

*"The LORD bless you and keep you; the LORD*
*make his face shine on you and be gracious to you;*
*the LORD turn his face toward you and give you peace."*
NUMBERS 6:24-26 NIV

As you head out the door in the morning, remember this blessing given by God to Moses for the Israelites. What wonderful words to begin any journey in your day, be it a commute to work, a drive to the supermarket, a ride to school, or wherever you're heading. Imagine the joy the Israelites must have felt to know that God blessed them with a reminder and reassurance of His protection, favor, kindness, approval, and peace.

You too can be confident in God and empowered by all His blessings, such as this one related by God to you through Jeremiah: "For I know the thoughts and plans that I have for you. . .thoughts and plans for welfare and peace and not for evil, to give you hope in your final outcome" (Jeremiah 29:11 AMPC).

Woman of God, the Lord knows your future and gives you peace and hope, even when you cannot see where your life may be heading. What better gift could there be to keep yourself standing tall and unshaken?

*Dear God, I thank You for the wonderful blessings You have*
*given me. I pray Your gift of peace would be with me, giving me*
*strength and courage to begin each day's journey.*

# LIFETIME GUARANTEE

*"And call on me in the day of trouble;*
*I will deliver you, and you will honor me."*
PSALM 50:15 NIV

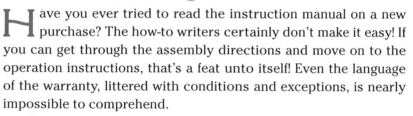

Have you ever tried to read the instruction manual on a new purchase? The how-to writers certainly don't make it easy! If you can get through the assembly directions and move on to the operation instructions, that's a feat unto itself! Even the language of the warranty, littered with conditions and exceptions, is nearly impossible to comprehend.

Take heart. For there is one manual you will never have trouble deciphering. It's found in Psalm 50, the ultimate, concise, and clear-cut instruction manual for what to do when you're troubled. Step 1: Call on the Lord. Step 2: Know the Lord will deliver you. Step 3: Give thanks to the Lord and honor Him. Then, simply repeat steps 1 to 3 as needed.

The relief you need is just that easy and guaranteed. But this is a guarantee like no other, for this one is backed 100 percent by the Manufacturer, the maker of all, the Lord God.

With God's guarantee, you have nothing to fear. When you're in trouble, just remember these three simple steps: call on God, have faith He will deliver you, and honor Him. What could be easier?

*Dear God, thank You for this incredible and*
*wondrous guarantee for my life! Because of You,*
*I know I can and will be safely delivered.*

# THE GREATEST

*"To love him with all your heart, with all your understanding
and with all your strength, and to love your neighbor as yourself
is more important than all burnt offerings and sacrifices."*
MARK 12:33 NIV

I f asked what the most important rule for living was, could you answer without hesitation? In Mark's Gospel, Jesus did just that. A teacher of the law asked Him which of God's Commandments was the most important. Jesus did not skip a beat. His answer is the key for a better life. Love. Love your God. Love your neighbor as you love yourself.

In 1 Corinthians 13, the apostle Paul speaks of love. In verse 13, he echoes the words of Jesus, writing, "And now these three remain: faith, hope and love. But the greatest of these is love."

Love is potent. Whether you're on the giving or getting end, there are few things more powerful. In loving God with all your heart and loving your neighbor as yourself, you too will reap the benefits. In keeping your thoughts positive and focusing on love, you eliminate the negative in your life.

Love does indeed conquer all because God *is* love (1 John 4:8 NIV).

*Dear God, it's so amazing that love is the key that unlocks
the door to a more empowered and godly life. Help me,
Lord, to closely follow Your command to love by better
loving You, my neighbor, and myself. Amen.*

# RENEWED

*Let me hear joy and gladness;*
*let the bones you have crushed rejoice.*
PSALM 51:8 NIV

No human is perfect. This is proven by King David, the author of Psalm 51. He, the apple of God's eye (Psalm 17:8), made his fair share of mistakes. One big error was committing adultery with Bathsheba. Sometime afterward, he felt crushed by the weight of sin and regret and guilt, all of which were a heavy load to bear. David describes the painful effects of his sin as crushed bones.

Although David's misstep did not take away from his greatness as a ruler or from his wisdom, it gnawed at him to the point that he felt compelled to ask forgiveness of God.

Years later, Matthew would write in his Gospel: "Ask and it will be given to you; seek and you will find; knock and the door will be opened to you" (Matthew 7:7 NIV). Jesus tells us that if it's forgiveness you seek, you just have to ask. God will never slam the door in your face. Instead, He will leave it wide open for you to humbly make amends.

David ends verse 8 of this psalm on an encouraging word: "rejoice." That's something you too can feel when you ask God to forgive you and you feel the burden of sin lifted.

*Dear God, I pray You will forgive me of my sins*
*and restore the joy and gladness in my heart.*

## HEART OF GOLD

*Create in me a pure heart, O God,
and renew a steadfast spirit within me.*
PSALM 51:10 NIV

Do you remember playing with clay or Play-Doh when you were a child? You could mold a blob into whatever you wanted—an animal, a flower, a person, wherever your mood took you. Or maybe you remember building things with Lego blocks. Again, you had the ability and freedom to create something amazing from individual interlocking blocks. But God, the Master Craftsman, has the ability to create something much more magnificent—a pure heart within you!

Yet that's not all! David tells us that the almighty God has the ability to "renew a right, persevering, and steadfast *spirit* within" (Psalm 51:10 AMPC, emphasis added) you.

No matter what you've done or where you've been, God renews you just as He has renewed "the ruined cities that have been devastated for generations" (Isaiah 61:4 NIV). He can restore to you "the joy of your salvation and grant [you] a willing spirit" (Psalm 51:12 NIV), one that will sustain you!

What a blessing! A pure heart and steadfast spirit and joy—all you need for a life of grace and happiness. It is yours for the asking. So why not ask today?

*Dear God, I ask that You create a pure heart within me, renew
and fortify my spirit, forgiving me my failures and sins. And,
Lord, I pray You would also restore the joy of my salvation
and bless me with a willing spirit. Amen.*

## STRONG ROOTS

*But I am like an olive tree flourishing in the house of God;*
*I trust in God's unfailing love for ever and ever.*
PSALM 52:8 NIV

Some people don't trust in God for their strength and protection. Instead, they trust in and find their confidence from the amount of money they make, their bank balance, and all the material possessions they have garnered.

But the woman of God is another person altogether. She likens herself to a green olive tree. She's planted in the house of God, with her branches extending outward and upward, reaching a height of 50 feet and a width of 20 feet. Because her root system is closer to the surface, she can easily absorb moisture and scant rainfall to survive drought conditions. Because she relies on God, trusting in His loving-kindness and mercy, she flourishes in His care.

Today, remind yourself who you are and *whose* you are. Realize where your confidence is best placed. Remember who has provided you with shelter from the storms, protected you from outside dangers, and nourished you. Allow God's love and care to give you unshakable strength and fortitude.

*Dear God, it is on You alone I rely. It's my trust in Your unfailing love that helps me flourish in Your heavenly house. Thank You for giving me the care and attention I crave and the unshakable strength and fortitude that keeps me growing. In You I pray, amen.*

## HEAVENLY EYES

*God looks down from heaven on all mankind to see if
there are any who understand, any who seek God.*
PSALM 53:2 NIV

A s a child, you likely remember your parents looking down on you, making sure you were safe and had all you needed. That is the role of a good parent. As a result, you felt safe and loved. There was no stress regarding how you would survive or where your next meal was coming from. There was just the knowledge that your needs were covered. And if you needed help, all you had to do was find your parents, look up at them, and ask.

Now that you're all grown up, your parents may or may not be around. But your heavenly Father definitely is. He looks down from heaven on you to see if you understand what He's doing in your life. He wants to see if you are seeking Him.

As God looks down from heaven, He wants you to know He has everything under control. All He asks is that you look to *Him* for all things. That You be faithful to Him, living your life in accordance with His teachings and striving to better understand His Word.

Today, look to God for what you may need (Psalm 121:1-2). And while you do so, remember God is looking down, watching over you.

---

*Dear God, look down on me as I, in turn, look upward,
seeking You and working to broaden my understanding of You.*

# RESCUED

*You have delivered me from all my troubles,*
*and my eyes have looked in triumph on my foes.*
PSALM 54:7 NIV

E veryone has them. Troubles. Adversaries. Foes.

In Psalm 54, David tells us that he has literally looked into the eyes of his foes because they were that close. And yet, the Lord delivered him from them *and* their evil.

Do you have troubles? Are you afraid? Do what David did. He first asked God to save Him, recognizing God had the power and strength to do so. Then he asked God to listen to his prayer, his complaint. He gave God the exact situation he was in and described his attackers as "people without regard for God" (Psalm 54:3 NIV).

At one point, David seemed to be talking to himself, reminding himself who God is, writing, "Surely God is my help; the Lord is the one who sustains me" (Psalm 54:4 NIV).

In the end of this psalm, David writes as if God has already delivered him, as He always has in the past—and acknowledged that his enemies will be the losers.

When you need help, remember that just as God delivered David from deadly peril, He will deliver you. All that is required is that you believe, that You have faith in God's power to conquer your foes.

*Dear God, I have faith that You will deliver me from*
*my troubles. Through You, I will triumph!*

## TERRA FIRMA

*Cast your cares on the LORD and he will sustain you;*
*he will never let the righteous be shaken.*
PSALM 55:22 NIV

I f you've ever experienced an earthquake, you know the feeling of being physically shaken. The ground is unsteady and unsafe. You have nowhere to turn, not knowing whether the ground is going to open up under you. It's a feeling of utter helplessness.

We can feel shaken by circumstances over which we have no control. The state of the world, a job situation, difficulties with friends or family—all can lead us to feel helpless. Our own thoughts and the words of others can also trouble and upset us. We may think that our only alternative is to fly away, to run to a place of shelter far from the storms assailing us within and without.

Yet we remember who we are. What our solution may be. We can say, "As for me, I call to God, and the LORD saves me" (Psalm 55:16 NIV).

When you start to feel some tremors coming on, pile your worries and woes onto God. He'll sustain you. He'll ensure His righteousness will not be shaken.

What does it mean to be "righteous?" Simply put, it's being the best person you can be, doing the right thing, and treating others as you would want to be treated. When you do that and transfer your worries to God, He'll make sure you remain unshaken.

*Dear God, allow me never to be shaken.*

# GOOD NEWS!

*"Don't be alarmed," he said. "You are looking for Jesus the Nazarene, who was crucified. He has risen! He is not here. See the place where they laid him. But go, tell his disciples and Peter, 'He is going ahead of you into Galilee. There you will see him, just as he told you.' "*

MARK 16:6-7 NIV

Three women—Mary Magdalene, Mary the mother of James, and Salom—went to the tomb to anoint Jesus' body. As they walked, they wondered who would roll the stone away from the tomb entrance. Imagine how surprised they were when they arrived at their destination and the stone had already been removed!

When the women entered the tomb, they were surprised to see an angel sitting there. He told them not to be afraid, that Jesus had risen—just as He said He would! And they would find Him in Galilee just as He'd told them.

There are times we forget what God has told us. And it's then—when we forget God's Word, His promises, His miracles, His blessings—that we find ourselves shaking. Fortunately, when fear starts gripping our hearts, we can simply reach for God's Word. There we can confirm what we know, what God has promised. Then we can stand once more, unshaken, unafraid.

*Dear God, thank You for Your wonderful Word. When I'm alarmed, remind me to reach out for your Book. May Your good news then keep me steady. In Jesus' name, amen.*

## IN GOD WE TRUST

*In God, whose word I praise, in the L*ORD*, whose word I praise—*
*in God I trust and am not afraid. What can man do to me?*
PSALM 56:10-11 NIV

I n 1861, Secretary of the Treasury Salmon Chase wrote a letter to the director of the U.S. Mint in Philadelphia, asking him to include the words "In God We Trust" on all currency. His letter stated, in part, "No nation can be strong except in the strength of God, or safe except in His defense. The trust of our people in God should be declared on our national coins."

By trusting in God, in His Word, fear is replaced by faith, trepidation by triumph. With God on your side, what is there to fear? God is in control, and no one can harm you. Why be afraid?

In times of weakness or discouragement, remember what God has done in your life, how He's delivered you and kept your feet from stumbling so that you can continue walking in His light (Psalm 56:13). When you're afraid, put your trust in the One who holds not just you but the entire world in His hands.

To help this message hit home, consider carrying a dime in your pocket or purse. If you need encouragement, take it out and read the phrase "In God We Trust"—four simple words with a huge meaning.

*Dear God, help me keep my trust in You.*

# IMPOSSIBLY BLESSED

*"Blessed is she who has believed that the Lord*
*would fulfill his promises to her!"*
LUKE 1:45 NIV

It's one thing to be told something amazing is coming your way. It's quite another thing to actually believe it.

In Luke 1:30-32, God sent the angel Gabriel to Mary to tell her she had been chosen to give birth to a son. He says, "Do not be afraid, Mary; you have found favor with God. You will conceive and give birth to a son, and you are to call him Jesus. He will be great and will be called the Son of the Most High."

When Mary asked how this would happen, Gabriel explained the Holy Spirit would come upon her and the power of the Most High God would overshadow her. To this Mary simply said, "I am the Lord's servant. . . . May your word to me be fulfilled" (Luke 1:38). In other words, Mary believed God's promise. And it was that belief that became a joyous blessing.

Woman of the Way, remember that God will *always* fulfill His promises! Take comfort and ease in that knowledge. Then, like Mary, you too can rejoice! You too are blessed by God's promises! No shaking, no doubt, no fear can enter that equation.

*Dear God, please bless me as You blessed Mary.*
*Help me to have faith, to ask that Your Word be fulfilled.*
*Help me to believe so that I may be impossibly blessed.*

# CHARLIE BROWN

*Fear not: for, behold, I bring you good tidings of great joy, which shall be to all people. For unto you is born this day in the city of David a Saviour, which is Christ the Lord.*
LUKE 2:10-11 KJV

I f you've ever seen *A Charlie Brown Christmas* on television, the above verses will sound familiar. They're part of Linus's response to Charlie Brown's question "Isn't there anyone who knows what Christmas is all about?" Linus said, "Sure, Charlie Brown, I can tell you what Christmas is all about." He then quotes Luke 2:8-14 from the King James Bible on national television. For many, this is the highlight of the show.

The truth is, these lines of dialog were almost never broadcast. Back in 1965, Peanuts creator Charles Schultz was asked to write a Christmas special in one day. Schultz complied, with several interesting features, the most prominent of which was the use of scripture. The television producers fought its inclusion, but Schultz insisted. After its triumphant premiere, this show won several awards for excellence *and* the hearts of millions.

Not only is Linus's speech a good answer to the question of what Christmas is all about, but it also reminds us that, as the angel said, we need never fear nor be shaken. Why? Because our God took human form on earth, then lived and died to save our lives—and His spirit is still with us today.

*Lord, all praise to You who brought joy, peace, and goodwill to all! Amen.*

# DELIVERY

*Deliver me from my enemies, O God; be my fortress
against those who are attacking me.*
PSALM 59:1 NIV

T he Lord's Prayer is likely the most recognized prayer in the
Christian world. And it continues to be learned early in the lives
of most people. Jesus used it to teach people how to pray. Part of the
Lord's Prayer includes the words "And lead us not into temptation,
but deliver us from the evil one" (Matthew 6:13 NIV). Sound familiar?

In Psalm 59:1, David wrote very similar words when Saul sent
men to watch David's house in order to kill him. God heard David's
prayer and protected him.

Although David needed deliverance from a physical attacker,
enemies can take many forms. Perhaps you're battling illness or
experiencing difficult times. Whatever or whomever your enemy
might be, raise your voice to God and He will deliver you.

Reciting the Lord's Prayer can bring peace to your mind and
calm to your soul. Give it a try. Based on Matthew 6:9-13 and Luke
11:2-4, here's the full prayer:

*Our Father, who art in heaven, hallowed be thy name; thy
kingdom come; thy will be done; on earth as it is in heaven.
Give us this day our daily bread. And forgive us our trespasses,
as we forgive those who trespass against us. And lead us
not into temptation; but deliver us from evil. For thine is the
kingdom, the power and the glory, for ever and ever.*

## A MOTHER'S HEART

*Then he went down to Nazareth with them and was obedient to them. But his mother treasured all these things in her heart.*
LUKE 2:51 NIV

Each year, the child Jesus traveled to Jerusalem with His family for Passover. One day, when He was twelve, He, unbeknownst to His parents, stayed behind when His family was returning home. When Joseph and Mary realized He was missing, they returned to Jerusalem, desperately searching for their Son. They finally found Him in the temple, sitting among the teachers, asking questions and conversing with a level of understanding and knowledge that amazed everyone.

Though Mary was told from the beginning that "He will be great and will be called the Son of the Most High" (Luke 1:32 NIV), this was her first real exposure to just how great her Son would be. While we can only speculate about Jesus' childhood years, this glimpse of the depth of His knowledge moves Mary. As a mother, she embraced this moment as one she would never forget.

There is little that's stronger than a mother's love for her child. Mary certainly showed this during Jesus' lifetime and after His death. Her belief in Him, in His teachings, and in His devotion to the Father are an inspiration to all women in good times and bad.

---

*Lord Jesus, may I look to Mary as my inspiration to have a steadfast belief in Jesus, knowing within Him and His teachings lie my strength and hope. Amen.*

# THE BANNER AMID THE BATTLE

*You have set up a banner for those who fear and worshipfully
revere You [to which they may flee from the bow], a standard
displayed because of the truth. Selah [pause, and calmly think
of that]! That Your beloved ones may be delivered, save with
Your right hand and answer us [or me].*

PSALM 60:4-5 AMPC

When we're in the midst of a struggle, there may be times during which we feel as if God has deserted us. It can seem as if there's no safe place to go or to be.

Yet, in the midst of our suffering, if we take our eyes off our situation and look for God, we may find Him. For He will set a flag up above the fray, a banner recognizable to those who worship Him and hold Him in awe. And it is to that flag that we may run and rally around. It's there we'll find the truth, the right course, the place of refuge, the safety we yearn for physically, emotionally, and spiritually.

When you're in a hard place, take your eyes off the mayhem around you and look for God's banner. Allow it to give you the guidance and courage you need. Then lift your prayer to God, asking Him to answer the one He loves.

*Dear God, help me to find You above the fray! Give me
the courage to persevere amid the battle as I await Your
deliverance. In Jesus' name I pray, amen.*

# VICTORIOUS

*With God we will gain the victory,*
*and he will trample down our enemies.*
PSALM 60:12 NIV

F ew things in life are guaranteed. As you venture through it, you may encounter many different situations, some more difficult than others. Adversity is inevitable. But in the verses of Psalm 60, you learn that with God in your corner, you'll eventually be victorious.

Earlier in this chapter, David speaks of the many obstacles he faced, fighting his many enemies. However, in the final verse of Psalm 60, he reminds you that with God, you will always come out on top.

During recent times, there may have been many days that you faced fear or doubt as the struggles of everyday life challenged you and caused you to suffer anxiety. It's during those difficult days that you want to remember God is in your corner and that no matter what or who your enemy might be, He will always bring you through victorious.

The words of Proverbs 30:5 (KJV) offer this assurance: "Every word of God is pure: he is a shield unto them that put their trust in him." *Trust.* That's the key word. Trust in God. Always. And you will be victorious.

*Dear God, how easy it is, in the thick of my daily battles,*
*to forget that I am* not *alone. Remind me that You are*
*with me always to defeat my enemies and keep me safe.*
*Help me put my trust and faith in You.*

## FOLLOW ME

*Then Jesus said to Simon, "Don't be afraid; from now on you will fish for people." So they pulled their boats up on shore, left everything and followed him.*

LUKE 5:10-11 NIV

Nothing was going right for Simon Peter and his fishing crew. They had fished all night, trying different locations, but every time they had let down their nets, they came up empty. They were at the point of despair. Exhausted, they had basically given up and headed back to shore.

As they were washing their nets, Jesus came up to the fishermen, directing them to row out a short way and cast their nets again. This would be like a coworker coming up to you after you had tried everything you could think of, telling you to try one more time. Surely, you would be slightly put off, certain you had exhausted all possibilities.

And yet, something must have told Simon Peter to listen to this Man. So he did as he was told and caught so many fish that his nets began to rip at the seams! Suddenly, the impossible proved possible. He knew immediately he should leave everything and follow Jesus.

And so it is with you too. Follow where Jesus directs, and your despair will morph into delight.

*Dear God, I know I can do great things if I follow You. Please inspire me to rely on Your direction always.*

## ALWAYS THERE FOR YOU

*Jesus answered them, "It is not the healthy who need
a doctor, but the sick. I have not come to call the
righteous, but sinners to repentance."*
LUKE 5:31-32 NIV

Years ago, doctors made house calls to visit sick patients. It
was comforting to know that the doctor was just a phone call
away. Of course, it was the sick who benefitted from this service. The
healthy had no need. Similarly, Jesus spent a good bit of His earthly
time visiting sinners. In so doing, He received a lot of pushback from
the Pharisees and scribes of His day, who didn't understand why He
sought out the troubled. But Jesus knew those who had misstepped
were the ones who most needed His compassion and forgiveness,
not the righteous.

Later in Luke's Gospel, Jesus tells the parable of the lost sheep.
He explains that if a shepherd has one hundred sheep and one goes
missing, he leaves the ninety-nine to search for that one. After all, it
is not the ninety-nine that need help but rather that one. Once it's
found, the shepherd rejoices.

Each person has, at one time or another, been that one lost sheep
whom Jesus has rescued. Each person has, at one time or another,
been that misstepper needing Jesus' compassion and forgiveness.
How comforting to know that, no matter what, Jesus will always be
there to come to your rescue.

*Good Shepherd, thank You for always being there for me.*

# IMPENETRABLE ROCK

*My salvation and my honor depend on God; he is my mighty
rock, my refuge. Trust in him at all times, you people;
pour out your hearts to him, for God is our refuge.*
PSALM 62:7-8 NIV

To say something is a rock speaks volumes. What better foundation, what more secure structure could there be? Certainly monuments like Stonehenge in England have withstood the test of time. Built more than 5,000 years ago, these stone structures are still standing strong. And then there is the Great Pyramid of Giza, about 4,500 years old. Again, built with rock. It, the oldest of the Seven Wonders of the Ancient World, remains sturdy and impenetrable.

With God as your personal and mighty rock, what could possibly stand against you? According to David in today's verse, God is your refuge in whom you can trust. Through your faith in Him, you will have salvation and honor.

Psalm 62:7 is one of the most uplifting and positive verses, one that you should always carry with you. Through good times and bad, remember that God is your "Rock of unyielding strength *and* impenetrable hardness" (PSALM 62:7 AMPC). You need no better refuge than He, the One on whom you can lean and rely.

*Dear God, thank You for providing me a safe haven, a refuge in Your loving arms. I praise You alone, my impenetrable rock on whom I can rely and my assurance of salvation.*

## JOYFUL PROMISES

*Looking at his disciples, he said: "Blessed are you who are poor,*
*for yours is the kingdom of God. Blessed are you who hunger*
*now, for you will be satisfied. Blessed are you who weep now,*
*for you will laugh. Blessed are you when people hate you,*
*when they exclude you and insult you and reject your*
*name as evil, because of the Son of Man."*
LUKE 6:20-22 NIV

I f ever there were uplifting words to take to heart, it is those above. Jesus was addressing a large gathering of poor, sick, and otherwise downtrodden people. This crowd was in desperate need of encouragement and help. Notice that Jesus addresses the crowd in the second person, using the word *you* instead of a more impersonal third person of *whoever*. He is speaking to each and every individual in that crowd that day, peppering His words with promises of hope. What a wonderful message to a despondent crowd!

Are you feeling downtrodden or fearful? Read Jesus' words again. The promise of better times is clear. For He follows the verses above with "Rejoice in that day and leap for joy, because great is your reward in heaven" (Luke 6:23 NIV).

Woman of God, rejoice! Leap for joy! God's promises are always fulfilled. Your reward in heaven is guaranteed!

*Dear God, thank You! I take heart in knowing that*
*I am blessed and that my reward awaits me in*
*Your kingdom! I rejoice and leap for joy!*

# THE ROCK

*"Why do you call me, 'Lord, Lord,' and do not do what I say?*
*As for everyone who comes to me and hears my words and puts*
*them into practice, I will show you what they are like. They are*
*like a man building a house, who dug down deep and laid the*
*foundation on rock. When a flood came, the torrent struck that*
*house but could not shake it, because it was well built."*

LUKE 6:46-48 NIV

What a wonderful blueprint for a solid structure! If you were to build a house, you might dig deep into the ground, finding the most solid rock possible on which to build. No matter what storms were to come your way, your house would stand tall, unshaken, never to be broken away from the love of God.

Jesus' message is clear. Call on the Lord and take His words to heart. If you do, you'll remain safe on the rock of your foundation because that Rock is God Himself! Like David, you'll sing, "The LORD is my rock, my fortress and my deliverer; my God is my rock, in whom I take refuge, my shield and the horn of my salvation. He is my stronghold, my refuge and my savior" (2 Samuel 22:2-3 NIV).

*Dear God, I know I can stand securely on Your firm*
*foundation. As I take Your words to heart, I know no storm*
*can ever shake me because You are my solid Rock.*

## NOTHING TO FEAR

*You may say to yourselves, "These nations are stronger than we are. How can we drive them out?" But do not be afraid of them; remember well what the LORD your God did to Pharaoh and to all Egypt. You saw with your own eyes the great trials, the signs and wonders, the mighty hand and outstretched arm, with which the LORD your God brought you out. The LORD your God will do the same to all the peoples you now fear.*

DEUTERONOMY 7:17-19 NIV

If you have ever faced overwhelming odds, you have probably experienced fear. Today's verse reminds you that when things seem hopeless, it's wise to remember that God does indeed answer prayers, just as He did when the oppressed Israelites called out to Him in Egypt. When Moses was finally able to lead the Israelites out of Egypt, things began to look bleak as Pharaoh was right on their heels. Yet God saved them by drowning the Egyptian army in the Red Sea.

When you hear words of fear echoing in your heart, remember that with God you're safe and secure. Just as He delivered His people from Egypt, He'll deliver you. Though sometimes you may feel like the underdog, with God on your side, you'll always be triumphant.

*Dear God, because You repeatedly perform miraculous deeds in delivering Your people, I know You will protect me from all that I fear and that no matter how bleak things may look, You will ultimately bring me to victory. Amen.*

# PLAN NOT SUBJECT TO CHANGE

*They plot injustice and say, "We have devised a perfect plan!"*
*Surely the human mind and heart are cunning. But God will*
*shoot them with his arrows; they will suddenly be struck down. . . .*
*The righteous will rejoice in the LORD and take refuge in him;*
*all the upright in heart will glory in him!*
PSALM 64:6-7, 10 NIV

P lans change all the time. Because of things out of your control, carefully crafted days may need to be rescheduled, pushed back, or even canceled—even though they may have been extremely important or maybe even reshaped your future.

Yet you can always find comfort that God's plans never change. His Will isn't based on what happens in this world. When the Israelites disobeyed the Lord, He still allowed their descendants into the Promised Land. When others made plans to destroy David, they were shot down by God's own power. As the world became more and more corrupted, God made sure John the Baptist would still be in place so he could prepare the way for Jesus.

You can plan all you want, but life circumstances will get in the way sometimes. Yet you can trust God has got everything worked out for your good, not because of who *you* are, but because of who *He* is. All His plans are good because He's good.

*Dear God, thank You for Your goodness. Thank You for*
*always looking ahead and never changing Your plans.*
*Because of Your constancy, I can trust You.*

## IN AWE

*And now, Israel, what does the Lord your God require of you but [reverently] to fear the Lord your God, [that is] to walk in all His ways, and to love Him, and to serve the Lord your God with all your [mind and] heart and with your entire being.*

DEUTERONOMY 10:12 AMPC

Two women stand on top of a great height with only a fence standing between them and the chance of falling. One fully trusts the fence. And because she trusts, she is able to take in the great beauty of the sights the view has to offer. The other woman doesn't trust the fence at all. Filled with fear, she can't focus and misses out on the spectacular scenes surrounding her.

This is what fearing the Lord is like. While others may be afraid of the presence of God, daughters of Christ are full of awe of Him. Instead of being scared into submission, they serve and follow the Lord because nothing brings them more pleasure.

May we follow the example of the tarnished woman who washed Jesus' feet (Luke 7:36-50). May our awe of the Lord be greater than our fear of what others might think.

*Lord, I stand in awe of You today. Thank You for who You are and what You've done for me. I choose to walk beside You and to serve You with every inch of my heart and soul. Amen.*

## LET IT SHINE

*"No one after lighting a lamp covers it with a jar or puts it under a bed, but puts it on a stand, so that those who enter may see the light. For nothing is hidden that will not be made manifest, nor is anything secret that will not be known and come to light."*
LUKE 8:16-17 ESV

You'd never cover a lit candle with a bowl or put it under your bed. If you did, chances are you'd either stub your toe in the darkness or your blankets would catch fire. The whole purpose of the candle's light is to help you and others see.

The Lord's presence within you is the same. Once Jesus ignites His truth in your life, it's impossible for you to keep it hidden. You'll need that light to keep you from stumbling in the dark and heading into trouble.

And once you have that light within, people will see something different about you and wonder why. When they ask, you can tell them about Jesus and the unshakable love and light He offers to every single one of His children. You can be that shining beacon of hope, peace, and truth that points others to God.

*I'm sorry, Lord Jesus, for the times I've tried to hide Your light because of my fear of what others might think. Help me to let my light shine freely. To be Your beacon for others. In Your name, I pray, amen.*

## THE RULE BOOK

*For you are a holy people [set apart] to the Lord your God;*
*and the Lord has chosen you to be a peculiar people to*
*Himself, above all the nations on the earth.*
DEUTERONOMY 14:2 AMPC

I t seems like everywhere you look there are more rules to follow. Guidelines for your workplace or educational institutions, social and political structures in your town, healthcare network protocols, or certain policies mandated by your state can seem overwhelming at times.

In Deuteronomy, the Lord placed many, *many* rules on the Israelites, but the bottom line for all of them was this: the Israelites were set apart to be a new nation chosen by and under God. Those rules helped set them apart from other nations that worshipped other gods.

You too are set apart. By Jesus. When you accept Him into your heart, your life is supposed to be different. Jesus sets the example for His followers on how they should act. When you follow Him with an open heart, He'll calm your storms and fight your darkness.

Your Savior is the ultimate rule book on how to live the best life you possibly can on this side of heaven.

*Lord Jesus, thank You so much for setting the awesome*
*example of how to live. Help me to walk in Your will*
*and way so that I can remain unshaken in You.*

## RIGHT ON TIME

*Then the woman, seeing that she could not go unnoticed, came trembling and fell at his feet. In the presence of all the people, she told why she had touched him and how she had been instantly healed. Then he said to her, "Daughter, your faith has healed you. Go in peace."*
LUKE 8:47–48 NIV

Every year, almost 386 million dollars are spent on planners and calendars. That represents a lot of people who would like to organize their lives! Yet no one can control every single one of her days no matter how much she tries.

God doesn't give anyone a specific timeline. Nor does anyone fully know His plans, when He'll heal, or even when He'll return.

One woman suffered for twelve years with an affliction. Then she had the chance to touch Jesus' clothes. A man with a sickly daughter heard news of his little girl's death moments after he'd asked Jesus for help. But in each situation, Jesus said that their faith would lead to their healing—faith in Him and His power, despite their circumstances.

Your heavenly Father is never late. He knows exactly what time will be best for the growth of His daughters.

*Father, I feel like I've been waiting forever for You to finally come through for me. Help me to place absolute trust in You. And comfort me today as I learn to trust Your timing.*

## A LOSS FOR WORDS

*But he most surely did listen, he came on the double when he heard my prayer. Blessed be God: he didn't turn a deaf ear, he stayed with me, loyal in his love.*
PSALM 66:19-20 MSG

There may be some seasons in life when God seems to be speaking directly to you every moment. Because of that close connection with Him, you're filled with confidence and the assurance of His presence. Yet there may be some seasons when God seems completely and utterly silent—and you may start to question whether He's even listening, leading you into areas of uncertainty and doubt.

Be assured that God does listen. To every prayer, every cry, every praise. When you can't find the words, He takes in the groans of your heart.

Your God is "loyal in his love." He is with you even when the world around you seems to be crumbling. God's with you even when you sin and fall short. God's with You even when He appears to be silent.

God has promised to never leave you (Deuteronomy 31:6). So place your trust in Him continually. Then you'll have a firm foundation to stand on when life starts quaking. Even if you can't find the words, spend time in His presence. He'll stay with you as long as you need.

*God, thank You for always being there, for always listening, for always being loyal in Your love. With You in my life, nothing can shake me.*

## LETTING IT GO

*Then he said to the crowd, "If any of you wants to be my follower, you must give up your own way, take up your cross daily, and follow me. If you try to hang on to your life, you will lose it. But if you give up your life for my sake, you will save it."*
LUKE 9:23-24 NLT

Have you ever watched a child forced to give up something? More often than not, when she gets the first taste of surrendering belongings or plans, her doing so comes with a lot of struggling, complaining, and crying. No one likes to give up what she is used to, has worked for, or thinks she deserves.

During His Transfiguration (Luke 9:28-36), Jesus demonstrated His divinity for three of His disciples. To them He revealed what He had given up to take on human attributes and the responsibility of healing this broken world. So it's no wonder He asks His followers to give up their previous lives to follow Him.

Jesus promises so many things to you if you're willing to let go of what you are used to, have worked for, or think you deserve. In exchange, He offers you peace, joy, comfort, and a way. Are you willing to be His follower and gain more than you ever had?

*Dear God, help me each day to let go of my life and follow You.*

## GOOD, GOOD PARENT

*Father of the fatherless and protector of widows is God in his holy
habitation. God settles the solitary in a home; he leads out the
prisoners to prosperity, but the rebellious dwell in a parched land.*
PSALM 68:5-6 ESV

When you were younger, you may not have liked all the rules you
were made to follow. But now that you're older, you may have
a greater understanding of why your guardians made you follow the
mandates they set before you. Your chores perhaps instilled within
you a work ethic and may have taught you responsibility. The set
allowance may have been a lesson in finance. The set curfew may
have been for your own safety.

Just as you had earthly parents or guardians, you have a spiritual
One as well. God is your parent in every sense of the word but not an
earthly parent that can make mistakes or be shaken. He's an amazing
One who loves boundlessly and endlessly. Everything He does is to
help shape your character and provide for your well-being. All the
rules He has devised are for your teaching and safety. Through your
circumstances, He's shaping you to be like His Son. He's recreating
you into the woman you were meant to be. He's solid, always there,
never changing. God is everything you need Him to be.

*Dear Father, You are so wonderful at being everything I need.
Thank You for loving me in a way like no other. Amen.*

## PROVIDES

*And when we cried to the Lord, the God of our fathers, the Lord
heard our voice and looked on our affliction and our labor and
our [cruel] oppression; and the Lord brought us forth out of
Egypt with a mighty hand and with an outstretched arm, and
with great (awesome) power and with signs and with wonders;
and He brought us into this place and gave us this land,
a land flowing with milk and honey.*
DEUTERONOMY 26:7-9 AMPC

The Lord provides so much in this life. He hears His children's cries. He sees what's happening in their lives and saves them. He fulfills His promises and employs His awesome power. He uses His outstretched arm to bring them to a place of abundance.

Knowing those things doesn't mean this world will be easy to walk through, but it hopefully reminds you that there's more to your life and this world than you see on the surface. It may perhaps bring you to the realization that God designed you for greater things. All you have to do in return is to choose to grab on to Him.

While God knows His provisions are plentiful, there are few who accept them and even less who spread them. Let yourself take hold of God and His provisions today and share them with those around you tomorrow.

*Lord, thank You for Your promises that never break
and Your blessings that I may take. Open my eyes
to those with whom I may share them.*

## WHO IS HE?

*Blessed be the Lord, Who bears our burdens and carries
us day by day, even the God Who is our salvation!
Selah [pause, and calmly think of that]!*
PSALM 68:19 AMPC

You may look through the pages of the Old Testament and wonder who is this God, full of curses and punishments? He isn't like His Son, who's celebrated on Palm Sunday. The Old Testament God doesn't seem to fit into the mold of a loving father and a peaceful guardian. But it's important to remember that in the days of Moses, the Lord was already paving the way to deliver His creation—not just out of Egypt but out of the bondage of sin.

God surpasses understanding in every way. No one will ever be able to wrap their mind around the entirety of who God is and the what and why of His actions. But one thing is sure: God is always working for your good.

In Luke 10:22 (NLT), Jesus proclaims, "My Father has entrusted everything to me. No one truly knows the Son except the Father, and no one truly knows the Father except the Son and those to whom the Son chooses to reveal him."

Jesus is the reason you can connect to the Lord of forever. The two can't be separated or placed into boxes that this world can define.

*Lord, when I'm confused about who You are, I'll still choose
to trust You for I know You are for me in every way.*

## CHOOSE HIM

*Now as they went on their way, Jesus entered a village. And a woman named Martha welcomed him into her house. And she had a sister called Mary, who sat at the Lord's feet and listened to his teaching. But Martha was distracted with much serving. And she went up to him and said, "Lord, do you not care that my sister has left me to serve alone? Tell her then to help me."*

LUKE 10:38-40 ESV

Sometimes your life may look like Mary's. You have the time and the motivation to spend a few moments with the Lord. But sometimes your life may look more like Martha's: you're bustling around, always on the go, upset that people aren't working as hard as you are.

When Martha complained to Jesus about her sister, Jesus actually reprimanded her, saying, "Martha, Martha, you are anxious and troubled about many things, but one thing is necessary. Mary has chosen the good portion, which will not be taken away from her" (Luke 10:41-42 ESV).

It's all about choice. Choosing to place your focus on Jesus despite what the world is doing around you is a choice for unshakable abundance, not anxiety.

*Dear God, thank You for letting me cast my burdens and my gazes upon You when life becomes too much to bear. On all days and in all ways help me choose to focus on You. To choose unshakable abundance over undermining anxiety!*

## BE STRONG. TAKE COURAGE.

*"Be strong. Take courage. Don't be intimidated. Don't give them a second thought because GOD, your God, is striding ahead of you. He's right there with you. He won't let you down; he won't leave you."*
DEUTERONOMY 31:6 MSG

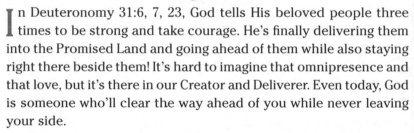

I n Deuteronomy 31:6, 7, 23, God tells His beloved people three times to be strong and take courage. He's finally delivering them into the Promised Land and going ahead of them while also staying right there beside them! It's hard to imagine that omnipresence and that love, but it's there in our Creator and Deliverer. Even today, God is someone who'll clear the way ahead of you while never leaving your side.

When the circumstances of this life seem overwhelming, God calls out to His beloved. Only in Him can you find true strength and courage. Relying solely on yourself or others could lead to disappointment and pain. But your heavenly Father is eager and ready to carry you *and* all the pain, all the baggage, and all the problems—despite what your past looks like or what you've done. He never ever meant for any of His children to live this life without Him.

*Lord, thank You so much for always being with me.*
*Help me keep my eyes open to the light You pour into my life.*
*Remind me of the times You carried me through hardships.*
*Let me be an example of strength and courage that*
*always directs others back to You. Amen.*

## INSIDE AND OUT

*Then the Lord said to him, "Now then, you Pharisees clean the outside of the cup and dish, but inside you are full of greed and wickedness. You foolish people! Did not the one who made the outside make the inside also? But now as for what is inside you— be generous to the poor, and everything will be clean for you."*
LUKE 11:39-41 NIV

Have you ever met people who were particularly beautiful or handsome, but once you got to know them, you realized they weren't very nice at all? Did their appearance become distorted once you saw who they truly were? Some people can be like a rotting fruit that looks delicious until the first squishy bite. What's on the inside affects the whole product, no matter how pretty the packaging.

Jesus warns His followers against living such a superficial life. While He wants you to take care of your body, He also wants you to take care of your inner self. This doesn't just mean exercising and eating right! He wants you to fill up on His presence, His Word, and on other things He deems good so others will see that You are good inside as well as out.

*Dear God, help me focus more on my inner self than my outer self. Lead me, Lord, to maintain a steady diet, filling myself up with You, Your Word, and Your goodness each day.*

# RAHAB'S MISSION

*"I know the L*ORD *has given you this land," she told them.*
*"We are all afraid of you. Everyone in the land is living*
*in terror. . . . For the L*ORD *your God is the supreme*
*God of the heavens above and the earth below."*
JOSHUA 2:9,11 NLT

E very woman has the chance to be a part of God's story—no matter how society views her or what sin she's committed. The Lord looks past all that to see only His beloved daughter.

Rahab, a prostitute in Jericho, the country the Israelites were to conquer, met up with some of Joshua's spies who were lodging in her house. Because she believed in the might of their God, she hid His people from harm when the king of Jericho's men came looking for them.

Because of her strength and courage, Rahab and her loved ones were given safety from Joshua's army.

It can't be said for certain why Rahab was a prostitute, but you can be sure that God used, protected, and loved her through it all. She became a part of the amazing story of ultimate deliverance—and an ancestress of Jesus Himself!

You have that same chance. When you place your strength and courage on the Lord, you gain the power to perform that immovable and unshakable mission He's placed on your life.

*Father, thank You for using me regardless of my past.*
*Today I choose Your strength and courage, knowing that*
*will make me mightier than I could ever be on my own.*

# GOOD FRIDAY

*Reproaches have broken my heart, so that I am in despair.*
*I looked for pity, but there was none, and for comforters,*
*but I found none. They gave me poison for food,*
*and for my thirst they gave me sour wine to drink.*
PSALM 69:20-21 ESV

The psalmist, David, wrote Psalm 69 centuries before Jesus was born. But as you honor and remember the events of Good Friday and what Jesus endured on the cross in your place, you know that Jesus understood these words well. He experienced them all.

It's hard to imagine what Jesus felt as He suffered all that physical and emotional pain. Before His crucifixion, Jesus had told His disciples, "Don't fuss about what's on the table at mealtimes or if the clothes in your closet are in fashion. There is far more to your inner life than the food you put in your stomach, more to your outer appearance than the clothes you hang on your body" (Luke 12:22-23 MSG). How can someone about to undergo such suffering say that with such conviction?

Because unlike His followers at the time, Jesus knew not only what life was *really* all about, He knew the end of the story. He knew death would not win. And today you get to share in that victory too.

*Thank You, Jesus, for Your sacrifice on the cross. I receive*
*the message of the Gospel once again today and rejoice*
*that I know the end of this story. For You have won!*

## THE REWARD

*So Joshua saved Rahab the harlot, with her father's household and all that she had; and she lives in Israel even to this day, because she hid the messengers whom Joshua sent to spy out Jericho.*

JOSHUA 6:25 AMPC

Rahab experienced a time of waiting. Would the spies of Israel whom she'd helped really keep their promise to save her and her family?

Have you ever ached in anticipation of an event that could either be life-saving or heart-wrenching? The promise made to Rahab was a promise made in God's name (Joshua 6:12-14). And God always keeps His promises to those who have faith and obey. Rahab believed in God and chose to believe she would be saved.

Rahab's anticipation reminds one of Holy Saturday, a day of mourning and waiting. It was the day after the crucifixion, the first day without Jesus. His disciples and female followers were mourning for the lives they'd led before His death. They were waiting to see what the future would hold without their leader and friend. But Jesus had promised that after His death He would rise again. And you know He always keeps His promises.

Like the servant waiting for his master to return, you can do the same. Believe and wait for Jesus' answer and His return—your reward.

*God, in the waiting, I'll praise You. When You answer, I'll praise You. Thank You for being my leader, friend, and reward!*

## EASTER SUNDAY

*But may all who seek you rejoice and be glad in you; may those*
*who long for your saving help always say, "The Lᴏʀᴅ is great!"*
Psᴀʟᴍ 70:4 ɴɪᴠ

T oday Christians everywhere praise God for the miracle of miracles. This is the day Jesus promised His disciples He would rise again. This is the day that changed everything for the entire world. This is the day Jesus rose from the dead in a triumphant return from the grave, leaving sin and death behind and offering us abundant life in Him. This is the day we acknowledge how great God is.

Yet that truth should be acknowledged every day!

God is great because He resurrected Jesus. God is great because He loves His creation enough to sacrifice His Son. God is great because He still works in believers' lives, sharing boundless and unshakable love, joy, and mercy. God is great because He does that not just on Easter Sunday—but every single day.

Jesus says in Matthew 7:7 (ɴʟᴛ): "Keep on asking, and you will receive what you ask for. Keep on seeking, and you will find. Keep on knocking, and the door will be opened to you." So keep on keeping on, woman of faith, And you will be eternally blessed with and rejoice in God's help, comfort, and presence.

*Lord Jesus, thank You for dying so that I can*
*live fully in You. Because of You, I will keep on*
*keeping on, rejoicing in our Abba! Amen.*

## IN THE DETAILS

*He also asked, "What else is the Kingdom of God like?*
*It is like the yeast a woman used in making bread.*
*Even though she put only a little yeast in three measures*
*of flour, it permeated every part of the dough."*
LUKE 13:20-21 NLT

Where is God? Where is His majesty, His miracles, the work of His hands in your life?

God is the morning sunrise when it's hidden by dewy fog. He's the oldest evergreen tree in the woods and the budding flower in spring. He's the comforting touch between spouses, the laughter with friends, and the kindness of strangers.

Jesus says the kingdom of God is in everything you see, touch, hear. His kingdom is in everything good. Like the yeast in bread, once it's added, it cannot be taken out or seen and counted, but you can see its effects. The dough rises with help from the yeast, whether it's seen or unseen.

God is like that yeast. He's always working in your life even when you don't see it or feel it. You simply have to trust His will, His hand, and His way are in the details.

*Dear God, I know You are with me. Even when I can't*
*see You. Even when I can't feel you. I trust that You have*
*gone ahead of me and are planning the way and guiding*
*my steps. I trust You, Lord, to know what is best. Amen.*

# REST

*Joshua fought against these kings for a long time. Not one town made peace with the People of Israel, with the one exception of the Hivites who lived in Gibeon. Israel fought and took all the rest.*
JOSHUA 11:18-19 MSG

After Joshua, as God had instructed, took control of the land and split the inheritance between the tribes, "Israel had rest from war" (Joshua 11:23 MSG). The word doesn't say the war was over. It doesn't say this was the ending wrapped up in a bow. It says Joshua and the tribes had rest. They were able to breathe, look around at this land that had been promised to them, and *rest*.

While God may call you to many things in this life, and it may feel as if you're fighting battles, remember that God allows times of rest for His children. This isn't just a good night's sleep or a day to treat yourself. This rest is meant to refill your spirit with the Lord's presence so you can continue doing God's work in your life. It's a time meant for worship and praise.

When you find it hard to slow down or take a break because of all that needs to be done, know that God asks you to spend time with Him for the unshakable strength and power to journey on.

*Father, please refill me with Your Spirit and Your strength.*
*In this time of rest, my eyes are on You.*

# MADE OF HONOR

*"When you are invited, take the lowest place, so that when your host comes, he will say to you, 'Friend, move up to a better place.' Then you will be honored in the presence of all the other guests."*
LUKE 14:10 NIV

Have you ever been a maid or matron of honor? It's the chance to not only stand with a loved one at her wedding, it's the opportunity to be right next to her as she says her vows. While this title adds that extra blessing, it also includes more duties than a bridesmaid. Usually the bachelorette party and shower are planned by the maid or matron of honor. She's also in charge of the wedding going smoothly while the bride gets to enjoy the day. And she does whatever else the bride requests! Although her position is a higher honor, more work is required.

The idea that Jesus wants you to live out is similar. When you choose the lowest place—when you choose to be humble and put someone else before you—you have actually gained an important place at the table. One that is right next to the Savior.

To be made of honor is to be like Jesus, humbly working every day to love and serve those around you.

*God, I know when I truly work on becoming more like Your Son, "You will increase my honor and comfort me once more" (Psalm 71:21 NIV). May I be made of honor for You. Amen.*

## PART OF THE PLAN

*These women came to Eleazar the priest, Joshua son of Nun,
and the Israelite leaders and said, "The Lord commanded Moses
to give us a grant of land along with the men of our tribe."
So Joshua gave them a grant of land along with their uncles,
as the Lord had commanded.*

Joshua 17:4 nlt

These five sisters were pretty brave for their time. The Bible—especially the Old Testament—is dominated by male characters. After all, it was a patriarchal society.

In the scene before you today, Joshua is handing out land lots according to the male descendants of each tribe. But Zelphehad had no sons to receive the lot from Joshua. So his five daughters approached the men in charge and asked for what the Lord had granted them (Numbers 27:1-7).

These women had no idea how the leaders would react. The elders could have laughed in the sisters' faces and spilt the tribe between the other male heirs. But Zelphehad's daughters trusted the Lord would fulfill His promise.

And Joshua agreed! Because God Himself commanded it.

This is only one example of how God *doesn't* work the way society does. He didn't change His plans just because there were no male heirs. These five daughters were *always* a part of the plan.

You can trust that, as a woman, you're a part of God's plan too. And that plan can't and won't be changed.

*Father, thank You so much for looking out for me.
I love being a part of Your plan!*

## THE ONE

*What man of you, if he has a hundred sheep and should lose one of them, does not leave the ninety-nine in the wilderness (desert) and go after the one that is lost until he finds it? And when he has found it, he lays it on his [own] shoulders, rejoicing.*

LUKE 15:4-5 AMPC

You may wonder why the shepherd cares so much for just one sheep. After all, he has ninety-nine others for wool or meat. Why should he worry if one goes missing? But the fact of the matter is that the shepherd bought or brought into the world each lamb. He loved and cared for it. The sheep are not just his flock but his companions as he is away from home. Even one means everything to him.

That's how your Lord views you. You were bought with a price and called by name into God's kingdom. Everything changes when you're lost to Him. Everything changes again when you're found by Him.

When you chose to follow Jesus, there was rejoicing in heaven. You. You were the one Jesus died and rose again for. You. You were the one He chases after. *You.* Rest in and receive that Good Shepherd's love, that passion He has for you today.

---

*Dear God, sometimes I forget how much You love me and cherish me. But today I acknowledge everything You've done in my life and what You will continue to do in my future. Amen.*

# THE OLDER SON

*"And he said to him, 'Son, you are always with me,*
*and all that is mine is yours.' "*
LUKE 15:31 ESV

In the story of the prodigal son, the older brother doesn't seem very happy when his sibling returns home. But he isn't really mad that his brother is back. He's upset that the father never threw him a party to honor his constant faithfulness to the family. The eldest son tells the father, "Look, these many years I have served you, and I never disobeyed your command, yet you never gave me a young goat, that I might celebrate with my friends" (Luke 15:29 ESV).

From a worldly perspective, it does seem unfair. Why should the one who went away and squandered his inheritance be rewarded when he returns? Yet the father answers that what belonged to him and was ultimately given to the lost son was always offered and available to his other son.

What are some blessings given by the heavenly Father that you haven't received yet? Do you feel like you deserve something more? Maybe the gifts weren't given in the way you imagined, but they're still good and meant for you. You're His daughter, and He longs to care for you. Why not open your arms to receive all He has to offer?

*Father, forgive me for not fully accepting my blessings because*
*I think I deserve something more. I thank You for everything*
*You've done for me and all You plan to do.*

## MONEY, MONEY

*"No one can serve two masters. Either you will hate the one and love the other, or you will be devoted to the one and despise the other. You cannot serve both God and money."*

LUKE 16:13 NIV

Before Joshua passed away he told the Israelites again and again that they can't go back to their old ways of worshipping idols. God knows they've done it before. As we all know, it's hard to leave something that was once a big part of your life without the Lord's help.

One modern idol that affects almost everyone is money. It's on a lot of people's minds. That's because to live in this world you need money. And there are a lot of people who want a lot of it. Yet when people do gain a truckload of money, those riches can change the recipients from the inside out.

Jesus warns that you can't worship both God *and* money. You may look at this scripture and claim that wanting to live comfortably isn't valuing money over God. But constantly worrying about finances can show you trust money to comfort and provide for you more than you trust the God who created you.

Money is fickle and always changing, but God is steadfast and unshakable. Rely on Him alone—for everything.

*God, I'm sorry for not always trusting that You'll provide for me. I give my worries about my finances to You todayfor I have put my trust in You. Thank You!*

## SETTLING

*Whenever the LORD raised up a judge over Israel, he was with that judge and rescued the people from their enemies throughout the judge's lifetime. For the LORD took pity on his people, who were burdened by oppression and suffering.*

JUDGES 2:18 NLT

In Judges 2, the Israelites once again strayed from God's plan. Instead of taking the land from the nations given to them, they decided to live among them. In verse 12, it's revealed that "they abandoned the Lord, the God of their fathers, who had brought them out of the land of Egypt" (NLT). They chose other gods before Him and worshipped them. God warned His people to beware because He knows their hearts. By settling in these nations, the Israelites settled into the temptation and then into sin.

Yet God always took pity on His people. He saw they were suffering in their sin and His heart ached for them. So He saved His people again and again. And He does the same with His children today.

As a daughter of Christ, you were made for more than settling into temptation and sin. When You're tempted again and again, the Lord offers you a way out, again and again. Your job is to find it. And then follow it, trusting He has your best interests at heart.

*Father, give me the unshakable strength to face my temptations the way Jesus did—armed with Your Word and faith. Amen.*

## SUPERWOMAN

*Jael, wife of Heber the Kenite, most blessed of homemaking women. . .grabbed a tent peg in her left hand, with her right hand she seized a hammer. She hammered Sisera, she smashed his head, she drove a hole through his temple. . . . He slumped at her feet. . . . Dead.*
JUDGES 5:24, 26-27 MSG

New movies come out every couple of months, highlighting ordinary people with extraordinary abilities, such as flying, invisibility, or super strength. And now women are getting the chance to take on the role of superhero, saving the day instead of being the damsel in distress.

Yet the book of Judges reveals God already knew the amazing powers of woman. As Israel cried out for a hero, He prepared several, including Deborah. When the Israelites' commander wouldn't go into battle without her, she said, "I will go with you. But you will receive no honor in this venture, for the LORD's victory over Sisera will be at the hands of a woman" (Judges 4:9 NLT). Cue the explosions, right?

Super women Deborah and Jael did things men had typically done. They both knew the Lord was behind them, and without His strength, they would falter. In the end, they gave the victory back to Him.

You're the same. When you rely on God, you can do anything.

*God, thank You for being my strength. Help me be a super woman and give the victory back to You. Amen.*

# GOD CALLS YOU

*And the Angel of the Lord appeared to him and said to him,*
*The Lord is with you, you mighty man of [fearless] courage.*
JUDGES 6:12 AMPC

Take a sheet of paper or mentally make a list of how you'd describe yourself. Start off with some physical attributes. Then add personality traits. Once you're finished, consider all the things you listed. Did you use the words *fearless* or *courageous*? Think about how God says He views His daughters. Does your list match His?

In the beginning of Gideon's story, he wasn't a judge or even a hero. But the angel who visited him called him a "mighty man of [fearless] courage." Other translations use the phrases "man of valor" (ESV), "mighty warrior" (NIV), and "mighty hero" (NLT).

When hiding from the Midianites, Gideon couldn't have felt like any of those descriptions. But God spoke of Gideon as He saw him, not as Gideon saw himself. And God knew the plans He had for him.

God does the same with you. He calls you loved. He calls you beautiful. He calls you a woman of fearless courage. Even when you don't feel that way. Allow yourself to be the woman God sees.

*Father, thank You for seeing me differently than I see myself.*
*On the days I don't like myself, remind me that You love me*
*and created me to do what You've called me to do.*
*Help me be the woman You see.*

## EVERY CHANCE

*"No chance at all," Jesus said, "if you think you can pull it off by yourself. Every chance in the world if you trust God to do it."*
LUKE 18:27 MSG

In the story of *Les Misérables,* the main character, Jean Valjean, a thief newly released from jail, seeks safety and rest at a Catholic church. After stealing from the priest who invited him in, Jean is caught by local authorities after he leaves. When they return him to the priest's house and ask the priest if the convict had indeed stolen his silver and gold, the priest answers that everything he had was given freely to Jean. In fact, the priest says, Jean left some of his best gifts behind. Seeing this compassion and forgiveness, the former convict turns his life around.

This is a wonderful image of how God responds to His children. No matter what you've done or how far away you may have run from Him, God still has so much to give you. Love and a second (third, fourth, every) chance at eternal life with Him. But no one can do it on her own. Only God can provide these chances with His unshakable love for you.

*Father, thank You again and again for welcoming me back every time I stray. Forgive me for fearing how You would treat me when I now know how You long to lavish Your love upon me. Help me, Lord, to grow my trust in and love of You. Amen.*

## MAKER

*The day is yours, and yours also the night; you established
the sun and moon. It was you who set all the boundaries
of the earth; you made both summer and winter.*
PSALM 74:16-17 NIV

L ike a sculptor making a masterpiece out of clay or a painter using
simple colors to create a canvas of life, God is a master maker. In
the verses above, the psalmist is remembering the creation story in
Genesis, rejoicing in the beauty and miracle of it. The Message version
of the creation account says, "First this: God created the Heavens
and Earth—all you see, all you don't see" (Genesis 1:1). The sun, the
moon, the sea, the land, the seasons were all made with perfection.
And when He was done, "God saw that it was good" (Genesis 1:10).

When God made you, He saw the same thing. *Good.* You're good
because He created you with a good purpose. While good things may
not always come in your life, you can trust that God will establish
it for good. Just as He sets the line of the horizon and the days that
turn winter to spring and spring to summer for good. You are His
masterpiece, "created. . .anew in Christ Jesus, so [you] can do the
good things he planned for [you] long ago" (Ephesians 2:10 NLT).

*God, You are the ultimate masterpiece maker.
Use the hard moments of my life and make
something good. In Jesus' name. Amen.*

# WORSHIP

*He said, "If they kept quiet, the stones*
*would do it for them, shouting praise."*
LUKE 19:40 MSG

Jesus is told by the Pharisees to rebuke His disciples for cheering and praising God's name when He enters Jerusalem on a colt. But Jesus declared that if no one worshipped the Lord, then the stones, once silent and stoic, would begin to cry out.

Jesus is telling us that everything on this side of eternity extols its Creator. If you don't worship God, nature can do it for you. But God longs for your praise of Him.

Perhaps you think it difficult to worship. You may be afraid of how others will think of you. You may worry others will treat you differently because of your faith. Jesus knows more than any one of us what it's like to suffer for, follow, and praise the Lord. But God promises to be beside you every step of the way.

It may be that you're in a praise slump. And that's okay. Perhaps it may help if you praise in a different way.

How do you worship God? Do you make art? Do you lift your voice in a church? Do you write your prayers in a journal or find a secret place to spend time with the Lord?

Try and praise your heavenly Father in a new way today. He can't wait to hear from You.

*God, today I praise Your name for who You*
*are and what You do and will do. Amen!*

## EVEN A RASH VOW

*And as soon as he saw her, he tore his clothes and said, "Alas, my daughter! You have brought me very low, and you have become the cause of great trouble to me. For I have opened my mouth to the Lord, and I cannot take back my vow."*

JUDGES 11:35 ESV

It's easy to believe God is in control and our faith unshakable when we are worshipping in church after a week of victorious devotional life and solid witnessing for Christ. It's more difficult to believe when one has been spiritually indiscreet, even with the right motive.

Here is a loving father who has only one beloved child, his daughter. He would do anything in his power for her good. And yet, in a moment of spiritual passion, he vows recklessly, not thinking through all the implications. He doesn't seem to consider that his daughter might be first to greet him.

Have you tried to do a good thing in your spiritual zeal and then discovered that it hurt someone you loved?

Take a breath. Hear God's voice. He is in control anyway: "When the earth totters, and all its inhabitants, it is I who keep steady its pillars. Selah" (Psalm 75:3 ESV).

It's best to vow with understanding. But remember it's *God* who keeps the earth steady, even in our moments of human faltering.

*God of heaven, I trust in Your strength today.*
*Give me wisdom in what I vow. Amen.*

## STRONGER THAN
## REBELLIOUS CHILDREN

*The woman bore a son and called his name Samson. And the young man grew, and the Lord blessed him. And the Spirit of the Lord began to stir him. . . . Then he came up and told his father and mother, "I saw one of the daughters of the Philistines at Timnah. Now get her for me as my wife."*

JUDGES 13:24-25; 14:2 ESV

Most women don't have an angel announce their upcoming pregnancy. But the barren wife of Manoah did. The angel even made a return trip to tell her husband the same news. Manoah was also seeking the Lord for guidance on how to raise a son who was to be set apart for God—a Nazarite. It was an honor but one that came with social stigma—a Nazarite was not to cut his hair or to enjoy any food or drink made with grapes, which were a fundamental part of Hebrew life. The babe they would name Samson would also have to be especially kosher in his diet.

Imagine the parents' dismay when, as a young adult, Samson demands that his father arrange a marriage with a Philistine woman.

Maybe you have raised a child who turned on you and your belief in God. Just remember, the redemption of God is stronger than rebellion. Don't give up.

---

*Lord God, You are the One who gives wisdom to earthly parents.*
*I ask for discernment and grace today. Amen.*

# WHEN YOU STAND ALONE

*"You will be hated by all for my name's sake.*
*But not a hair of your head will perish."*
LUKE 21:17-18 ESV

One of the most heartening practices in the courtroom is the tradition of having the defense lawyer stand beside his client as the verdict is handed down. The defendant, whether innocent or guilty, does not stand alone to hear his or her fate. He or she is supported by the person who knows the most about the case, the motives, the angles, the minute details.

In His earthly life, Jesus often spoke to peoples' fears of the future. He knew that humans were apt to worry about what's coming and be anxious about how to handle it. When His disciples questioned Him, Jesus supplied the answers. His listeners didn't always understand the descriptions He gave them because they weren't used to looking at life through the lens of a heavenly kingdom. But Jesus tried to prepare them for the fall of Jerusalem and the destruction of the temple, for wars and future conflict.

It's encouraging to realize we'll never stand alone in the defense of our faith. Although it may appear as if there's no one else in the well of the courtroom with us, our spiritual eyes can recognize the empowering presence of Jesus standing beside us.

*Dear Lord, I am trusting in You for the strength and confidence*
*I need when my time comes to stand up with and for You. Amen.*

## WATCH FOR TRAPS

*"Heaven and earth will pass away, but my words will not pass away. But watch yourselves lest your hearts be weighed down with dissipation and drunkenness and cares of this life, and that day come upon you suddenly like a trap."*
LUKE 21:33-34 ESV

The old saying goes that nothing is sure in life but death and taxes. And, at times, we must admit that seems true.

Yet, Jesus reminded His disciples that the Word of God is a sure thing. It will never pass away. And because we know that, we are able to trust it to help us avoid the traps of living in this temporal world.

Jesus warned us that deliberate sins, spiritual carelessness, and ordinary busyness can be traps for our souls. The only way to live a truly unshakable life in any generation, any culture, is to have an intentional and regular focus on the eternal Word.

Psalm 76:9 (ESV) says that "God arose to establish judgment, to save all the humble of the earth." A sign of real humility is being willing to accept words of wisdom from a trusted Source. When we hear its admonitions and obey it, our eyes become aware of the traps that lay before us. And we will be empowered by the Holy Spirit to walk in spiritual freedom.

*Dear God, I want to avoid traps the enemy may have laid for me. Guide me as I read Your Word and walk in Your freedom. In Jesus' name, amen.*

## WONDERS OF OLD

*Then I said, "I will appeal to this, to the years of the right hand
of the Most High." I will remember the deeds of the LORD;
yes, I will remember your wonders of old.*
PSALM 77:10-11 ESV

A t times, it seems our generation has the corner on grisly murders and rampant sexual sins. But there has been corruption of God's plan for humankind since the first sin in the perfect Garden.

Judges 19-20 contains a horrific account—an account of betrayal, family feuding, rape, intrigue, perversion, murder, heartless people. It caused a national uproar and a war between Israel and the men of Gibeah, the perpetrators.

When we read of things like this in scripture and then read the reports of what's happening in today's world, we're tempted to give in to spiritual discouragement, fear, or anxiety. But we must remember that, when the psalmist saw the evil around him, he chose to focus on the track record of the One he served—not the human race to which he belonged.

Today is the National Day of Prayer in the United States. Although we may often be appalled at the sins of our nation, the dysfunction in our families, and the seeming powerlessness of our churches, we need not despair. Instead, we may appeal and look to the Most High of America. The God who performed "wonders of old."

*Lord God of wonders, today we pray for our nation and its people.
Turn us back to You and Your Word. In Jesus' name, amen.*

## THE SIFTER AND OUR FAITH

*"Simon, Simon, behold, Satan demanded to have you, that he might sift you like wheat, but I have prayed for you that your faith may not fail. And when you have turned again, strengthen your brothers."*

LUKE 22:31-32 ESV

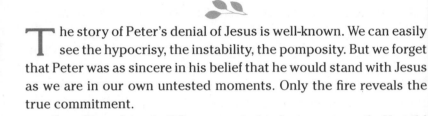

The story of Peter's denial of Jesus is well-known. We can easily see the hypocrisy, the instability, the pomposity. But we forget that Peter was as sincere in his belief that he would stand with Jesus as we are in our own untested moments. Only the fire reveals the true commitment.

Jesus knew how frail Peter was in his human strength. He told Peter that Satan wanted to *sift* him like wheat. The Greek phrase used here means "to shake in a sieve" or "agitate." Satan wanted to put Peter into a situation where he would totally reverse his decision to follow Jesus.

Satan desires to have you today. He's maliciously planning what situation he can create in your life that will make you turn on Christ and give up your discipleship. He's looking for a way to sift you.

But don't let him. Claim Christ's power and resist the temptation! And if you do give in, don't let that be the final word. Repent and go strengthen others.

*Lord Jesus, give me the strength of the Holy Spirit today so I can stand strong in You when Satan tries to sift me. I ask this in Your holy name, amen.*

## PARABLES OF OLD

*"The Lord repay you for what you have done,
and a full reward be given you by the Lord, the God of Israel,
under whose wings you have come to take refuge!"*
RUTH 2:12 ESV

This story of a widowed woman from a foreign nation who was given a second chance at love and then became part of the line of Messiah has captured imaginations and hopes down through time. We thrill to the tale of the rich landowner Boaz whose eyes and heart are captured by the destitute immigrant. We rejoice when he marries her and she bears a child, a "grandson" to Naomi in her old age, a blessing this grandmother probably thought she'd never see after the death of her sons.

Ruth was determined to adopt the homeland, the people, and the God of her mother-in-law, Naomi. Ruth took refuge under His *wings*. This Hebrew word denotes a covering and can mean the corner of a skirt. This is especially meaningful to the story when we remember that Ruth asked Boaz to spread the skirt of his robe over her, a figurative request for his protection and provision in marriage.

We too can come to the heavenly Kinsman-Redeemer, Jesus, and ask for His mercy and grace and strength. And as we do so, He'll cover us with His wings of love, and we'll discover an unshakable refuge there.

*Lord Jesus, I pray for Your forgiveness, protection,
and guidance. Please be my Redeemer today. Amen.*

# A MOTHER'S GREATEST RESOURCE

*There followed him a great multitude of the people and of
women who were mourning and lamenting for him. But turning
to them Jesus said, "Daughters of Jerusalem, do not weep for
me, but weep for yourselves and for your children." . . . And all
his acquaintances and the women who had followed him
from Galilee stood at a distance watching these things. . . .
The women who had come with him from Galilee followed
and saw the tomb and how his body was laid. Then
they returned and prepared spices and ointments.*
LUKE 23:27-28; 49; 55-56 ESV

These women who were friends of Jesus must surely have felt
that their world was coming to an end. The One they believed
to be the Messiah had been sentenced and executed. There was
no worse death, no greater shame, no crueler ending of life. Their
foundation was shattering.

Today is Mother's Day. What in your life today seems like the end?
Although we can't know exactly how those women felt in Jerusalem
that day, we know how desperate we are at times with the challenges
of our relationships, professions, homes, and families.

Yet, by faith, we know the other difficulties we face cannot
and will not triumph over us if we latch on to Jesus' grace. He is a
mother's greatest Resource.

---

*Lord, when I feel abandoned and hopeless, I ask You,
by Your grace, to give me strength, wisdom,
and the courage to keep going. Amen.*

# THE ORDERED WORLD

*Then Hannah prayed: "My heart rejoices in the LORD! The LORD*
*has made me strong. Now I have an answer for my enemies; I*
*rejoice because you rescued me. No one is holy like the LORD!*
*There is no one besides you; there is no Rock like our God. . . .*
*For all the earth is the LORD's, and he has set the world in order."*
1 SAMUEL 2:1-2, 8 NLT

Little girls still love the Nancy Drew books by Carolyn Keene. Some may have even imagined themselves as the titian-haired girl detective. Fans know that every now and then, Nancy is described as "nonplussed." Being nonplussed, unable to figure something out, was unusual for Nancy and thus it merits a statement.

Sometimes those who do not believe in God are nonplussed. They prefer a theory of randomness over the concept of intelligent design. And yet they discover in the created world that God brought into being a structured and disciplined world, a universe that runs on a rhythm, an earth that circles the sun and experiences seasons, a vast array of atoms and cells that operate according to certain rules, and a species of humankind with bodies that regenerate and reproduce according to a prescribed pattern.

We are not adrift in a random twilight zone. We have a God who holds the earth in His hands.

*Creator God, thank You for the beautiful and orderly things*
*You create. I trust You, my Rock, with my life. amen.*

# THE UNFAILING ONE

*For the law was given through Moses, but God's unfailing love
and faithfulness came through Jesus Christ. No one has ever
seen God. But the unique One, who is himself God, is near to the
Father's heart. He has revealed God to us.*
JOHN 1:17-18 NLT

One day a Sunday school teacher told a boy to draw a picture in class. As he was busily working, the teacher asked him what he was drawing.

"A picture of God."

"But no one knows what God looks like."

He smiled. "They will when I'm done!"

This story makes us smile because all of us want to know what God looks like. At least we think we do.

A vision of God would be one thing. But His actual *presence* would be too much for us to take. That's why God would only allow Moses to see a shadow of a shadow of His glory. And even then, Moses had to veil his face so other people could look at him afterward.

Jesus came to show us what the Father looks like. In human flesh, God looks like Jesus. He talks like Jesus. He loves like Jesus. He redeems like Jesus. Jesus is God. And He was sent from heaven to show us the Father's unfailing love and faithfulness. Within Him, we find our unshakable security!

*Father, thank You for sending Jesus, Your Son, in the flesh,
representing Your unfailing love and faithfulness.
In Him I find my unshakable security! Amen.*

# GOD ABOVE IT ALL

*Then Samuel said to all the people of Israel, "If you want to
return to the LORD with all your hearts, get rid of your foreign
gods and your images of Ashtoreth. Turn your hearts to the
LORD and obey him alone; then he will rescue you from the
Philistines." So the Israelites got rid of their images of Baal
and Ashtoreth and worshiped only the LORD.*

1 SAMUEL 7:3-4 NLT

The presence of God dwelled in a tangible way with the Israelites.
The Ark of the Covenant was a holy piece of furniture, symbolic
of the glory of God among them. The pagan nation of Philistia
discovered this in a dramatic way. It happened when they carried
the Ark off as a trophy of war. They brought it into the temple of
their idol Dagon. Later they found Dagon had fallen face down and
broken apart in the presence of Jehovah.

After the Ark was returned to the people of Israel, Samuel
commanded them to rip out the idols in their homes and in their
hearts and return wholly to the one true God.

Through this story, God tells us the same thing. We don't need
the Ark today. We ourselves are the temples of the Holy Spirit if we
have received Christ as Savior. And we are made holy by allowing
only His presence within us.

*Almighty God, thank You for sending Your Holy Spirit
to dwell in me. Shine Your presence through
me to others. In Jesus' name, amen.*

# UNSEEN KING AND KINGDOM

*Samuel was displeased with their request and went to the LORD
for guidance. "Do everything they say to you," the LORD replied,
"for they are rejecting me, not you. They don't want me
to be their king any longer."* . . .
*"Dear woman, that's not our problem," Jesus replied.
"My time has not yet come." But his mother told
the servants, "Do whatever he tells you."*
1 SAMUEL 8:6-7; JOHN 2:4-5 NLT

I n the Old Testament, the people of Israel, who were chosen as the
earthly channel through which the Messiah would come, often
envied other nations—their visible gods and their visible kings. The
history of the Hebrews repeats ad nauseum the cycle of idolatry
and repentance. One of the more notable stories was the creation
of the golden calf by Aaron. Having finally grown weary of Jehovah
God as their invisible, heavenly King, the Israelites demanded one
they could see.

In the New Testament, the followers of Jesus, even His very
apostles, could not recognize that He was working for a heavenly
kingdom. They wanted a Messiah who would conquer in earthly ways.
But Jesus knew the time hadn't yet come, as He told His mother at
the wedding in Canaan.

Look for the unexpected and invisible ways in which God is at
work in your world. But don't reject it if it doesn't align with your
imagined sequences.

*Lord, I know You are at work. Help me
trust Your eternal, unseen plan. Amen.*

# BIRTH MATTERS

*Jesus replied, "I assure you, no one can enter the
Kingdom of God without being born of water and the
Spirit. Humans can reproduce only human life,
but the Holy Spirit gives birth to spiritual life."*
JOHN 3:5-6 NLT

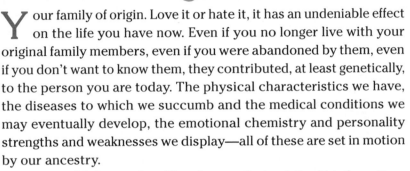

Your family of origin. Love it or hate it, it has an undeniable effect on the life you have now. Even if you no longer live with your original family members, even if you were abandoned by them, even if you don't want to know them, they contributed, at least genetically, to the person you are today. The physical characteristics we have, the diseases to which we succumb and the medical conditions we may eventually develop, the emotional chemistry and personality strengths and weaknesses we display—all of these are set in motion by our ancestry.

Jesus told the teacher, Nicodemus, that spiritual birth matters the most. While human beings can only reproduce earthly life that will someday die, God can produce eternal life in us through the Holy Spirit. And that genetic code results in the nature of God being reproduced in our attitudes, actions, words, and opinions. It will ground us in holiness, help us remain unshakable in the extremities of life, and usher us at last into the everlasting Kingdom.

*Father God, thank You for making the way through Jesus
for me to be born again of the Spirit. My true place
in Your family is what matters most. Amen.*

## CONTINUALLY SATISFIED

*Jesus replied, "If you only knew the gift God has for you
and who you are speaking to, you would ask me,
and I would give you living water."*
JOHN 4:10 NLT

In the Old Testament, the people of God are continually searching for a place to belong. They want to live in peace, raise their families, tend their land, and leave a legacy for the next generation. Over and over, all these things seem denied to them. In fact, in Psalm 78, the history of the Israelites is told—and it's a tale of wandering indeed. Both literally and spiritually.

In New Testament days, the Samaritans were living proof that often the quest for happiness did not turn out well. The result of intermarriage, the people of Samaria were considered "dogs" by full Jews. And the Samaritans returned the favor by hating the Hebrews as well.

When Jesus purposely stopped by Jacob's well to talk to a Samaritan woman, He acted completely out of character for a Jewish man. But He went a step further. He even offered her the same redemption He came to bring to His own people. He invited her to drink the living water of relationship with God. He welcomed her to enjoy fulfillment with everyone else who puts their trust in Him.

*Father, often I forget how great a gift it is that I have a
relationship with You to satisfy my deep longing! Thank
You for this continual drink of refreshing, living water. Amen.*

# WORSHIPPING BOTH WAYS

*God is a Spirit (a spiritual Being) and those who worship*
*Him must worship Him in spirit and in truth (reality).*
JOHN 4:24 AMPC

Y ou've no doubt heard someone say, "I will be there in spirit!"
    That means that, though it's not possible to be physically
present at an event, the person will be thinking about the ones
gathered and will be "there" in a vicarious way through the longing
to be so.

Yet being "there" in spirit is not a good substitute for actually
being present. We are flesh and blood entities who enjoy concrete
interaction and relationship. But we are also spirit-beings who have
the eternal breath of our Creator in us; our spirits will live forever
in either heaven or hell.

God sent His Son to take on flesh and show us what He's like.
And then, on the day of Pentecost, He sent the Holy Spirit to indwell
believers. Thus, we have both the bodily example of Jesus and the
Spirit-guidance from heaven. We can worship our God with our
bodies and in our spirits.

We can pray, sing, raise our hands, and engage in other outward
expressions of worship.

We can lift our spirits to God in submission and devotion at any
time and in any place.

*Father, there is no God like You, who created me, loved me, and*
*sacrificed for me. Today I worship You in spirit and in truth. Amen.*

## BETTER THAN SACRIFICE

*Samuel said, Has the Lord as great a delight in burnt offerings and sacrifices as in obeying the voice of the Lord? Behold, to obey is better than sacrifice, and to hearken than the fat of rams. For rebellion is as the sin of witchcraft, and stubbornness is as idolatry and teraphim (household good luck images). Because you have rejected the word of the Lord, He also has rejected you from being king.*
1 SAMUEL 15:22-23 AMPC

Some Christian women have this mom-rule for their children: no "witchy" movies. It's a healthy fear of everything paranormal and demonic that prompts these parents to install strict boundaries along these lines.

Whatever your own viewing standards, we have to recognize that God was very severe on dealing with "familiar spirits." Because this spiritual activity was not holy but originated with the fallen angels of Satan, God wanted His people to have nothing to do with it.

In today's passage above, the prophet Samuel likens King Saul's disobedience toward God to the sin of witchcraft, a sin God abhorred. This is the reason we need to teach children to obey, to respect the authority of a parent. If children are allowed to rebel against Mom or Dad, they may more easily rebel against God someday.

*Dear Lord, search my heart and show me if there is any hint of rebellion in it so that I can repent and make it right. In Jesus' name, amen.*

## THE GLORY THAT AWAITS

*The person whose ears are open to My words [who listens to My message] and believes and trusts in and clings to and relies on Him Who sent Me has (possesses now) eternal life. And he does not come into judgment [does not incur sentence of judgment, will not come under condemnation], but he has already passed over out of death into life.*

JOHN 5:24 AMPC

When you were a child, one of the joys of looking forward to Christmas may have been imagining the thrill of owning a new toy. Perhaps you saw a picture of a desired gift or the real thing itself and imagined yourself playing with it for hours on end. Of course, your anticipation may have been more satisfying than the reality. Though you may have loved some of the Christmas gifts received, you may have realized you'd experienced the most joy in going to sleep at night and dreaming of the joy that awaited in those packages around the tree.

Fortunately, we don't have to imagine we'll have the gift of eternal life someday. Jesus tells us His gift of eternal life *is already ours!* Yet we *do* anticipate the complete fulfillment of it.

How wonder-filled we can be as we live this life, knowing that now and forever, we will always have God within and with us.

*Heavenly Father, thank You for giving me eternal life through Your Son. I rejoice in that knowledge today! Amen.*

## SHINING STRENGTH

*Turn us again, O God, and cause thy face
to shine; and we shall be saved.*
PSALM 80:3 KJV

On an overcast day, our energy can be at a low ebb. It feels dark and limp, even with bright lights in the home or office. Of course, we all like a rainy day now and then, but it does seem to fit better with huddling under a quilt than with tackling energetic projects. But notice the difference to your mood when the clouds start to split and a ray of sunshine beams through.

In school we learned the sun is always shining just above the clouds. But that doesn't seem possible when all we can see is the dark, menacing atmosphere around us. Yet when the sun starts to dance and glitter in happy rays, there is suddenly a lift to everything.

In scripture, the imagery of God causing His face to shine on someone is symbolic of His blessing. The psalmist acknowledges that the only way Israel will be saved from her calamities and her transgressions is for the mercies of God to shine down on her.

Are you under a spiritual cloud today?

Does it seem that all is dark?

Do you need mercy for sin or grace for trials?

Remember God is above all.

Turn to Him and ask Him to turn His face to you. He will. He promised.

*God, today please turn Your face to me and
shine down grace for my need. Amen.*

# WALKING ON THE SEA

*And the sea arose by reason of a great wind that blew. So when
they had rowed about five and twenty or thirty furlongs, they see
Jesus walking on the sea, and drawing nigh unto the ship: and
they were afraid. But he saith unto them, It is I; be not afraid.*

JOHN 6:18-20 KJV

Sea stories capture the imagination. Tales like *Moby Dick* recount
the harrowing times sailors endured at sea and relate legends
of sea monsters lurking in the depths, dragging great ships down,
and swallowing men thrown overboard.

Surely many of the disciples, those who'd lived by the sea all
their lives, had heard their share of such stories. And there's nothing
that makes fear arise more than a violent storm on the water. Then,
in the middle of their panic and chaos, while furiously rowing, they
saw an apparition walking on top of the water. And they were afraid.

We've all experienced figurative storms in our lives. Tossed
about in ferocious waves, driven by gale-force winds, sometimes
we didn't recognize Jesus when He came.

That's why we need to hear His voice by reading His Word. In
it, He tells us, just as He told His disciples, not to be afraid. Jesus
reminds us that He's in charge of all. He brings calm to the chaos.
We can continue rowing.

*Lord Jesus, just as You brought peace to the sea,
bring peace to me in this moment of now. Amen.*

# WIDE MOUTHS AND MANY BLESSINGS

*I am the Lord thy God, which brought thee out of the*
*land of Egypt: open thy mouth wide, and I will fill it.*
PSALM 81:10 KJV

The small-town dentist had a needlework plaque on his wall with these fitting words: "OPEN THY MOUTH WIDE AND I WILL FILL IT." It seems a scripture readymade for a such a profession.

But, humor aside, there is another truth for us to discover.

This psalm speaks of the history of the Hebrew people, recounting how God led them out of Egypt and through the wilderness. In this verse, the Lord is telling them that He has delivered them into the promised land. He admonishes them to open wide—to anticipate the good things that He would do for them.

Sometimes we are afraid to expect good things from God. It seems presumptuous. But remember that God says to have an open mouth, not open hands. He is not responding to a "gimme" attitude but rather is, as a mother bird, nourishing His child with good things. We cannot expect unhealthy pampering, but we can expect delight as God meets our needs in good ways.

*Father God, You are good and wise in all You do.*
*Today, I open my mouth like a child in a snowfall and*
*expect You to give me all I need. In Jesus' name, amen.*

# RESPECT GOD'S ANOINTED

*And he [David] said unto his men, The LORD forbid that I should*
*do this thing unto my master, the LORD's anointed, to stretch forth*
*mine hand against him, seeing he is the anointed of the LORD.*
1 SAMUEL 24:6 KJV

It was usually considered bad form for either side to target officers in a military engagement during the American War for Independence. There was a sense of honor for the role of being set apart to lead, an honor for honor. The gold braid and epaulets and other distinguishing folderol sent a clear message—this person carries authority.

David, running for his life from the maniacal King Saul, recognized this very important fact. And though he did nothing that harmed the anointed leader of Israel, David was assaulted by his conscience after even a symbolic act against the man God had appointed to guide the Hebrews.

It's tempting for us to find fault with our spiritual authority today. But it will serve us well to remember David's deep conviction and refuse to stretch out our hands, even figuratively, against someone whom God has called and placed. And if there is actual wrongdoing in that person, God will, as He did in the case of Saul, deal with it justly and rightly.

*Lord, help me always remember to show honor for those You*
*have called into spiritual leadership. In Jesus' name, amen.*

## SECURING THE INSECURE

*Defend the poor and fatherless: do justice to the*
*afflicted and needy. Deliver the poor and needy:*
*rid them out of the hand of the wicked.*

PSALM 82:3-4 KJV

The greatness of a nation can be determined by how it treats its less fortunate. Those who understand the need to defend those who cannot defend themselves experience a security that others do not.

Standing up for the poverty-stricken and the orphaned is more than giving handouts. It's defending their privilege of defending themselves. It's enabling them the opportunity to gather and gain for themselves (seen in the Old Testament laws about letting the indigent glean in the fields; e.g., Leviticus 19:9-10), to become in a way unshakable themselves. It's affording them the right to live by protecting those who are medically fragile or yet unborn. It's acknowledging that they are capable and valuable and deserve what everyone else deserves—not a subsidy but an opportunity.

Jesus modeled compassion. And often, He allowed the needy to expend effort as well—washing in the pool of Siloam, removing the graveclothes, picking up the bedroll.

Defending the needy is standing in the gap when they cannot and then equipping them to take your place in the line. This understanding of God's economy assures us that things will be well.

*Dear God, please grant me wisdom and compassion so*
*that I may wisely help to empower those who are poor,*
*fatherless, and needy. In Jesus' name, amen.*

## SOLID RESTORATION

*When Jesus had lifted up himself, and saw none but the woman,
he said unto her, Woman, where are those thine accusers? hath
no man condemned thee? She said, No man, Lord. And Jesus
said unto her, Neither do I condemn thee: go, and sin no more.*
JOHN 8:10-11 KJV

In the well-known story of the woman caught in the act of adultery, Jesus knows very well what she has done—she has sinned egregiously and intentionally. He also knows what the hypocritical Pharisees want Him to do with her—condemn her then stone her.

Instead, Jesus does what no one expects.

He forgives her.

He convicts them.

She is not expecting mercy. The Law was clear on her punishment. But Jesus fulfilled the Law because He was soon going to pay the price for her sin. So, He forgave her.

The Pharisees were not expecting to feel convicted of their own sins. But, ironically, the One who could legitimately cast the first stone—the sinless Son of God—reminded them that they were not qualified to carry out an execution based on their own merits.

Jesus was always doing the unexpected. Not because He didn't value norms but because He came to reinvent them—with grace.

*Dear Father, please give me eyes to see others through Your lens
of mercy. Instead of rejecting them, prompt me to point them to
the Source of forgiveness and restoration. In Jesus' name, amen.*

# THAT WORD "INDEED"

*If the Son therefore shall make you free, ye shall be free indeed.*
JOHN 8:36 KJV

L ittle children often want extra security as reassurance.
"Do you promise?"
"Cross your heart and hope to die?"
"Pinky promise?"

Yet there are times when all of us—adults and children alike—want and need reassurance. In a world where promises are sometimes lightly kept and commitment is elusive, we crave confirmation about important matters. We want to know that the people important to us aren't going to abandon us. We want to know that the things that matter in life will stay the same. We want to know that a certain medication will have the desired results or that a product will live up to its advertising. We examine reviews for online purchases and peruse the comments before trying new restaurants. We are a society that likes to know what we're getting.

Jesus made sure everyone would know He has power to free us from any type of bondage. Through Him, we can be not only free but free indeed. For sure.

There are many types of bondage—emotional, spiritual, sexual, relational, chemical, behavioral, and more. But He is the Master locksmith. He has the key to any type of chain that binds you. Today, Jesus beckons you to find out for yourself that *He* is the great Emancipator.

*Jesus, I rejoice that You set captives free. Help me*
*to live in Your unshakable freedom. Amen.*

## STRENGTH FROM ABOVE

*Blessed are those whose strength is in you, in whose heart are the highways to Zion. . . . For a day in your courts is better than a thousand elsewhere. I would rather be a doorkeeper in the house of my God than dwell in the tents of wickedness. For the LORD God is a sun and shield; the LORD bestows favor and honor. No good thing does he withhold from those who walk uprightly. O LORD of hosts, blessed is the one who trusts in you!*
PSALM 84:5, 10–12 ESV

In ancient times, many people groups worshipped the sun. In primitive settings, without the benefit of scientific discovery, guided by superstition, the bright star in the sky seemed to them the most powerful force at work. It seemed to control the seasons and the weather, and it brought either warmth or lack of it to the earth; it caused things to grow. To this sun god, they sacrificed and paid homage. And yet it shone all the while because of the goodness of the God of the universe.

The psalmist tells us that our Lord God is a sun and shield. He is both the brightness and the shade on our souls. He, not the star He created in the heavens, bestows favor and honor on the earth and its dwellers. And in that truth, there is unshakable confidence.

*Creator God, Your power is above the heavens and beyond my imagination. Thank You for making this world and for sustaining me in it. Amen.*

## DRAWN TOWARD TRUTH

*But David answered Rechab and Baanah his brother,*
*the sons of Rimmon the Beerothite, "As the LORD lives . . .*
*How much more, when wicked men have killed a righteous*
*man in his own house on his bed, shall I not now require his*
*blood at your hand and destroy you from the earth?"*
2 SAMUEL 4:9, 11 ESV

As we read the Old Testament, we encounter practices that appear barbaric, relational systems that look dysfunctional, and a people who seem too unstable to be the earthly channel for the coming of Messiah. But we must remember that God was leading them and working with them in direct and often immediate ways of guidance and judgment.

This instant retribution for the sin of Rechab and Baanah may appear to us to be hasty and unmerciful. But we must remember that their law was "life for life, eye for eye, tooth for tooth" (Exodus 21:23-24 KJV). It was only when Jesus came to fulfill the law that mercy shaped the way we interpret sentencing today. Now, although God's judgment is still certain, it is delayed until the end of life.

Difficult to understand passages in scripture may tempt us to doubt the integrity of God. But we must remember that God does and will always reveal the full truth of His sovereignty through time.

*Father God, You have opened up the truth to us through the*
*revelation of Your Son. Today, I thank You for the secure*
*foundation I have in this knowledge. Amen.*

## TRUST HIS CHARACTER

*Yes, the LORD will give what is good, and our land*
*will yield its increase. Righteousness will go before*
*him and make his footsteps a way.*
PSALM 85:12-13 ESV

Moms sometimes say to their children, "You'll understand this someday when you're a parent." Oh, how true those words are! And although this truth cannot be used as a reason for everything we require of our children, it is an important point. Some things cannot be understood until one has reached maturity and had comparable life experience.

Perhaps this is just a tiny glimpse into how we should process the workings of God in our world and lives. Of course, we will never "mature" into being just like God, but perhaps, with our heavenly minds and understanding, we will see just a bit more.

For now, we can understand that much of the sorrow and pain we bear is the result of the curse that sin brought onto the human family and even nature itself. For now, trust is the action to which we are called. Trust that the God of holy character can only do holy things. Trust that we don't need to understand everything right now.

Because God is righteous and just, He will do, as this psalm says, what is good, even if we can't fully understand it.

*Heavenly Father, I trust You today to do what is good.*
*Give me grace to have an unwavering trust in You*
*and to rest in You. In Jesus' name, amen.*

# EVOLUTION AND SHEPHERDS

*"I am the good shepherd. The good shepherd lays down his life*
*for the sheep. . . . For this reason the Father loves me, because*
*I lay down my life that I may take it up again. No one takes it*
*from me, but I lay it down of my own accord. I have authority to*
*lay it down, and I have authority to take it up again.*
*This charge I have received from my Father."*
JOHN 10:11, 17-18 ESV

Charles Darwin's book, *The Origin of the Species,* became an anthology for new ways of thinking about the universe and its beginnings, purporting the existence of life by chance, at random. If this is so, there is no purpose, no overarching reason for us or our world and no need for any type of guidance in our lives.

Yet God's Word does not affirm this belief. And neither did Jesus when He came to fulfill the Word. God says we need a Guide, a Caretaker, a Provider, a Savior, a Redeemer, a Shepherd. And that's why Jesus came. He came to lay down His life of His own free will, of His own authority. That's what good shepherds do. The despair of evolutionary teaching has nothing to compare to the unfaltering love that Jesus showed and continues to show His people.

*Lord Jesus, I claim You as my Shepherd.*
*Thank You for laying down Your life for me. Amen.*

# THE CONSEQUENCES OF MISSTEPS

*Nathan said to David, "You are the man! Thus says the Lord,
the God of Israel. . . 'The sword shall never depart from your
house, because you have despised me and have taken the
wife of Uriah the Hittite to be your wife.'" . . . David said to
Nathan, "I have sinned against the Lord." And Nathan said to
David, "The Lord also has put away your sin; you shall not die.
Nevertheless, because by this deed you have utterly scorned
the Lord, the child who is born to you shall die."*
2 Samuel 12:7, 10, 13-15 esv

The tale of King David's sin with Bathsheba has been told and retold for generations, and rightly so. But it will only do us good if we remember that what David discovered is true in our own lives. Our sins will end up backfiring on us, making us suffer for our missteps.

Numbers 32:23 (esv) says, "Be sure your sin will find you out." About this verse, Matthew Henry wrote, "It concerns us now to find our sins out, that we may repent of them, and forsake them, lest they find us out to our ruin."

Like David, we may try to hide our sins. But they are sure to bubble up to the surface. So it's better to fess up now, ask for God's forgiveness, and change our way, lest our sins lead to our ruin.

*Lord God, examine my heart and show me any sin within it. Amen.*

# THE INEVITABILITY OF ETERNITY

*Jesus said to her, "I am the resurrection and the life.*
*Whoever believes in me, though he die, yet shall*
*he live, and everyone who lives and believes in*
*me shall never die. Do you believe this?"*
JOHN 11:25-26 ESV

A child may first become acquainted with suffering and death through pets. A youngster may become a firsthand witness to a beloved animal—whether it be a kitten, dog, or even a goldfish—becoming injured or losing its life in myriad of ways and having to be either lovingly nursed or returned to the earth.

For a wise mother, the death of a pet can be an opportunity to teach her child that humans don't disintegrate into nothingness. Although our bodies may decompose, we're created with never-dying souls that live on and on.

To the grieving sister of Lazarus, Jesus said that the person who believes in Him for salvation will never die! Because Jesus is the very embodiment of resurrection and life.

Today is Memorial Day in the United States. As we remember those who gave their lives for freedom, let us also remember the One who made eternal life in heaven possible for anyone who believes in Him.

*Dear Lord, thank You for eternal life in Your Son.*
*May my life today be a witness to the unending and unshakable*
*hope I have in You, and help me find a way to share*
*that hope with others. In Christ's name, amen.*

# THE GREATEST DECLARATION

*The large crowd that had come to the feast heard that
Jesus was coming to Jerusalem. So they took branches of
palm trees and went out to meet him, crying out, "Hosanna!
Blessed is he who comes in the name of the Lord, even the
King of Israel!" And Jesus found a young donkey and sat on it,
just as it is written, "Fear not, daughter of Zion; behold,
your king is coming, sitting on a donkey's colt!"*

JOHN 12:12-15 ESV

There are fewer words more exhilarating than the declaration, "And the winner is. . . !"

All of us love to win. And Jesus is the greatest Victor of all time.

When the crowds gathered in Jerusalem, they were looking for an earthly king. They saw in Jesus a pathway to liberation from the Romans, a route to importance and prosperity, a chance to come out on top.

What they didn't know was that this wasn't the biggest win. Someday, Jesus will return in the heavens, on a white horse, with a vesture dipped in blood and a sword in His hand and every eye will see Him and every knee will bow, and every tongue will confess that He is Lord (Philippians 2:11). On that great day, the declaration will be complete.

*Lord Jesus, I crown You in my heart and life today and wait with
unshakable expectation for the day I can acknowledge You with
all the rest of creation as King of kings and Lord of lords. Amen.*

## WHAT SHALL WE SAY?

*"Now my soul is troubled, and what shall I say?*
*'Father, save me from this hour'? No, it was for this very*
*reason I came to this hour. Father, glorify your name!"*
JOHN 12:27-28 NIV

Very soon, Jesus would be betrayed, abandoned, arrested, and crucified. Innocent though He was, He would take the punishment for *all* sin. His soul was troubled, and no wonder! Things couldn't get worse than that.

In our lives, when worse seems headed toward worst, our only prayer may be for rescue. *Get me out of this mess. Spare me from this trouble.* How many of us have the faith to pray, *Father, in this hour, bring glory to Your name*? Yet that's exactly what Jesus modeled. He knew the path ahead would be dark, but it would also lead to glory. So the Savior submitted; the Son put His confidence in the Father's will.

God's ways are not our ways. His *whys*—His reasons—are often not clear. But His providence is beyond question, whether that means we walk through the valley one step at a time or march triumphantly through a parted sea. We can put our troubled souls into His hands because our souls can trust in the One who glorifies His name again and again—and again (John 12:28).

---

*I pray for detours around the difficult parts of life,*
*but I believe You have a purpose even in the worst times.*
*So, Father, glorify Your name!*

## LOVE SONG

*Your love, GOD, is my song, and I'll sing it!*
*I'm forever telling everyone how faithful you are.*
PSALM 89:1 MSG

What is our song when times are tough? What refrain flows from our mouths? If we're focusing on the problems, we tend to harp on the problems, don't we? We tend to complain and lament. It might even seem that we only ever talk about the bad in our world. But what if we changed our tune? What if we sang a song of love instead?

Jesus was an earthly picture of God's love. The apostle John wrote of Jesus, "Before the Passover celebration, Jesus knew that his hour had come to leave this world and return to his Father. He had loved his disciples during his ministry on earth, and now he loved them to the very end" (John 13:1 NLT). Another translation says that Jesus loved His disciples "to the last and to the highest degree" (John 13:1 AMPC)—exactly the way God loves us. Think of it: God loves to the full. His love is never absent and never lessened. We have this love to carry us through any and all circumstances. And that's worth singing about—yes, in any and all circumstances!

Like the psalmist, let's sing of the Lord's love and never stop.

*Lord, I feel like a broken record, stuck on what's wrong.*
*Transform my words of woe into songs of praise.*
*Open my mouth to share Your love.*

## FAITHFUL IN THE STORM

*O LORD God of hosts, who is mighty as you are, O LORD,*
*with your faithfulness all around you? You rule the*
*raging of the sea; when its waves rise, you still them. . . .*
*The world and all that is in it, you have founded them.*
PSALM 89:8-9, 11 ESV

Perhaps nothing in creation can make us feel smaller than nature in the fury of a storm. Winds topple trees. Floods engulf entire towns. Once-solid land slides away. Waves higher than buildings leave rubble in their wake. Normally, nature soothes us—think gentle rains, lulling waves, and grounding earth—but when the storms roll in? Nature shakes us. . .unless we keep our minds fixed on God.

As mighty as nature's power seems, God is mightier. He is the Power that controls creation itself. The Bible tells us that God rules over the raging sea. He stills the waves. What's more, our mighty God, who founded everything that exists, radiates faithfulness. He will not leave us alone in the storm.

And that's as true of nature's storms as it is of life's storms. God is in charge of the raging seasons that threaten to overwhelm us. He can still the waves of rising fear. Nothing is mightier, no one more faithful, than He.

*Lord, with such an almighty God as You in my life,*
*I have no reason to be afraid. Remind me of Your*
*faithfulness when storms threaten to shake me.*

# DESTINATION: HEAVEN

*"Don't let your hearts be troubled. Trust in God, and trust also
in me. There is more than enough room in my Father's home.
If this were not so, would I have told you that I am going to
prepare a place for you? When everything is ready, I will come
and get you, so that you will always be with me where I am.
And you know the way to where I am going."*

JOHN 14:1-4 NLT

Imagine setting out on a road trip with no destination in mind. You could drive aimlessly for miles!

Most of the time, travelers like to know where they're going. In life, we like to know where we're headed too—in our relationships, in our careers, in our retirement. For many, planning ends with death. Their destination after this life is over is unknown.

As Christians, we don't need to wonder or worry. Jesus says, "Don't be troubled. Your future is secure. Trust Me." God has prepared a place for us, and we know the way. That should steady our hearts and our steps through life. Regardless of how "aimless" our earthly journeys may be at times, our ultimate destination is known—and we can depend on God to get us there.

*Lord, thank You for the assurance of heaven. I don't know
where my tomorrows will lead me on earth or what they
will be like. But I know where I'm headed for eternity.*

## PEACE, PLEASE!

*"Peace I leave with you; my peace I give to you.*
*Not as the world gives do I give to you. Let not your*
*hearts be troubled, neither let them be afraid."*
JOHN 14:27 ESV

What is peace? Peace can mean freedom from conflict between nations. Peace can mean harmony among people. Peace can mean calmness following chaos.

But the peace Jesus spoke about goes beyond the peace of this world. Our world is broken, so any peace we create by human effort is fragile. Not so with Jesus' peace. Jesus' peace means conflict and animosity and chaos can happen all around us, yet we remain secure, unafraid, and calm. How is *that* kind of peace possible?

Only through Christ. He can accomplish in us what we cannot do ourselves. Jesus even said, "Apart from me you can do *nothing*" (John 15:5 ESV, emphasis added). The opposite also holds true: when we abide in Him, nothing is out of our reach, including peace in our hearts.

Life may be like a smooth sea for you right now. But maybe there's something on the horizon or already surrounding you that's lapping at your peace. Abide in Jesus. Stay close to Him. He's holding out His peace. It's yours for the taking. So grab hold!

*Lord, I've been relying on the peace the world gives,*
*and it's no surprise my heart is troubled. Thank You for*
*the peace You offer—peace that is ever possible.*

# MERCIFUL

*David said to Gad, "I am in deep distress. Let us fall
into the hands of the L ORD, for his mercy is great."*
2 S AMUEL 24:14 NIV

D avid was a man after God's own heart, but he was only human. He sinned, sometimes greatly. While we might think of Bathsheba as David's greatest failure, 2 Samuel records another great failure. (Breathe a sigh of relief that *our* sins are not recorded for generations to come!) Scripture says that David was incited to number Israel and Judah. The result? David chose to sin.

But why was the census bad? What did David do that was so wrong? After all, God once commanded Moses to take a census. Unlike Moses, David wasn't acting in obedience. Maybe he wanted to boast about his military power (= pride). Maybe he needed a boost in confidence and forgot that his strength came from God (= lack of trust). In any case, David counted the people, and he was soon struck by guilt.

Ever been to that place of guilt? You gave in to temptation. Then, like it did for David, reality hit, and you realized how greatly you had sinned. So what did David do next? He prayed, confessing and asking forgiveness. He left his fate in God's hands, punishment and all. He had faith that nothing, not even great sins, can negate God's mercy—for His mercy is great indeed.

*God, please forgive my sin. I'm throwing
myself on Your mercy today.*

## HE WHO PROMISED

*How long, LORD? Will you hide yourself forever? . . . Lord,
where is your former great love, which in your
faithfulness you swore to David?*
PSALM 89:46, 49 NIV

God had made promises. Israel was His covenant nation; the Davidic throne would continue forever. But toward the end of Psalm 89, it's clear the psalmist was wondering what had happened to God's promises—because what was happening in his world seemed to contradict those promises. The psalmist described rejected people, breached walls, ruined strongholds. There was plunder going on. Exalted foes. Vanished splendor (Psalm 89:38–45 ESV). Hardly the setting for God's chosen people. Had God reneged?

So, confused and a tad frustrated, the psalmist cried out, "Where are You, God? Where is Your love?" God and His love were right where they had always been. Despite the circumstances, nothing had changed. God had even predicted the current state of affairs and reaffirmed His promises: "I will punish their transgression with the rod and their iniquity with stripes, but I will not remove from him my steadfast love or be false to my faithfulness" (Psalm 89:32–33 ESV).

God may seem missing in our lives. When the situation says one thing, we must fall back on what scripture says. And scripture says that He is a God of His word.

*God, at times it's hard to hold on to Your promises.
But I choose to believe You for every last one.*

## STABILITY IN A ROCKY WORLD

*"I'm not asking you to take them out of the world,*
*but to keep them safe from the evil one."*
JOHN 17:15 NLT

When Jesus left this earth, He would leave His disciples behind in a hostile world. They were not of the world, yet living in it, and that made for rocky days ahead.

Although our lives are filled with things that Peter, James, and John never heard of, we're in the same world as those first disciples. A fallen world. A world that wants to carry on unhindered by God and opposes believers. We may face extreme persecution, or we may just be the butt of jokes, excluded, or criticized. But Jesus didn't pray for us to be taken *out* of this mess. He prayed for stability *in* the mess. He prayed for protection—and something more: "I pray that they will all be one. . .as you are in me, Father, and I am in you. And may they be in us. . . . May they experience such perfect unity that the world will know that you sent me and that you love them as much as you love me" (John 17:21, 23 NLT).

Our world can be an unholy mess. Even so, we can be grounded in the One who loved us before this world ever existed!

*Father, a three-strand cord is not easily broken (Ecclesiastes*
*4:12). United with You and Jesus, I am not easily shaken!*

## CAUSE FOR GLADNESS

*Satisfy us in the morning with your unfailing love,*
*that we may sing for joy and be glad all our days.*
PSALM 90:14 NIV

Psalm 90 was written by Moses, "the man of God," a man who had likely seen good days, joyous days, triumphant days. We know he had also seen many hard days. He had watched his fellow Hebrews suffer oppression in Egypt. He had witnessed God's wrath over Israel's disobedience. He had led an unruly group through the wilderness for forty years. Moses' prayer here is one we might relate to: "Make us glad for as many days as you have afflicted us, for as many years as we have seen trouble" (Psalm 90:15 NIV).

When the grim days stack up, we long for just *one* glad day, let alone enough to balance the scales. Like Moses, we pray for those glad days, and God often gives us more glad days than we can count. But even if our prayers seem unanswered, we can look forward to the endless glad days that God guarantees in heaven. That future glory blots out every present trouble (Romans 8:18).

Moses included another request in his psalm—that God would so satisfy His people that they could rejoice *all* their days. Good or bad. Rain or shine. Even when our seasons seem darkest, we are not without God's light and love.

*Lord, thank You for being with me*
*and making me glad every day!*

## A MIGHTY FORTRESS

*Those who live in the shelter of the Most High will*
*find rest in the shadow of the Almighty. . . .*
*He will shelter you with his wings.*
PSALM 91:1, 4 NLT

We don't need to scroll through a news feed to know that our world isn't safe and sound. Danger isn't just on the other side of the world; sometimes it's right outside our front door. Biblical times were dangerous too. Yet the psalmist makes a bold claim: "You will not fear the terror of the night, nor the arrow that flies by day, nor the pestilence that stalks in darkness, nor the destruction that wastes at noonday. . . . It will not come near you" (Psalm 91:5–7 ESV). How does he back this up? "Because you have made the LORD your dwelling place. . .no evil shall be allowed to befall you" (Psalm 91:9–10 ESV). Believers aren't immune to trouble, but when we abide in our God, *only* what He permits touches us. And we can be sure that it fits into His good, pleasing, and perfect will.

The psalmist called the Lord "my God, in whom I trust" (Psalm 91:2 ESV). It's difficult to trust someone we aren't close to. It's even more difficult to find shelter when we're not near. For the one who remains with God, though, trust and fearlessness are easy.

*God, draw me close so that I am forever*
*in Your guarding presence.*

## WORDS TO LIVE BY

*When the soldiers crucified Jesus, they took his clothes,*
*dividing them into four shares, one for each of them, with the*
*undergarment remaining. This garment was seamless,*
*woven in one piece from top to bottom. "Let's not tear it,"*
*they said to one another. "Let's decide by lot who will get it."*
*This happened that the scripture might be fulfilled.*
JOHN 19:23-24 NIV

How did Jesus' followers react as they watched His crucifixion? Some were probably brokenhearted at the sight of the Savior's suffering. Still others probably panicked, thinking all their hopes were dying on that cross. But the ones who were paying attention would have seen that everything was going as expected.

God foreknew every detail of that dreadful day—down to the soldiers divvying up Jesus' clothes. Centuries earlier, David had written, "They pierce my hands and my feet. . . . They divide my clothes among them and cast lots for my garment" (Psalm 22:16, 18 NIV).

In trying times, we may be so focused on the trouble that we miss God's messages. No, the details of our particular troubles aren't predicted in the Bible, but God has given us details about who He is in *any* trouble—He is omniscient, trustworthy, all-powerful, compassionate—and those details see us through the trouble. Rest in His Word. All is going according to His plan.

*God, make Your messages clear to me as I read*
*the Bible. Encourage me with Your words.*

# PRAISE & WORSHIP

*It is good to give thanks to the LORD, to sing praises to
the Most High. It is good to proclaim your unfailing love
in the morning, your faithfulness in the evening. . . .
I sing for joy because of what you have done.*
PSALM 92:1-2, 4 NLT

A melody preps the audience for a poignant scene in a movie. A band blasts a rousing tune to pump up the crowd at a stadium. . . . Music has the ability to move us. If we choose to, praising God will set the tone for our lives.

God is worthy of worship. Our praises rise to Him and please His heart. *Our* hearts are affected by praise too, especially in our difficulties. Note the psalmist's words of praise that sandwich troubling reality: "O LORD, what great works you do! . . . The wicked sprout like weeds and evildoers flourish. . . . But you, O LORD, will be exalted forever" (Psalm 92:5, 7-8 NLT). Praise reminds us of truth. Our God is greatest even when evil seems to be greater. The wicked run riot now, but God will repay—He reigns forever.

It's good to sing praises to God. It's good morning and evening. It's good *any*time. Out loud or in your heart, sing of God's faithfulness. Sing of His love. Sing of how great He is!

*God, evil may clamor, but You will
hear my praise. Great are You!*

## VOICE RECOGNITION

*[Jesus] asked her, "Woman, why are you crying? Who is it you are looking for?" Thinking he was the gardener, she said, "Sir, if you have carried him away, tell me where you have put him, and I will get him." Jesus said to her, "Mary." She turned toward him and cried out in Aramaic, "Rabboni!"*
JOHN 20:15-16 NIV

Mary Magdalene made her way to Jesus' tomb before daybreak. If she had been asked what the weather would be like once the sun rose, she might have said "overcast"—weather to match the sadness inside her. She wasn't expecting to find an empty tomb. Later, she saw a man she didn't recognize—that is, until He spoke her name. Imagine the relief that replaced her distress!

Earlier in John's Gospel, Jesus said He was the Good Shepherd. As Shepherd, He calls His sheep by name, and we know His voice and follow Him into green pastures (John 10:1-18; Psalm 23:1-2). With our Shepherd is where distress dissolves. In His presence is where we thrive: "The righteous will flourish like a palm tree. . . they will flourish in the courts of our God" (Psalm 92:12-13 NIV). Sometimes distress pulls us toward God; but other times we become so distracted that we wander away. Our Shepherd is calling us back.

*Lord, may I hear Your voice over my weeping as You call me to Your side, a place of safety and love.*

## MIGHTY PEACEFUL

*On the evening of that day, the first day of the week,*
*the doors being locked where the disciples were for fear*
*of the Jews, Jesus came and stood among them and*
*said to them, "Peace be with you."*
JOHN 20:19 ESV

T he disciples were hiding out. In their place, we might well have done the same. How many times have ordinary troubles made us want to hide under the covers rather than face the day? These were extraordinary troubles. Jesus had been executed, and the disciples could be too. But suddenly Jesus was in the room, greeting them as He would more than once: "Peace be with you."

Jesus, who stood in that room with the disciples, is the same mighty God that the psalmist described: "The LORD reigns; he is robed in majesty. . . . The floods have lifted up, O LORD. . .the floods lift up their roaring. Mightier than the thunders of many waters, mightier than the waves of the sea, the LORD on high is mighty!" (Psalm 93:1-4 ESV). Isn't it interesting that the God who is so mighty so often brings peace? The thundering waters of the mightiest wave cannot compare to Him, yet He comes beside us and says, "Peace be with you." The flood's roaring can be deafening, yet it cannot drown out God's power or His words "Peace be with you."

*Thank You for Your peace, Lord, peace that*
*surpasses anything I'm going through.*

## SETTLED PLANS

*Jesus replied, "If I want him to remain alive until I return,
what is that to you? As for you, follow me."*
JOHN 21:22 NLT

J esus questioned Peter about his love. . .then Jesus predicted martyrdom for his future. Peter's total commitment to Jesus would be a *total* commitment. Close on the heels of Jesus' words, Peter looked around, saw John, and asked Jesus, "What about him?" The verses don't give us clues about Peter's tone, whether he was petulant, dismayed, or just curious. But Jesus' response is clear: "Leave that in My hands. Concentrate on following Me."

God's plans for us are not factory produced and one size fits all. They are handmade and carefully tailored. That fact is a delight when His plan is something we would have chosen ourselves. But what if it isn't? What if our hopes and dreams never come true? What if we receive an unwanted diagnosis? What if we start looking around and asking, "But what about them?"

The only way to be steady in God's plans for us individually is to leave the planning in His hands and concentrate on following Him. We trust God with our eternal lives. Can we not trust Him with our earthly lives too?

*God, Your plans for me may not be my first choice, but I choose
to rest in Your will. When I begin to wonder why my life isn't like
others', remind me that You never make mistakes.*

## WHO?

*When I said, "My foot is slipping," your unfailing love,*
*LORD, supported me. When anxiety was great within me,*
*your consolation brought me joy.*
PSALM 94:18-19 NIV

The psalms are packed with verses that describe the proliferation of evil and the suffering of saints. But you don't have to be besieged by enemies or held captive in a foreign land to sense wickedness all around. Coworkers spread damaging lies. Hackers attempt to steal. A walk through your own neighborhood may seem risky as violence increases. And what about the devil's attacks?

With threats on every side, we might feel like sitting ducks. We might ask in our hearts, as the psalmist did, "Who will rise up for me against the wicked? Who will take a stand for me against evildoers?" (Psalm 94:16 NIV). There's always an answer to those questions, even when it seems there's nothing between us and harm. Apparently the psalmist was in such a spot. Had *the Lord* not helped him, he would have died (Psalm 94:17)!

Though God does not take us out of evil's way every time, we can be sure that He has not left us to endure alone. At the moment we begin to lose our footing, His love reaches out to hold us up. Just when we think we cannot bear another ounce of anxiety, His Spirit uplifts ours.

*Lord, You are always here beside me right when I need You.*
*Thank You for Your ever-present presence.*

## KING OF KINGS

*Come, let us worship and bow down. Let us kneel*
*before the LORD our maker, for he is our God.*
*We are the people he watches over.*
PSALM 95:6-7 NLT

W hile reading through the Bible's lengthy history books (like 1 Kings), do you ever think, *What practical purpose does this serve in my life?* The names may not be familiar, and we may need a chart to keep track of who reigned when, but the biblical records remind us that no matter which kings rose and fell, God remained— the King continued to reign! Looking deeper, we see that although difficult times came along in every king's life, the ones who had hearts committed to God experienced His faithfulness. Conversely, the kings who did what angered God reaped what they sowed and forfeited God's blessing.

That's an important lesson, whether we're rulers on thrones or just an average Jane. It's a lesson woven throughout the Bible. Even the psalmist pleads for people to heed God: "If only you would listen to his voice today! The LORD says, 'Don't harden your hearts as Israel did at Meribah, as they did at Massah in the wilderness' " (Psalm 95:7-8 NLT). When we soften our hearts toward God and His ways, we can be confident that He calls us His own. Difficult times or carefree times, we are the people He watches over.

---

*Help me be loyal to You, my Father, my King.*

# SPIRIT-ENABLED

*Declare his glory among the nations,*
*his marvelous works among all the peoples!*
PSALM 96:3 ESV

66 S ing to the LORD, praise his name; proclaim his salvation day after day," the psalmist said (Psalm 96:2 NIV). But, let's face it, some days we don't feel much like singing. We know God is great, yet our burdens seem greater. We lug their heavy weight with us everywhere until the burdens are the biggest thing in our lives. They would stay that way too if we were left on our own. But we are not on our own, not since one day centuries ago.

It was the day of Pentecost. Earlier, Jesus told His followers that they would be baptized with the Holy Spirit. Just what He meant they likely didn't know. Then on that day they heard a sound like rushing wind, and flaming forked tongues rested on each of them. They were filled with the Holy Spirit! If that wasn't amazing enough, they also began speaking in different languages as the Spirit prompted them, declaring God's mighty works (Acts 2:1-4, 11). What they never imagined doing, the Spirit enabled them to do.

Still today, the Holy Spirit fills believers. Still the Spirit enables us to declare God's glory even in the bleakest times. Still He who is in us is greater than anything we encounter in life (1 John 4:4).

*Holy Spirit, fill me so full that I can't help but sing out!*

# TRIED AND TRUE

*"This promise is to you, to your children, and to those far away—all who have been called by the Lord our God."*
ACTS 2:39 NLT

W hen Peter preached a sermon at Pentecost, he drew from the scriptures, which had stood the test of time. Peter quoted David's inspired words: "I saw the Lord always before me. Because he is at my right hand, I will not be shaken. Therefore my heart is glad and my tongue rejoices; my body also will rest in hope, because you will not abandon me to the realm of the dead. . . . You will fill me with joy in your presence" (Acts 2:25-28 NIV). People were yearning for stability, for peace, hope, and joy. David was a king who had seen much trouble in his life, some self-inflicted, some not. Yet he was a man who loved God despite the trouble. And he was a child of God—God, who had held him through the trouble. Because God was near, David would not be shaken.

God's promise of a restored relationship with Him was not for David alone. It is to everyone He calls to Himself. He wants to be ever before us, ever at our side, so that we will not be shaken. That's a promise that stands the test of time.

---

*God, sometimes I depend on temporary things to provide stability. Open my eyes to see You— my eternal Rock—before me.*

## POWER-FILLED

*"Repent therefore, and turn back, that your sins may be blotted out, that times of refreshing may come from the presence of the Lord."*
ACTS 3:19-20 ESV

How mighty is our God! How utterly powerful! At His command the universe was formed out of nothingness. In His presence the same creation shakes: "The earth sees and trembles. The mountains melt like wax before the LORD, before the Lord of all the earth" (Psalm 97:4-5 ESV).

That same powerful God chooses to funnel His power into us. Imagine! His power that makes the earth tremble and mountains melt is the power that makes us new. A beggar in Jerusalem experienced this firsthand. The man had been unable to walk since birth and was carried to the temple each day, where he would remain all day, asking for alms. But God performed a miracle through Peter and John—the man's legs were healed *instantly*.

Peter was just as quick to give credit where credit was due. To the crowd he said, "Why does this take you by such complete surprise, and why stare at us. . . . The God of Abraham and Isaac and Jacob, the God of our ancestors, has glorified his Son Jesus" (Acts 3:12 MSG). It is our God also who restores us, who strengthens us, who steadies us. It is our God who makes crippled souls whole to dance and praise Him. Imagine.

*Lord, emotionally, I feel like a blob on the floor. I turn to You, the One whose power can make me stand again.*

## WHAT ABOUT EVIL?

*Let those who love the LORD hate evil, for he guards the lives of*
*his faithful ones and delivers them from the hand of the wicked.*
*Light shines on the righteous and joy on the upright in heart.*
PSALM 97:10-11 NIV

W e can pretend it isn't there. We can soften its blow by looking on the bright side. We can even escape it for brief moments via entertainment. But evil still exists—an undeniable, sad fact of a fallen world. If we can't deny it, how do we deal with it?

While we will never be okay with evil—we are in fact told to *hate* it—evil doesn't have to make us quake in our boots. When confronted with evil, we can find comfort in God. The Most High is watching over us. He is a guarding presence, a source of light and joy. He is the *only* lasting answer to evil. Social programs fail. Leaders let us down. The "gods" of money and ambition and stuff leave us empty. But those who trust in the Lord will not be put to shame.

Hold fast to the God who takes evil and redeems it (Genesis 50:20). Hold fast to the God who treads the heights and will one day trample evil for good.

---

*Lord, these days it seems there's no stopping evil,*
*yet evil is no match for You. Keep us safe in the*
*evil days and hasten the good days ahead.*

## CONTROLLING FORCE

*"Now, Lord, consider their threats and enable your servants to speak your word with great boldness."*
ACTS 4:29 NIV

With God's power behind them, Peter and John had healed a man. The witnesses kept spreading the news about the miracle throughout Jerusalem. And the Sanhedrin, the top judicial honchos, were not pleased. So the Sanhedrin told the apostles to say no more about this Jesus fellow. But that didn't make a dent. . . so they made threats and sent Peter and John on their way.

Back with the other believers, away from onlookers, the apostles could have been shaken. They could have scrambled to come up with a plan B, a way to preach without ruffling feathers. Instead, they prayed for more boldness. They knew they could be so bold because they knew who was in control. They had ancient—and recent—history to prove it. When the people plotted against Jesus, their actions had been threads in God's carefully woven design. All that had happened was only "what [God's] power and will had decided beforehand should happen" (Acts 4:28 NIV). And all that would happen in the coming days? It would be no different.

It is no different *now*. Where we feel threatened and shaky, we can pray for boldness, knowing who is in control.

*Lord, give me the boldness to live out Your will for me.*
*Even when circumstances seem against me, You are still*
*for me, and You have everything under control.*

## GOD AND FATHER

*The LORD reigns, let the nations tremble; he sits
enthroned between the cherubim, let the earth shake.*
PSALM 99:1 NIV

G od is our heavenly Father. He is a God who dries tears, who
sends His Spirit to comfort us, who enfolds us in the shelter of
His wings. He calls us to His side as a dad calls his children, and we
can call back, "Abba—Daddy!" Yet He is more. He is God Almighty.
"Great is the LORD," the psalmist wrote; "the LORD our God is holy"
(Psalm 99:2, 9 NIV). God is lofty, and down here entire nations tremble
and the earth shakes as a result.

When the Bible speaks of fearing God, it doesn't mean better-
run-and-hide fear; it means the awe and respect that overcome us
in God's presence. And that kind of fear actually ends the run-and-
hide kind, no matter where it surfaces in our lives. How can that
be? Because God is *both* mighty God and loving Father. He has the
ability and desire to hear us whenever we pray—as well as the power
and compassion to answer. He is holy and He is forgiving. He is the
steady pillar that points out the way, all the while reminding us that
we are not alone along the way. There's just no other God like Him!

*God, I am amazed by all You are. And I am so glad
that You are my God and Father.*

# THE LORD WORKS
# IN INCREDIBLE WAYS

*When Elisha arrived, the child was indeed dead,*
*lying there on the prophet's bed.*
2 KINGS 4:32 NLT

Weren't some of God's Old Testament miracles just plain odd? A dinky jar of oil fills many jars (2 Kings 4:1-7). Poisoned stew is made edible with flour (2 Kings 4:38-41). Then there's the incident of the Shunammite's son.

Elisha had foretold the child's birth, but then the child died. So Elisha prayed to God. He stretched out over the child twice, pacing the room in between. After that, the boy sneezed seven times and was alive and well. What was that all about?

The ways God works—either solo or through people—are sometimes surprising, not what *we* would expect or imagine. God simply isn't confined to convention. Still, how often do we feel unsettled looking at our situations because we are hoping for conventional solutions? We pray for God to intervene, but in the back of our minds we think there's no way things can change. Yet when Jesus told us that with faith we can say, "Mountain, move!" and it will move, He didn't spell out *how* the mountain would move (Matthew 17:20). We don't know how God will work either. And that should give us even more reason to hope.

*God, You can do anything—even in this*
*"hopeless" situation. I will trust You. And I*
*will watch for You to work in incredible ways.*

## STEER CLEAR OF EVIL

*I will be careful to lead a blameless life.*
PSALM 101:2 NIV

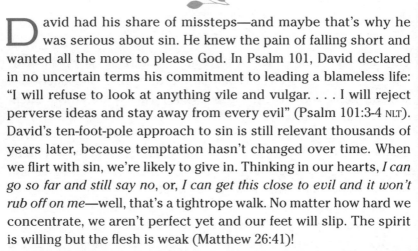

David had his share of missteps—and maybe that's why he was serious about sin. He knew the pain of falling short and wanted all the more to please God. In Psalm 101, David declared in no uncertain terms his commitment to leading a blameless life: "I will refuse to look at anything vile and vulgar. . . . I will reject perverse ideas and stay away from every evil" (Psalm 101:3-4 NLT). David's ten-foot-pole approach to sin is still relevant thousands of years later, because temptation hasn't changed over time. When we flirt with sin, we're likely to give in. Thinking in our hearts, *I can go so far and still say no*, or, *I can get this close to evil and it won't rub off on me*—well, that's a tightrope walk. No matter how hard we concentrate, we aren't perfect yet and our feet will slip. The spirit is willing but the flesh is weak (Matthew 26:41)!

What's the better tactic? No compromises, just commitment that settles our souls. No giving the flesh an inch, just pressing in close to God. There, we can walk a level path with plenty of room to put one steady foot in front of the other.

*Lord, my desire is to lead a blameless life, but I need You leading the way. Help me shun evil and keep in step with You.*

## "LEAN ON ME"

*Elisha replied, "Listen to this message from the LORD! . . .*
*By this time tomorrow in the markets of Samaria, six quarts*
*of choice flour will cost only one piece of silver."*
2 KINGS 7:1 NLT

The people in Samaria were going through a *terrible* time. The Syrians had besieged the city, which resulted in a famine. Prices skyrocketed: a donkey's head cost eighty pieces of silver; dove's dung cost five pieces of silver. Things were so desperate that mothers were eating children (2 Kings 6:28-29). Good, godly leadership was needed, but Israel's king gave up on God: "All this misery is from the LORD! Why should I wait for the LORD any longer?" (2 Kings 6:33 NLT). And his captain—a man "on whose hand the king leaned" (2 Kings 7:2 ESV)—doubted God despite Elisha's prophecy of relief. "That couldn't happen even if the LORD opened the windows of heaven!" he said (2 Kings 7:2 NLT).

But relief *did* come; God saw to that (2 Kings 7:3-20). Where the leaders lost hope in God, Elisha saw his Rock, his Rescuer, the God on whom the people could lean and never be let down. In the most terrible times imaginable, God is still God. His promises are still His promises. Lean on that truth today.

*Lord, thankfully I have not seen such terrible times.*
*But in any amount of trouble, Lord, relief is found in You!*

## GOD IN US

*"You stubborn people! You are heathen at heart and
deaf to the truth. Must you forever resist the Holy Spirit?
That's what your ancestors did, and so do you!"*
ACTS 7:51 NLT

Stephen could perform great wonders, but he wasn't making many friends among the Jewish officials. They argued with him, but Stephen's Spirit-infused wisdom bested them every time. So, failing to out-talk him, they decided to take him out instead. They dragged him before the Sanhedrin. A few false witnesses later and Stephen was in the hot seat. All eyes were on him. Would he cave? Cry? Call their bluff?

This man who was "full of God's grace and power" (Acts 6:8 NLT) began a history lesson! From Abraham to Jesus, Stephen spoke of the people's stubbornness despite God's faithfulness. He didn't defend himself so much as condemn those who refused to see and hear what God so plainly did and said.

Eloquent speech notwithstanding, things did not end happily for Stephen on earth—he was martyred. Yet he wasn't shaken. Stephen, a man so full of God's grace and power in his life, was upheld to his last breath. But Stephen isn't special in that he had some special access to divine power. He shows us that we *all* can be as unshakable—because we also have God Himself at our side and in our hearts.

*Lord, thank You that I don't face trials defenseless.
I face them with faith in You.*

# ROCK OF AGES

*Of old you laid the foundation of the earth, and the heavens are the work of your hands. They will perish, but you will remain; they will all wear out like a garment. You will change them like a robe, and they will pass away, but you are the same, and your years have no end. The children of your servants shall dwell secure; their offspring shall be established before you.*

PSALM 102:25-28 ESV

People live and die while this old world keeps spinning. Natural disasters may scar the planet we call home, but the foundation beneath us is the same foundation the forebearers walked on. Yet even the earth is not as permanent as our God. The earth and the heavens have an expiration date; God, the great I Am, will always be. They will get tattered like a well-worn garment and God will toss them away; God Himself will never change.

God's foreverness and unchangeableness are amazing enough to contemplate. But wait. . .there's more! Anyone who calls God her God will have a home in His presence—not just today, not just for a lifetime—for *all* time. He is the firm foundation for our lives and our souls. As the hymn goes, on Christ the solid Rock we stand. In Him we can trust when everything else sinks like sand underneath us.

*Lord God, there's nothing sturdier than You.*
*I am never more secure than I am with You.*

## DON'T FORGET

*Praise the Lord, my soul; all my inmost being, praise his holy name. Praise the Lord, my soul, and forget not all his benefits.*
PSALM 103:1-2 NIV

The phrase "praise the Lord" is found scores of times in the psalms, whether things were good—*or bad*. How is praise possible when our world is in turmoil? How is praise possible when all that meets our eyes is negative? We must choose to keep God's blessings in mind, to think on all God does. That's what David did. He told his soul to praise and to forget not. . . .

Forget not that God forgives every sin—even the ones we have a hard time letting go of ourselves. Forget not that God heals us, body and soul. Forget not that God redeems lives from the deep, dank, dark pit. Forget not that God then crowns us with love, with compassion that we don't deserve but that we need desperately. Forget not that God satisfies our desires with good things—yes, the *best* things—so that we are renewed like eagles soaring high above it all. (Psalm 103:3-5.)

In light of God's benefits, nothing on earth can douse our praise if we don't allow it. And nothing on earth can take God's benefits away.

*God, whatever happens around me or to me,*
*Your benefits are for sure. Praise the Lord, my soul—*
*and there is so much to praise You for!*

## LOVE ME STEADY

*For his unfailing love toward those who fear him is as*
*great as the height of the heavens above the earth.*
PSALM 103:11 NLT

To err is human, and when we're slumped in the aftermath of our latest sin, there's nothing we'd like more than a clean slate. The trouble is the devil likes to whisper in our ears. He tells us that heap of shame is where we belong. Worse yet, he tells us God prefers we stay there because a holy God can't look on us with love. Not now.

But that isn't God's truth. Not ever. If you are a trembling heap today, hear God's whispers. Imagine Him speaking His Word to you: "I have not dealt with you according to your sins; nor rewarded you according to your iniquities. For as the heaven is high above the earth, so great is My mercy toward you who fear Me. As far as the east is from the west, so far have I removed your transgressions from you. Like a father pities his children, so I pity you. For I know your frame; I remember that you are dust" (based on Psalm 103:10-14 KJV).

Ask forgiveness—for the God of mercy and compassion gives it freely. Then stand up—for His love can certainly bear your weight.

*God, I don't understand why You love me, but I'm so grateful*
*that You do. Forgive my sins. Help me rise tall and steady.*

# ANSWERS TO PRAYERS

*Ananias. . .laid his hands on him and said, "Brother Saul,
the Lord Jesus, who appeared to you on the road, has sent
me so that you might regain your sight and be filled with the
Holy Spirit." Instantly something like scales fell from
Saul's eyes, and he regained his sight.*
ACTS 9:17-18 NLT

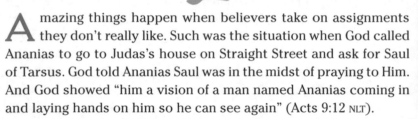

A mazing things happen when believers take on assignments they don't really like. Such was the situation when God called Ananias to go to Judas's house on Straight Street and ask for Saul of Tarsus. God told Ananias Saul was in the midst of praying to Him. And God showed "him a vision of a man named Ananias coming in and laying hands on him so he can see again" (Acts 9:12 NLT).

Ananias had already heard about Saul, how he had breathed out murderous threats against believers in Jesus. And so Ananias shared those fears with God. But God reiterated His command, saying that Saul was His chosen instrument to give the good news to the Gentiles.

So Ananias left the relative safety of his home, found Saul, and laid his hands on him. Because Ananias obeyed God, he too became God's chosen instrument *and* Saul's answer to prayer.

When God asks you to do something, you move out in unshakable confidence that you too can become God's chosen instrument and the answer to another's prayer.

*Thank You, Lord, for using me. Tell me, what would
You have me do for You today? Amen.*

## CLING ON

*Hezekiah trusted in, leaned on, and was confident in the Lord,*
*the God of Israel; so that neither after him nor before him was*
*any one of all the kings of Judah like him. For he clung and held*
*fast to the Lord and ceased not to follow Him, but kept His*
*commandments, as the Lord commanded Moses. And the Lord*
*was with Hezekiah; he prospered wherever he went.*
2 Kings 18:5-7 AMPC

When a child sees the ocean for the first time, there's a bit of wonder mixed with fear in his eyes. He automatically increases his grip on his mother's arms and pulls his body even closer against hers.

With whispers, the mother may try to push her child away from her, just a little bit, so she can dip her child's toe in the cold saltwater. Yet even with the wonder of the wet wave, the child cannot help but continue to cling to his mother, knowing being in her arms is the safest place to be.

Just as children cling to their mother, God would have you cling to Him. For when you rely on God for everything you need, confident He will come through, you will not only stay safe but prosper because you're living in God's will and way.

*It is You alone I trust with my life and my loved ones, Lord.*
*So I'm holding fast to You, knowing that in Your arms I will*
*not only be safe but prosper. To Your glory! Amen.*

## POWER TOOLS

*Tell Hezekiah, the leader of My people, Thus says the Lord. . .*
*I have heard your prayer, I have seen your tears; behold,*
*I will heal you. . . . Cornelius. . .has been instructed by a holy*
*angel to send for you to come to his house; and he has*
*received in answer [to prayer] a warning to listen*
*to and act upon what you have to say.*
2 KINGS 20:5; ACTS 10:22 AMPC

You have tools at your fingertips, tools to be sharpened, honed, refigured, tools that will help you not only gain God's ear but bring answers to your prayers.

When King Hezekiah became gravely ill, God told him to set his affairs in order for he would soon die. "Then Hezekiah turned his face to the wall and prayed to the Lord" (2 Kings 20:2 AMPC). After Hezekiah presented his case to God, God told him He'd heard his prayer and would heal him.

Centuries later, Peter received a vision from God. While he was meditating on what it meant, the Holy Spirit directed him to greet the men at his door, to go with them to see Cornelius. For he had received instructions by an angel in answer to his continual prayers.

Your tools are prayer, visions, meditation, and obedience, tools that connect you to God, Jesus, and the Spirit. Which will you work on sharpening today?

*Thank You, Lord, for the power tools You've put at*
*my disposal. Help me learn to use them wisely and*
*in line with Your will and way. Amen.*

# A WONDER-FILLED WORLD

*What a wildly wonderful world, GOD! You made. . .earth overflow with your wonderful creations. . . . All the creatures look expectantly to you to give them their meals on time. You come, and they gather around; you open your hand and they eat from it. If you turned your back, they'd die in a minute.*

PSALM 104:24, 27-30 MSG

July 4 is when citizens in the United States celebrate the signing of the Declaration of Independence. By signing that document, the thirteen American colonies declared they would no longer be subject to the rule of Britain's King George III.

In remembrance of this day, people celebrate with firework displays, parades, family reunions, picnics, baseball games, speeches, and much more. A nation celebrating its independence from a tyrant is one thing; but one can never celebrate her independence from God. For God is the One who provides for her, gives her life, breath, spirit, and a purpose. Without God, woman and man would cease to exist.

As you celebrate your nation's independence, remember to celebrate your dependence on God as well. Thank Him for the wonder and variety of His amazing creation. Thank Him for the breath, spirit, life, and provisions He has gifted you. Praise your Lord!

---

*Lord, I thank You for the wonder of Your creation, as well as my breath, life, soul, spirit, and smile. Help me be to the earth as You are to me—a loving caretaker and friend. Amen.*

## FAITH-FILLED BELIEVERS

*Peter was kept in prison, but fervent prayer for him was*
*persistently made to God by the church (assembly). The very*
*night before Herod was about to bring him forth, Peter was*
*sleeping between two soldiers, fastened with two chains,*
*and sentries before the door were guarding the prison.*
*And suddenly an angel of the Lord appeared.*
ACTS 12:5-7 AMPC

King Herod had killed John's brother James. He then imprisoned Peter under the guard of sixteen soldiers. But there was one thing the king hadn't counted on: the fervent prayers of believers, an invisible and invincible power of God that no obstacles can bar.

A faith-filled Peter, lying in chains between two soldiers, slept the sleep of a confident believer. Suddenly an angel appeared. Surrounded by a heavenly light, he stood beside Peter, woke him, and told him to get up. The chains fell away. In a stupor, Peter followed the directions of the angel, dressing himself and allowing the spirit to lead him out past guards and to the city gates. As they walked along a street, the angel left him. It was then Peter woke as if from a dream and knew God had sent the angel to rescue him.

When it seems as if there's no hope left, take heart. Sleep the sleep of one who has full faith in God. Remember, others are praying for you, and God has sent angels to lead you to safety.

*Help me, Lord, to become an unshakable*
*faith-filled believer. Amen.*

# SEEKING

*Honor his holy name with Hallelujahs, you who seek God. Live a
happy life! Keep your eyes open for GOD, watch for his works; be
alert for signs of his presence. Remember the world of wonders
he has made, his miracles, and the verdicts he's rendered.*
PSALM 105:3-5 MSG

When worries are overloading you, when you feel you cannot
catch a breath, when you wonder where God has gone,
don't hide under the covers. Instead, honor God. Praise His name.
Shout out hallelujahs. And seek the One who holds your life and
breath in His hands.

For when you seek God, you will find Him. That's a vow God
makes repeatedly, the first such appearing in Deuteronomy 4:29
(AMPC): "If. . .you will seek (inquire for and require as necessity) the
Lord your God, you will find Him if you [truly] seek Him with all your
heart [and mind] and soul and life."

"Seeking" doesn't mean a quick morning glance at the Bible or a
short hum of a hymn. This is an all-in kind of seeking, a looking for
Him with *all* your heart, mind, soul, and life.

And once you start seeking Him, keep your eyes open for
where He's working. Watch carefully for signs of His presence. Stay
aware of all the wonders He's performed, the promises He's kept,
the judgments He's made.

Today, praise and seek Your God. And all His power, strength,
and wonders will uphold you.

*Lord, I come with open eyes seeking You with all I am.*

## SHAKE IT OFF

*The Jews. . .stirred up persecution against Paul and Barnabas,*
*and drove them out of their district. But they shook off the dust*
*from their feet against them and went to Iconium. And the*
*disciples were filled with joy and with the Holy Spirit.*
ACTS 13:50-52 ESV

God knows there will be days when people will mock you for your faith or even stir up a crowd against you. But Jesus would have you simply shake off their remarks, disregard their looks, shrug off their attitudes, and go on your way.

There may be times when you want to do more than try to shrug off those who will not receive you and your message. But Jesus would have you follow His guidance in this area (Matthew 10:14-15). For, as in all things, when you handle rejection Jesus' way, you will find yourself not only blessed but continually and completely full of joy and the Spirit.

Remember that those who the Spirit has readied will willingly hear your message. So by spreading the Word either by mouth or example, you've done your part. Now it's up to the Holy Spirit to do His. So leave the results of your efforts in God's hands, and continue on your joy-filled way!

*Lord, when I share my faith in word or by example,*
*help me leave the results in the hands of You and*
*Your Spirit and go merrily upon my way. Amen.*

## UP ON YOUR FEET!

*There was a man in Lystra who couldn't walk. . . . He heard Paul*
*talking, and Paul, looking him in the eye, saw that he was ripe*
*for God's work, ready to believe. So he said, loud enough for*
*everyone to hear, "Up on your feet!" The man was up in a flash—*
*jumped up and walked around as if he'd been walking all his life.*
ACTS 14:8-10 MSG

I f someone looked at your face during a sermon, regardless of the topic, would he see a woman tired of life, looking at her watch, idly chewing her gum, or drawing a picture on an offering envelope? Or would he see a woman with fire in her eyes, hanging on every word, eating up God's Word, ready for whatever God had in mind for her?

One of the best ways to not get crushed by the worries and woes of this world is to be on fire for God, eager to hear and read His Book, faithful to His truths, and excited about *being* the Word, not just reading it.

Woman of the Way, dig into God's Word with all your heart, soul, spirit, and mind! Then get up on your feet! Look for where God is working—and head in His direction, knowing He'll give you all you need to further His will and way.

*Here I am, Lord! Up on my feet with faith and Your*
*Word in hand. What would You have me do?*

## EVIDENCE OF GOD AND GOODNESS

*"We have come to bring you the Good News that you should. . .
turn to the living God, who made heaven and earth, the sea,
and everything in them. In the past he permitted all the nations
to go their own ways, but he never left them without evidence of
himself and his goodness. For instance, he sends you rain and
good crops and gives you food and joyful hearts."*
ACTS 14:15-17 NLT

When you feel the weight of the world pressing down upon your shoulders, take a break from whatever you're doing and look for the evidence of God that surrounds you. Look for the One who sends believers *and* nonbelievers rain and good crops, food and joyful hearts. See His wonderful creation with the delight of a child—which you are in God's eyes.

Look up to the sky. Revel in the sun, rain, and moon, the stars, fog, mist, light, and night. Step outside and touch a tree. Feel the bark, leaves, nuts, or pinecones. Find a flower. Feel its stem and petals and thorns, if it has any.

Allow yourself to see the world God has made—it's wind, waves, rainbows, and people. Permit His joy to enter into your heart, you, another wonder of His own making, a woman of love and light.

*Lord, help me to see Your world and wonders with new eyes so
that I may see You and the evidence of Your goodness. Amen.*

## GO-TO GUIDE

*The LORD spread a cloud above them as a covering and gave
them a great fire to light the darkness. . . . He split open a
rock, and water gushed out to form a river through the dry
wasteland. For he remembered his sacred promise to his servant
Abraham. So he brought his people out of Egypt with joy,
his chosen ones with rejoicing.*

PSALM 105:39, 41-43 NLT

Feel like you're living in a world of lack? Now's the time to change that mindset. Why? Because you have a God with and in you who provides for you, protects you, and not only makes amazing promises but actually keeps them!

God didn't just help His people escape slavery in Egypt. He spread a cloud over them to protect them by day. He gave them a pillar of fire to light up their darkness. When they grew thirsty, He split open a rock from which water gushed out and formed a river! And He came through on every single promise He made to His people, turning their trials into triumphs and their vexations into victories.

Got a problem? Go to the One who knows how to salve all wounds and solve all problems. The One who will not only help you escape your trouble but bless you with an unshakable joy!

*You, Lord, are my go-to Guide. Help me constantly
and continually remember Your blessings and banish
my banes. In Jesus' name I pray, amen.*

## CONTINUALLY SAVED

*After our parents left Egypt, they took your wonders for granted, forgot your great and wonderful love. They were barely beyond the Red Sea when they defied the High God—the very place he saved them!—the place he revealed his amazing power! He rebuked the Red Sea so that it dried up on the spot—he paraded them right through!—no one so much as got wet feet!*

PSALM 106:7-9 MSG

Have there been times in life when, amid a crisis, you prayed for God to help you? And then when He did something amazing to lift you up out of trouble you soon forgot all about it?

That's what happened to the Israelites. Time after time, God delivered them from some oppressing force by performing a miracle. But then, as time went by, His people forgot about it. Instead of taking comfort, courage, and confidence from all those past lifesaving experiences, the Israelites focused on the next obstacle, the next problem that was before them. Sound familiar?

Today, look back over your own life. Consider how many times God saved you from despair and difficulty. Make a list of all He has done for you. And take comfort, courage, and confidence He will do so again, no matter what lies before, beside, or behind you.

*Thank You, Lord, for continually saving me. Help me take comfort, courage, and confidence from all You have done for me. In Jesus' name, I pray and trust. Amen.*

# SHAKEN UP

*Around midnight Paul and Silas were praying and singing hymns to God, and the other prisoners were listening. Suddenly, there was a massive earthquake, and the prison was shaken to its foundations. All the doors immediately flew open, and the chains of every prisoner fell off!*

ACTS 16:25-26 NLT

I magine being dragged before authorities, attacked by a crowd, having your clothes torn off, being beaten, then put in a prison "for your own safety," with your feet clamped in leg irons—all because you were doing what God called you to do!

What would your next move be? Would you protest, cry, or crumble?

Paul and Silas didn't do any of those things. They simply prayed and sang hymns of praise to God. As they did so, other prisoners listened to them. Then suddenly a big earthquake shook the jail all the way down to its foundation. The doors of the prison flew open, and everyone's chains broke off!

What does this prove? That prayer and praise are two very powerful weapons you hold in your hands and upon your lips. When you have been wronged, beaten, and ripped apart, fold your hands and move your lips in prayer. Sing songs of praise. And God will use His power to shake the foundations of your imprisonment and release you from bondage!

*Help me, Lord, to turn to power and praise when I'm in trouble. For no matter how dire my situation appears, You can and will save me! Amen.*

# BREAKTHROUGH

*David asked God, "Should I go out to fight the Philistines?
Will you hand them over to me?" The Lord replied, "Yes, go
ahead. I will hand them over to you." So David and his troops
went up to Baal-perazim and defeated the Philistines there.
"God did it!" David exclaimed. "He used me to burst through
my enemies like a raging flood!" So they named that place
Baal-perazim (which means "the Lord who bursts through").*
1 CHRONICLES 14:9-11 NLT

Hearing David had been made king over Israel, the Philistines
came out to test his mettle. But David, the new king and
seasoned commander, didn't go out against them until he'd first
checked in with God. David asked if he should fight them. If he did,
would God hand them over to him. God said, yes and yes! Only then
did David step out, for he had God and his faith, the best weapons
for any battle. When David defeated the Philistines, he named the
battleground Baal-perazim, which means "The Lord Who Bursts
Through!"

When you're in a tight spot, don't do anything until you've
checked in with God. Ask Him if He's going to support you in your
endeavors, if He'll help you have a breakthrough. Then, and only
then, step out in the power of God's Word and your faith.

*Lord of all power, it is to You I run when I need
advice and direction. For You are my Chief
Strategist and Baron of Breakthroughs. Amen.*

## THE ANSWER

*Seek the Lord and His strength; yearn for and seek His
face and to be in His presence continually! [Earnestly]
remember the marvelous deeds which He has done,
His miracles, and the judgments He uttered [as in Egypt]. . . .
Honor and majesty are [found] in His presence;
strength and joy are [found] in His sanctuary.*
1 CHRONICLES 16:11-12, 27 AMPC

F eeling directionless, weak, alone? Beginning to doubt? Thinking
that the magic you once felt in your relationship with God has
diminished? Are you a bit down in the mouth—and heart?

God has the answer for you, the remedy to what ails you. It's
a solution He shared with David and that David then shared with
His peeps. It's the remedy that the chronicling scribe then left in
writing for you.

The answer to all your ailments is to simply and heartfully
thank God for all He's done. Call on Him. Sing to Him. Rejoice in
Him. And most importantly, seek His face and strength. Long to be
in His presence—not just during your prayer and praise time but
*all. . .the. . .time*! Remember who He is, everything He has done for
His people—including you! Then you will find strength and joy and
peace in the presence of your God—the God of all gods!

*You, Lord, are my answer. I yearn to seek Your face,
to spend time in Your presence. In You I find unshakable hope,
strength, joy, power, and peace. Amen.*

## HE'S NEAR

*"God. . .doesn't live in custom-made shrines or need the human race to run errands for him, as if he couldn't take care of himself. . . .He made the entire human race and made the earth hospitable. . .so we could seek after God, and not just grope around in the dark but actually find him. He doesn't play hide-and-seek with us. He's not remote; he's near. We live and move in him. . . !"*
ACTS 17:24-25, 27-28 MSG

God isn't lost. Nor is He hard to find. It's not like He's on one side of the continent and you're on the other, with no chance of either of you running into each other. No. God has set up His world—both earthly and heavenly—so You can easily seek, find, and call on Him. It's not as if He is hiding in the shadows, hoping you'll never discover Him. He's in that bright light, the glow that brightens up your world within and without.

Every moment, know that God is all around You. He's so near, you can feel His breath on your neck, see His light in your corner, touch His Spirit with your own, feel His heart beating in rhythm with yours.

Today, reach out to God. Know He's there—to secure and to save, to enlighten and to love.

*In You, Lord, I live, move, and have my being.*
*Thank You for always being near. Amen.*

# GODSPEED, WOMAN OF THE WAY

*"God-speed as you build the sanctuary for your God, the job God has given you. And may God also give you discernment and understanding. . .so that you will rule in reverent obedience under God's Revelation. That's what will make you successful, following the directions and doing the things that God commanded. . . . Courage! Take charge! Don't be timid; don't hold back."*
1 CHRONICLES 22:11-13 MSG

God has given you a specific job, a purpose, something only you can do to further His kingdom. Just as He did with the kings and queens of old, God makes available His wisdom so you'll be able to walk in His will and follow His way.

Just as God helped and blessed the wise King Solomon to rule His people and build His sanctuary, God can and will help and bless you. All you need to do is follow His directions. To live as He would have you live.

Yet to do so, you'll need courage. And faith. No matter how dark the future seems, no matter how unbendable those you are given to lead and love are, be confident in the knowledge that God walks with You. That His light and love are at your disposal. Then pray, ask, and believe.

Godspeed, Woman of the Way. He's got you.

*In You, Lord, I find wisdom. Give me the confidence and courage to do as You will Your way. In Jesus' name, amen.*

## DIVINE ENCOURAGEMENT

*"Do not be afraid, but go on speaking and do not be silent,
for I am with you, and no one will attack you to harm you,
for I have many in this city who are my people." . . . And he
entered the synagogue and for three months spoke boldly,
reasoning and persuading them about the kingdom of God. . . .
And God was doing extraordinary miracles by the hands of Paul.*
ACTS 18:9-10; 19:8, 11 ESV

P aul, a one-time Pharisee and persecutor of Christians, had many challenges ahead of him when Jesus called him. At times, he must have been riddled with fear. For why else would the Lord come and encourage him, telling him that not only was He standing with the apostle but assuring him he would come to no harm—because God had His own people nearby?

Because of God's encouragement, Paul was able to speak with great boldness and persuasion. *And* God was able to work amazing miracles through him.

God calls each of us to be His servant, His hands and feet in this world. Know that He is with you. That He has people who will help you do what you need to do. And as you go forward in His name, know that the closer and more confidently you follow God, the more miracles He will perform through your hands.

*Thank You, Lord, for Your words of encouragement. With and
through You, I can do what You've called me to do. Amen.*

## YOUR DESIRED HAVEN

*They. . .are at their wits' end [all their wisdom has come to nothing]. Then they cry to the Lord in their trouble, and He brings them out of their distresses. He hushes the storm to a calm and to a gentle whisper, so that the waves of the sea are still. Then the men are glad because of the calm, and He brings them to their desired haven.*
PSALM 107:27-30 AMPC

S eamen know of God's great power. When they sail in great waters, they see sights few landlubbers will ever witness. Between sea creatures, endless horizon, eddies, and great winds and waves, they are witnesses to God's great works and wonders.

Yet when these same sailors are caught in a horrific storm, there are times when "their courage melts away because of their plight" (Psalm 107:26 AMPC). These seafarers know that all their wisdom cannot save them. They know there will be times when all they can do is cry out for God's help, praying He will bring them to safety.

Woman of the Way, be assured that God can hush your storms and calm your waves. Trust Him with all you are and have. Know that once you attain that heavenly peace amid earthly peril, you too will be glad as He brings you to your desired haven.

*Lord, calmer of wind and waves, still my soul.*
*Bring me to my desired haven. Amen.*

## AT YOUR SIDE

*"Know the God of your father and serve him with a whole heart and with a willing mind. . . . Be strong and courageous and do it. Do not be afraid and do not be dismayed, for the LORD God, even my God, is with you. He will not leave you or forsake you, until all the work. . .is finished."*
1 CHRONICLES 28:9, 20 ESV

Have you ever worried that you won't have enough time or enough provision to accomplish all God has asked you to do? The young King Solomon may have thought his completing the temple for God was a monumental task. What if he got something wrong? What if God got busy helping someone else on a major project and was no longer around to answer Solomon's questions?

If you know God, you know He'll never desert you until your work is finished for Him. All He really wants from you is to know who He is so intimately that you will never question Him nor worry about what may or may not happen.

So aim to seek God every day. To serve Him with your entire being. Then take from Him the strength, courage, and faith you need, knowing He's always at your side, working not to hinder but to help you.

*Thank You, Lord, for giving me what I need to do what You would have me do. In Jesus' name, amen.*

## TURN TO GOD

*He turns a desert into pools of water, a parched land
into springs of water. And there he lets the hungry dwell,
and they establish a city to live in; they sow fields
and plant vineyards and get a fruitful yield.*
PSALM 107:35-37 ESV

God is always looking out for the common person, the one who doesn't put on airs. His heart is attracted and fixed on the woman who cares about others but may have only one pair of shoes.

For people like His Son, those who have no place to lay their heads nor their own home in which to abide, God turns a desert into a land that will yield fruit. For those who follow His will and way, those who love Him, seek Him, and thirst for His presence, He will provide deep wells of living water.

When you need help, when you feel you are crushed, forsaken, when you have a heart that you feel will never heal, turn to the One who lost His only Son, watched Him beaten, abused, mocked, and then crucified upon a cross. Go to the One who knows what suffering is. And you will find a well of release and relief, a friend and mentor, an unshakable Rock and refuge like no other.

*I need You, Lord. Quench my thirst for love, my craving
for kindness. Lift me up, Lord, into Your arms, until I
can stand firmly on my feet once more. Amen.*

# TURNED OVER TO GOD

*I'm turning you over to God, our marvelous God
whose gracious Word can make you into what he
wants you to be and give you everything you could
possibly need in this community of holy friends.*

ACTS 20:32 MSG

S ome days are harder than others. Some days the obstacles
before us seem insurmountable. We are like the newly freed
Israelites, with the Red Sea on one side and a magnificent army of
warriors with horses and chariots on the other. We think, *There's
no way I'm getting out of here unscathed!*

And then we remember whose children we are.

We're children of the God who can divide seas, split rocks, and
make the earth shake. We've an All-Powerful Being on our side who
hears our cries, however faint, however pained. We're the daughters
of an eternal King of kings who'll never leave or abandon us.

With God in our lives, we can leave our obstacles in His hands,
confident He'll remove them. He's the One who has already rescued
us from death and loves us like no other ever could.

Today, remember who you are and who God is. Immerse yourself
in His Word, put yourself in His hands, and you will become all you
were ever made to be and have all you could ever possibly hold.

*I put myself into Your hands today, Lord. Make me
what You want me to be and grant me all I could
possibly need. In Jesus' name, amen.*

## PROMISES, PROMISES

*God, O God of Israel, there is no God like you in the skies above or on the earth below, who unswervingly keeps covenant with his servants and unfailingly loves them while they sincerely live in obedience to your way. You kept your word to David my father, your promise. You did exactly what you promised—every detail. The proof is before us today! Keep it up, God, O God of Israel! Continue to keep the promises you made.*
2 Chronicles 6:14-16 MSG

People break their promises all the time. You may have done so yourself. Perhaps you missed a project deadline at work or forgot to take the kids to the park on the day you said you would.

Because people seem to break promises so easily, you may think God will break His too. Can you really trust Him to do what He says He'll do?

Time and again, scriptures tell us God is not like humans. What He says He will do, *He will do*. Why? Because He cannot break His word. (Numbers 23:19; Joshua 23:14; Psalm 89:34; Hebrews 6:18-20; 2 Peter 1:4.)

Once you understand God will keep His promises no matter what, seek out those promises when you need strength, encouragement, and hope. Trust God will do what He says He will do. Then rest easy, knowing you and your life are in His hands—just as promised.

*Thank You, Lord, for always keeping Your promises! Amen.*

## GO. PRAY. SEEK.

*If my people who are called by my name humble themselves,
and pray and seek my face and turn from their wicked ways,
then I will hear from heaven and will forgive their sin and
heal their land. Now my eyes will be open and my ears
attentive to the prayer that is made in this place.*
2 CHRONICLES 7:14-15 ESV

When's the last time you humbled yourself before God, bowing, getting down on your knees, or prostrating yourself, realizing who He really is, what He's done in the past, and what He's now doing in your life?

When's the last time you truly prayed from the heart, not the mind, with no holds barred, putting all the good, bad, and ugly about your world or even yourself before Him?

When's the last time you sought God's face with all your heart, mind, soul, spirit, and body? When's the last time you humbly asked the Lord of lords for forgiveness?

God wants you to know He's waiting to hear from you, ready to see you before Him. Are you ready to be open—totally open—to Him?

Open yourself to God today, in this moment, before your duties take you into that material realm. Know He's as open to you as you are to Him. Remember that you've been chosen by Him, that Jesus has paved the way for you to appear before Him. Go. Pray. Seek. And be continually changed.

*To You, Lord, I come, I pray, I seek. . .You.*

## OF THE WAY

*"I persecuted the followers of the Way, hounding some to death,*
*arresting both men and women and throwing them in prison. . . .*
*I was blinded by the intense light and had to be led by*
*the hand to Damascus by my companions. . . .*
*[Ananias told me], 'The God of our ancestors*
*has chosen yo . . .to be his witness.' "*
ACTS 22:4, 11, 14-15 NLT

Whenever you're unsure whether God can perform a miracle in your life or redirect it, remember what He did in the life of Paul.

Paul's name used to be Saul. As Saul, he admits to hounding Christ followers to their death or having them thrown into prison.

The cries of praying churches facing persecution must've gotten God's attention because the next thing Saul knows, Jesus is stopping him in his tracks, generating an intense bright light that blinds him. Jesus tells Saul to go to Damascus. Once there, Ananias lays hands on Saul, gives him God's new direction, and suddenly Saul can see! And Saul the persecutor becomes Paul the apostle!

God, the miracle maker and life planner, has a mission for you. And He'll do anything to make that mission clear. When you need redirection, trust God to show you His way.

*Lord, show me the way You would have me go.*
*Share Your plans with me. Make all things clear so I*
*can be sure my way lines up with Yours. Amen.*

## LISTEN CAREFULLY

*"Listen carefully. . . . God will stick with you as long as you stick with him. If you look for him he will let himself be found; but if you leave him he'll leave you. For a long time Israel didn't have the real God, nor did they have the help of priest or teacher or book. But when they were in trouble and got serious, and decided to seek God, the God of Israel, God let himself be found."*
2 Chronicles 15:2-4 msg

There will be days when life doesn't seem to go your way—at all. There will be days when you wonder where God is, and you wish He would just show up and do something miraculous, like take down your obstacles and show you a clear path, perhaps even erect a neon sign with a big arrow saying, Go this way! I will be with you!

Yet you *do* have something miraculous at your fingertips. It's something you can hold in your own two hands. It's where you can find all the wisdom you could possibly want or need to help you navigate your way through this life. It's the Word.

Woman of the Way, open God's Book. Read it carefully. Listen to its wisdom. You will find God and so much more.

*Lord, I need help, direction, wisdom, clarity, confidence, and so much more. Reveal Yourself and Your Way as I seek You through Your Book. In Jesus' name, amen.*

# FIRST RESOURCE

*"Because you went for help to the king of Aram*
*and didn't ask GOD for help, you've lost a victory over*
*the army of the king of Aram. Didn't the Ethiopians*
*and Libyans come against you with superior forces,*
*completely outclassing you with their chariots and cavalry?*
*But you asked GOD for help and he gave you the victory."*
2 CHRONICLES 16:7-8 MSG

King Asa had started out as a good king. When in trouble, he turned to God as his first resource. But then he began looking for help from his fellow humans *before* God. Doing so led to his downfall first on the battlefield, then in his health. "In the thirty-ninth year of his reign Asa was diseased in his feet—until his disease became very severe; yet in his disease he did not seek the Lord, but relied on the physicians" (2 Chronicles 16:12 AMPC).

Hanani the seer didn't mince words when he told Asa, "GOD is always on the alert, constantly on the lookout for people who are totally committed to him. You were foolish to go for human help when you could have had God's help" (2 Chronicles 16:9 MSG).

When you're in trouble, make God your first resource. Ask Him for help, advice, and guidance before all others, knowing He'll give you not only aid but victory.

*Creator, Maintainer, and Sustainer of all, help me turn*
*to You before I look anywhere else. Amen.*

## NEVER SHAKEN

*Happy is the man who fears the Lord, taking great delight in His commands. . . . He will never be shaken. The righteous man will be remembered forever. He will not fear bad news; his heart is confident, trusting in the Lord. His heart is assured; he will not fear.*
PSALM 112:1, 6-8 HCSB

God is a Creator who longs for His creation to revere Him, to worship Him with her entire being. This God who shaped your body and molded your mind is thrilled when you delight in His Word, wisdom, will, and Way!

The woman who is so trusting, loving, and reverent of God will never be shaken, disturbed, or perturbed. Her nerves will not be jangling, making her jumpy or stressed. She'll be long remembered as a gentle, calm, cool, and collected woman of God, an example to every other woman she meets.

When bad news comes down the pike, she won't lose her poise, scream in alarm, or fall away in a faint. She will be confident that whatever happens in her life, her God has a plan for her good. That somehow, in His wisdom, everything will work out alright. She needn't fret nor fear. Would that you would be that woman.

---

*Lord, help me become the woman who reveres You and remains unshaken no matter what comes her way. Make me a true daughter of the true King. Amen.*

# EYES ON GOD

*Jehoshaphat feared, and set himself [determinedly, as his vital
need] to seek the Lord. . . . And said. . . we have no might to
stand against this great company that is coming against us.
We do not know what to do, but our eyes are upon You.*
2 CHRONICLES 20:3, 6, 12 AMPC

I magine the leader of your country being told a huge army was
coming against her. Now imagine this same leader immediately
seeking God's help and guidance. Imagine her being so humble as
to admit publicly that there's no way she and her people can stand
against this powerful force. In fact, they don't know what to do! But
one thing she does know: her eyes and those of her nation will be
on God.

That's the kind of leader of people and follower of God the Lord
wants—one who admits her weakness and God's strength.

In response to King Jehoshaphat's prayer, God said, "You shall
not need to fight in this battle; take your positions, stand still, and
see the deliverance of the Lord [Who is] with you. . . . Fear not nor
be dismayed. Tomorrow go out against them, for the Lord is with
you" (2 Chronicles 20:17 AMPC). For a godly prayer and attitude
deserves a calming, confident, and comforting response.

*Lord, it's You I need and seek. I have no might to
stand against what's coming. I don't know what to do.
But my eyes are on You. Amen.*

## GOD YOUR ALLY

*Jehosheba, the daughter of the king, took Joash [infant] son*
*of Ahaziah and stole him away from among the king's sons*
*who were to be slain, and she put him and his nurse in a*
*bedchamber. So Jehosheba daughter of King Jehoram, sister of*
*Ahaziah, and wife of Jehoiada the priest, hid [Joash] from*
*[his grandmother] Athaliah, so that she did not slay him.*
2 CHRONICLES 22:11 AMPC

J ehosheba had to think fast. Her brother, King Ahaziah, had died. Now his mother, the murderous Athaliah, decided to kill all her grandchildren and rule in her son's place!

Athaliah was able to kill all the heirs of the throne of Judah but one—Joash. For his aunt Jehosheba took the infant, secreting him and his nurse in a bedroom. While Athaliah ruled Judah, Joash hid in the temple with his aunt and uncle for six years. He was crowned king at age seven. "Throughout the time of Jehoiada the priest, Joash did what was right in the LORD's sight" (2 Chronicles 24:2 HCSB).

There may come a time when you'll have to summon up your courage to right a wrong. When that time comes, remember you'll have all the help you need from God, the great Lord who is your ally (Acts 26:22) in all things, great and small.

*Help me remember, Lord, that with You as my ally, I can*
*and will do all You call me to do. In You, I'm unshakable.*

## HELP AND VICTORY

*"Do not let Israel's army go with you, for the LORD is not with Israel. . . . But if you go with them, do it! Be strong for battle! But God will make you stumble before the enemy, for God has the power to help or to make one stumble."*

2 CHRONICLES 25:7-8 HCSB

King Amaziah of Judah hired warriors from Israel for 7,500 pounds of silver. But then a prophet told him if he took those warriors with him, his army would be defeated. Amaziah protested. If he told the soldiers to go back home, he'd suffer a financial loss. The prophet assured him, "The LORD is able to give you much more than this" (2 Chronicles 25:9 HCSB). So, Amaziah sent the warriors back to Israel and, as God promised, won the battle.

Yet then Amaziah came home with the idols of the Seirites, the people he'd just vanquished—and he worshipped them! That's when another prophet told him God intended to destroy him.

Psalm 115:9 (NLT) warns against trusting and worshipping idols who are merely the work of human hands. Instead, God's people are urged to "trust the Lord! He is your helper and your shield."

Remember who can grant you victory or defeat, who can help or hinder. The Lord your God! He alone has the power to make you walk tall or stumble.

*Lord, it is You I worship, You I obey.*
*For You alone are my help and victory!*

## DON'T GIVE UP

*"Last night God's angel stood at my side, an angel of*
*this God I serve, saying to me, 'Don't give up, Paul.*
*You're going to stand before Caesar yet—and everyone*
*sailing with you is also going to make it.' So, dear friends,*
*take heart. I believe God will do exactly what he told me."*
ACTS 27:23-25 MSG

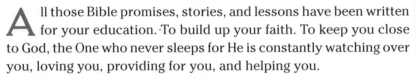

All those Bible promises, stories, and lessons have been written for your education. To build up your faith. To keep you close to God, the One who never sleeps for He is constantly watching over you, loving you, providing for you, and helping you.

God has sent His angels to keep you safe. He does this so that you'll receive His message: "Woman of the Way, don't give up. You're going to be able to do what I've created you to do. You and all those who walk with you are going to make it, going to see Me face-to-face, one day."

So take heart, Woman of the Way. Have courage. Ask God for help when you need it, and expect God to deliver. Believe God will do exactly what He has promised today and tomorrow.

*Thank You, Lord, for giving me the confidence to do what*
*You would have me do. I won't give up. I know all Your*
*promises will and already are coming true. Amen.*

## LISTEN TO ME

*I love the Lord because he hears my voice
and my prayer for mercy.*
Psalm 116:1 nlt

I t can be hard to talk to someone you love during an intimate moment or to friends when you're seated at a crowded table or to business associates during a meeting. There may be moments when you feel like you aren't actually being heard. Maybe others are talking over you or simply not understanding how you feel or what you're trying to say. Maybe they simply reject your words altogether. During those moments, you may begin to feel lonely and isolated. You might start thinking your voice doesn't matter.

If anyone has ever told you that you or your voice doesn't matter, know that those words are untrue and come straight from the enemy. You are under no obligation to receive or believe them.

Woman, God listens to you. Every day. Every moment. Because you're important to Him. Your Lord wants nothing more than to completely connect with His daughters. Your voice, your ideas, and your feelings are important to Him. Take them to Him at any hour, and He will be there to listen.

*Dear God, my relationships—even with those I love—are imperfect on this side of eternity. But You, Lord, are forever perfect. And whereas some people may ignore my words or hurt me with their own, I know You'll always listen to me and never harm me. For this I thank and praise You. Amen.*

## BY FAITH

*It's news I'm most proud to proclaim, this extraordinary
Message of God's powerful plan to rescue everyone who trusts
him, starting with Jews and then right on to everyone else!
God's way of putting people right shows up in the acts of faith,
confirming what Scripture has said all along: "The person in
right standing before God by trusting him really lives."*
ROMANS 1:16-17 MSG

Paul wanted the Romans to understand that Jesus dying on a cross
for the sins of the world and rising from the grave three days
later reveals that people cannot outdo their sinful nature on their
own. Only faith in Jesus and the belief in the Gospel will save them.

God knows how dangerous it can be when His children rely on
themselves for salvation. Because this world is broken and that
brokenness touches everything, what someone does on any given
day can be affected by many different factors such as her mood
and circumstances. Works can be tainted by motives and attitudes.

Yet *God* cannot be affected. Your faith in Him and the truth of
the Gospel is what will set you right before Him. Jesus has already
done all the work to pay for the sins of this world.

Trust God. And you will truly live.

*Father, I know I can't rely on the works I do for my salvation.
Only Your Son, Jesus, is the way. Strengthen my faith, Lord of
love and life, until it is as unshakable as You. Amen.*

## THE SHORTEST PSALM

*O praise the Lord, all you nations! Praise Him, all you people!*
*For His mercy and loving-kindness are great toward us,*
*and the truth and faithfulness of the Lord endure forever.*
*Praise the Lord! (Hallelujah!)*
PSALM 117:1-2 AMPC

P salm 117 (containing only two verses) is the shortest psalm and the shortest chapter in the Bible. But it's so full of wonderful truths that can spark more than a million and one words of praise. It first tells God's people to worship Him, the whole world to sing praises. Then it explains why: because the Lord's mercy and love for you is never-ending and unchangeable. God wants you to know this and believe it!

Isn't the idea of a stable and strong heavenly Father so comforting to hear when this life feels anything but normal? God doesn't have mood swings or change His mind. His love for His daughters doesn't shift because of what they do. It is entirely based on who He is.

This is a comfort that will hopefully push you to seek Him and His will. God wants to say to every one of His daughters today, "Loving you is so easy." Embrace this goodness and praise Him for His everlasting care.

*Lord, I'm so thankful for Your mercy and love for me.*
*I don't think I'll ever be able to define fully what it*
*means for You to always be there for me. But I praise*
*You, my Rock and Refuge, all the same!*

# SECOND CHANCE

*He prayed to him, and God was moved by his entreaty and heard his plea and brought him again to Jerusalem into his kingdom. Then Manasseh knew that the LORD was God.*

2 CHRONICLES 33:13 ESV

King Manasseh was a bad dude. He built altars and idols of other gods in the house of the Lord. He dealt with black magic and led all of Judah to follow his ways. But worse than all these, Manasseh sacrificed his own sons to a bogus god. Does a man like this deserve a second chance?

Before he became the apostle Paul, Saul persecuted and killed many Christians. He was a murderer. Does a man like that deserve a second chance?

If you look at worldly justice, the answer is no. These men would go to prison for a long, long time. But in each of these cases, God revealed Himself to them, knew their hearts, and accepted their repentance. Would you be able to do that?

If you find it hard to accept the remorseful words of others, don't be discouraged. God's plan and His unending love and mercy are impossible for His people to fully understand. And while He has forgiven the remorseful and given them a new purpose, He does the same for you.

*Father, I find it hard to forgive those who have done wrong in this world. Remind me that You love everyone I meet. Soften my heart to remember that I can forgive because You first forgave me. Amen.*

## TWO TRUTHS

*This righteousness is given through faith in Jesus Christ
to all who believe. There is no difference between Jew and
Gentile, for all have sinned and fall short of the glory of God,
and all are justified freely by his grace through the
redemption that came by Christ Jesus.*

ROMANS 3:22-24 NIV

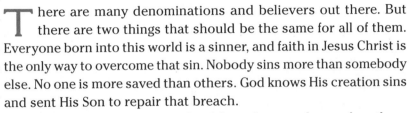

There are many denominations and believers out there. But there are two things that should be the same for all of them. Everyone born into this world is a sinner, and faith in Jesus Christ is the only way to overcome that sin. Nobody sins more than somebody else. No one is more saved than others. God knows His creation sins and sent His Son to repair that breach.

The focus for believers should not be on what makes them different from other believers or nonbelievers. Instead, they should be focused on the unshakable foundation of Jesus Christ and what that truth can do for the world.

Spreading the Gospel, no matter our denomination, church, location, ethnicity, or social status, is what God calls His children to do. Embracing the differences of His children is to embrace the majesty of God as a Creator.

*God, thank You so much for creating Your children with
differences that can be celebrated. I trust You know what
You're doing and how everyone fits into Your wonderful plan of
redemption. All I ask is that You let me be a part of it. Amen.*

# UNDERDOG

*Abraham never wavered in believing God's promise. In fact, his faith grew stronger, and in this he brought glory to God. He was fully convinced that God is able to do whatever he promises.*
ROMANS 4:20-21 NLT

Everyone loves a good underdog story. The Bible is full of them. Moses versus the Pharaoh. David versus Goliath. Abraham versus time itself. Jael versus Sisera. What these heroes have in common is that the world counted them out, but God counted them in. The world said it couldn't be done, but God said, "Watch Me."

Paul explains to the Romans that Abraham never lost faith in God's promise to him. Even though God's timeline didn't match Abraham's, he still chose to believe. And this faith brings glory to God and gives Him immense joy.

What are you waiting on? What do you feel will never happen in your life? Let God take care of it. Let God take care of you. Although you may feel like the underdog, that is exactly where God wants you to be. Because now you can trust Him to do something miraculous.

*Lord, give me faith today, a faith that cannot be moved. Although the world may seem bleak, I trust completely in You. I know You know best. I know I am exactly where I need to be to see You moving and working in my life. And I trust You to do as promised. Amen.*

## THE HARD TIMES

*Not only so, but we also glory in our sufferings,*
*because we know that suffering produces perseverance;*
*perseverance, character; and character, hope.*
ROMANS 5:3-4 NIV

A blacksmith knows how much heat it takes to create a sword. A jewelry-maker knows all the pressure a diamond goes through before it becomes beautiful. A glassblower knows the timing of how long her creation must stay in the fire for it to become exactly how she wants it. God knows the same about you.

The Message says it like this: "There's more to come: We continue to shout our praise even when we're hemmed in with troubles, because we know how troubles can develop passionate patience in us, and how that patience in turn forges the tempered steel of virtue, keeping us alert for whatever God will do next" (Romans 5:3-4).

God doesn't cause your struggles and the hard times, but you can be sure He will use them to help transform you into the precious daughter He created you to be. The hard times were never supposed to be a part of the story, but that's why Jesus came. He's rewritten the story.

*God, thank You for taking what's hard in my life and*
*making it good. I don't know why things happen, but I do*
*know that You love me deeply and will do what is best for me.*
*This is what gives me hope, boosts my faith, and lifts*
*my voice in praise of You. Amen.*

## AGAINST FEAR

*I have stored up your word in my heart,*
*that I might not sin against you.*
PSALM 119:11 ESV

You expect to experience fear in a haunted house. You know people in masks and costumes will be hiding, waiting for the perfect moment to jump out. And they'll probably do so when your back is turned and you're not expecting it. But you also know that nothing in the haunted house can hurt you. So, in that situation, you can either control your fear or let your fear control you.

Dealing with the enemy works the same way. He'll tempt you at your weakest. He'll try and get you when your back is turned. But as a daughter of Christ, you know he can't really hurt you. You also know the truth of God and who He is can come to your defense.

If you lean on God for strength, the enemy cannot harm you or even scare you. But you have to have God's Word already stored in your heart. That way, when the time does come to fight against fear, you'll know exactly what weapon of truth to use.

*Lord, I believe that You're strong. I believe that You're for me. Thus, when the enemy comes my way, I'll turn to You. Continually remind me that my own fear, which the enemy uses against me, has no place in my heart beside You. I pray You would fill that space with Your presence and strength instead.*

# X = JESUS

*Thank God! The answer is in Jesus Christ our Lord.*
ROMANS 7:25 NLT

In chapter 7 of Romans, Paul's words read like a long-winded and complicated word problem in a math textbook. Paul + Law + Sin = Bad. Paul + Law - Sin = Good. He continues to say he knows what's right, but his human nature forces him to do wrong. It's an unending cycle of Good to Bad to Redemption to Good again and so on. Paul asks helplessly if anyone will save him from this vicious circle of misery and death.

Then the apostle shares the answer he's found. The missing part of every equation Paul posed is Jesus. Jesus can save Paul from the cycle. Jesus + Paul = Forgiven and Saved. Jesus is the x, the cross that changes everything.

Jesus can be your answer too. He can be the answer to the grasp a sin has on your life. He can be the answer to that unending cycle of heartbreak, loneliness, anger, or sadness. He can encourage you toward the help you may need and the comfort you crave.

All you have to do is start adding Jesus to the equation.

---

*Father, thank You for Jesus and what He's done, saving*
*me from eternity without You. And He now wants to save*
*me from the brokenness of this world. Lord, although I*
*might not get every answer I want on this side of life,*
*I know Jesus is the ultimate solution. Amen!*

## GOD KNOWS YOU

*The Spirit helps us in our weakness. For we do not know
what to pray for as we ought, but the Spirit himself
intercedes for us with groanings too deep for words.*
ROMANS 8:26 ESV

Your heavenly Father knows your heart. He knows your dreams. And He knows when those dreams are shattered. He empathizes and cries with You. The heartbreak you have to endure was never supposed to be a part of His plan. That's why He sent Jesus to save this world and the Spirit to reside with you in it.

When life is too hard for words, the Spirit is able to speak for you. You don't have to know what to pray. You can just call on the Lord and He'll listen. In a world that seems to be full of talking heads on phones, televisions, and computers and in crowded stores or restaurants, you can still feel extremely lonely.

Time with God in solitude and silence may not be a quick fix for this feeling of aloneness, but it can be a reminder that God is here with you and for you. And He knows you well enough that you don't even have to speak a word.

*God, thank You for knowing me so deeply that I don't have to
explain my pain and hurt to You. Instead, I'll rest in the silence
with You, garnering Your strength and peace.*

## SUFFERING

*My comfort in my suffering is this:*
*Your promise preserves my life.*
PSALM 119:50 NIV

Shortly after the shortest psalm and chapter of the Bible (Psalm 117) comes the longest (Psalm 119). While many are unsure of who the author of these psalms could be, readers soon realize that whoever wrote 119 has experienced what others have encountered time after time: suffering. Yet the pain-filled psalmist also makes clear that no matter what his trials and troubles, he finds comfort by leaning on God and His promises.

The idea of finding solace amid suffering sounds similar to the apostle Paul's experiences. He writes again and again in his letters that to endure suffering is to be like Christ. Yet he adds that to find solace *amid* that suffering, we are to look to Christ. In Romans 8:38-39 (NIV), he writes, "For I am convinced that neither death nor life, neither angels nor demons, neither the present nor the future, nor any powers, neither height nor depth, nor anything else in all creation, will be able to separate us from the love of God that is in Christ Jesus our Lord."

Suffering directs you to trust God, to lean on Him for strength and peace instead of on yourself. It can be a reminder that even during down times, your God can and will lift you up.

*God, although I may at times encounter suffering,*
*I remain unshakable in the fact that You're*
*working all out for my good. Amen.*

## PRAYER AND CIRCUMSTANCES

*"O Lord, God of heaven, the great and awesome God who
keeps his covenant of unfailing love with those who
love him and obey his commands, listen to my prayer!"*
Nehemiah 1:5-6 nlt

If you grew up in a Christian household, you were probably taught the simple goodnight prayer of "Now I lay me down to sleep. . . ." Or maybe the dinner-time prayer of thankfulness: "Thank you for the food we eat. Thank you for the world so sweet. . . ." But as you got older and your life became more complicated, you've found those childhood prayers don't cover everything you want to say to Jesus, much less reflect what you're currently going through.

Nehemiah had a moment in his life when he needed to reach out to God with a drastic prayer. After hearing his homeland of Jerusalem was being destroyed, Nehemiah prayed on behalf of Judah. He also prayed for forgiveness of the sins committed against God by himself and his fellow Judeans. Furthermore, he asked for God's help and success to make things right.

Prayer helps you determine the difference between what you want and what is God's desire. It's a chance to ask God back into your circumstances to perform the miracles only He can. He's waiting for you to ask!

*Father, You're an amazing and merciful God. I ask You back into
my life and circumstances. Point me in the direction for Your will.*

# BELOVED

*As indeed he says in Hosea, "Those who were
not my people I will call 'my people,' and her
who was not beloved I will call 'beloved.'"*
ROMANS 9:25 ESV

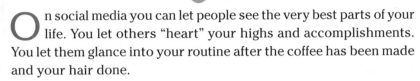

On social media you can let people see the very best parts of your life. You let others "heart" your highs and accomplishments. You let them glance into your routine after the coffee has been made and your hair done.

But do you let them see you when you first wake up after a long night of tossing and turning? Do you show them the messy hair, blemishes, and grumpiness?

You live in a world that has a dozen filters. If you don't like something about yourself, you can change it! But you aren't actually changing anything. You're just hoping someone won't look close enough to see what you're hiding.

Every single person has parts they feel they must hide from the eyes of others. But God doesn't look at His daughters the way the rest of the world looks at them. He doesn't even view you the same way you view yourself. He loves and desires the unfiltered version of you. What the world casts away as imperfect, God calls His beloved.

*God, thank You for reminding me that You love and desire every
part of me. Not only the good parts I show to the world, but the
parts I try to hide. Thank You for calling me Your "beloved."*

## WITH GOD

*They were all trying to frighten us, thinking, "Their hands will get too weak for the work, and it will not be completed." But I prayed, "Now strengthen my hands."*
NEHEMIAH 6:9 NIV

W hen you're doing exactly what you're supposed to do for the Lord, the enemy will create opposition through others to make you feel inadequate. His goal? To get you to quit. And he thinks the best way to do that is to make you feel discouraged and alone.

When others told Nehemiah that he and his fellow workers were too weak to finish the temple, he prayed to God for unshakable strength that wouldn't wither when others tried to dissuade him. And he got it!

Is there something in your own life that others may be opposing? If this "something" has been put on your heart by God, the good news is you have a heavenly Father who's bigger than the opposition. When you look to the Lord and ask Him to come through, He will. And He'll then go further than you ever imagined.

When others say you can't do it, reach out and ask God in. He'll reveal what you can do through Him.

*Lord, I ask You to fight any opposition that comes against me today. Remind me that I can do anything with Your strength and ability within me. Take my fear and turn it to courage. I'm ready to show them what You have planned.*

# CONVICTION

*And Nehemiah continued, "Go and celebrate with a feast of rich
foods and sweet drinks, and share gifts of food with people who
have nothing prepared. This is a sacred day before our Lord.
Don't be dejected and sad, for the joy of the LORD is your strength!"*
NEHEMIAH 8:10 NLT

G od's people were sad because they were being convicted of their
sin. The Law, God's Word, was doing what it was supposed to. It
was revealing how they'd all misstepped in their walk with the Lord.

Sometimes that kind of truth can hurt. And God's people
were definitely feeling the guilt and shame associated with their
wrongdoing.

But Nehemiah didn't want the people to linger upon this hurt.
He knew God was more than willing to rescue them from their sin.
He wanted to remind them that the most important part of God's
Word isn't that His people are sinners but that God is a Savior.

You can find joy from the Lord in this truth too. Even when you're
feeling convicted and sad, you can rejoice in the fact that God is
transforming you into the woman you were meant to be. From this
joy can come the unshakable strength to move forward in God's Will.

*God, thank You for correction and compassion. Even though
acknowledging my missteps is uncomfortable, it brings me
closer to You and Your plans for me. Amen.*

## SHINING LIGHT

*Your word is a lamp to my feet and a light to my path.*
PSALM 119:105 ESV

What if your car didn't have working headlights on foggy mornings or during midnight drives? Unable to see the road or anything ahead of you, you wouldn't be able to drive anywhere. That's how it was in the early days of the automobile. The first headlights contained a small flame that was easily extinguished by wind and rain. But later, as cars became more popular, electric headlights were developed to better help direct a driver along the road, to shine a light in the darkness.

Just as car manufacturers created headlights to help get people from point A to point B from dusk to dawn, God gifted you with His Word to help you get to where you need to be when the road ahead is dark. God's Word is a lamp with an inextinguishable flame that was created to show you the way and light your path. Neither wind nor rain can ever put it out or hide it. With God's Word firmly fixed in your mind and heart, you're able to see the next step ahead of you as you work your way to Him.

*Lord, thank You for the light of Your Word. May the study of it make the glow grow continually brighter, unquenched by wind or rain. And may Your Word always be my source of courage for today and my bright hope for tomorrow.*

# SHARE IN THE MOMENTS

*Rejoice with those who rejoice; mourn with those who mourn.*
ROMANS 12:15 NIV

It can be hard to be happy for your best friend who's getting married when you're still single. It can be tough to celebrate with your sister who's pregnant with her second child when you're still waiting for those double pink lines to appear in your own life. It can also be difficult to understand the pain of someone who's gone through a tragedy you've never experienced.

Jesus calls you to share your life with the lives of others, through all the ups and downs. Yet because of our humanness and the brokenness of this world, riding those waves with others may be harder than you think. It may mean being happy for someone when you may be feeling sorry for yourself. Or having to cry with a friend when you have no real concept of what she's going through.

Yet being there for others is what Jesus wants most from you. He asks you to love others above all else. Sometimes that may mean sacrificing your own comfort. No worries: Jesus will be there with His own personal comfort, peace, and assurance to help you along the way.

*Lord Jesus, give me Your comfort and guidance in what to say to others—and what not to say. Help me to care for others as well as You care for me, and to share with them, as You share with me.*

## FULFILLING LOVE

*The commandments, "You shall not commit adultery,*
*You shall not murder, You shall not steal, You shall not covet,"*
*and any other commandment, are summed up in this word:*
*"You shall love your neighbor as yourself." Love does no wrong*
*to a neighbor; therefore love is the fulfilling of the law.*
Romans 13:9-10 esv

It may be hard to understand how love and law go together. But love fulfills every law God created for His children to follow. What does that mean? It means you can follow each one of the Ten Commandments by choosing love first.

When you have love that is gifted from the One who first loved, you can do "no wrong to a neighbor." And although the way you love may sometimes be imperfect, the agape way of Jesus' love fills in the cracks. It's fulfilling in a way that nothing else in this world can be. Nothing can change this. Nothing can shift this from you.

The moment you accept Jesus into your life as your Savior, this love is available to you in every situation. And this love calls you to use it on others in a way that will ultimately point them back to Him.

*Jesus, You performed the ultimate act of love when*
*You sacrificed Yourself for the whole world. Thank You*
*for making this agape love available to me.*
*Help me to use it to direct others to You.*

## ROLE REVERSAL

*This man had a very beautiful and lovely young cousin, Hadassah, who was also called Esther. When her father and mother died, Mordecai adopted her into his family and raised her as his own daughter.*

ESTHER 2:7 NLT

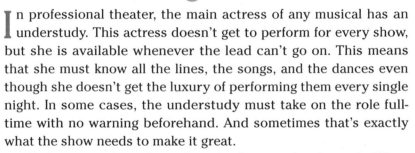

I n professional theater, the main actress of any musical has an understudy. This actress doesn't get to perform for every show, but she is available whenever the lead can't go on. This means that she must know all the lines, the songs, and the dances even though she doesn't get the luxury of performing them every single night. In some cases, the understudy must take on the role full-time with no warning beforehand. And sometimes that's exactly what the show needs to make it great.

Esther seemed to take on the role of a type of understudy. When a new queen was needed in Persia, they searched the country high and low, "auditioning" every eligible woman to fill this new role. Each one was expected to already know how to act like a royal. As it turned out, Esther, with the help of her uncle and a palace eunuch, was able to win the role of King Xerxes's queen.

God knew Esther's role would enable her to help save His people. He made the way and prepared her for His purpose. He's doing the same with you.

*Lord, thank You for always going before me and preparing me for what You need me to do.*

# THE SHOW MUST GO ON

*"For if you keep silent at this time, relief and deliverance*
*will rise for the Jews from another place, but you and your*
*father's house will perish. And who knows whether you*
*have not come to the kingdom for such a time as this?"*
ESTHER 4:14 ESV

G od will never make you do anything you don't want to do. He
will never force your decision in any situation. He will open
doors for you and show you the way. He can show you His will as
you spend time in His presence. But just like His Son, who lets His
beloved children choose or not choose Him, God will not force you
to do what He's asked you to do.

In today's verse, Mordecai tells Esther that if she chooses to
stay silent, deliverance will come from someone else because it's
God's will. If Esther stays silent, the show must go on. For God's
plan *will* succeed.

God loves you. He wants you to say yes to Him even if you're
fearful. He not only promises to be with you every moment but to
supply you with unshakable courage.

---

*Father, when I'm afraid to step into the role*
*You've assigned me, I'll look to You for the endless*
*courage I'll need to step on that stage. Continually remind*
*me that You created me with a purpose and a passion.*
*That I was made for this time and this place. Amen.*

## PRAY FOR ME

*I urge you, brothers and sisters, by our Lord Jesus Christ
and by the love of the Spirit, to join me in my
struggle by praying to God for me.*
ROMANS 15:30 NIV

It can be hard asking others for help, to let loved ones and friends into the difficult areas of your life, especially when you feel like you've already lost the battle yourself. Asking others to pray for you in that type of situation can be like adding salt to an already open wound.

Yet the believers God used in the Bible asked for prayer from others. Paul writes to the Romans and asks for joy, peace, and protection. Jesus asks His disciples to stay and pray for Him on the night of His arrest (Matthew 26:36).

Prayer is powerful. When you humbly let others into your life, share what's going on, and ask for prayer, you're allowing them to come before God with their active and energized love for you. You are, in effect, increasing your prayer power.

The enemy wants you to feel isolated and alone. He wants you to believe you can handle your problems without help from others, including God. But God has made you for connection with Him and fellow believers. Today, reach out and share your concerns with those you trust. Chances are, they'll open up to you in return.

*Lord, give me the courage to share my life
with those You've put in my path. Amen.*

## LOOK UP

*I look up to the mountains—does my help come from there?*
*My help comes from the LORD, who made heaven and earth!*
PSALM 121:1-2 NLT

D o you have a journey ahead of you? Maybe God has called you into a new chapter of your life and you are stepping into a new job, another chance at love, or into motherhood. The trip could be even more emotional if you're entering into a time of grief, uncertainty, or change. Whatever may be ahead, whether exciting or nerve-wracking, you may feel like a traveler about to scale a mountain. Have you packed enough? Have you prepared enough?

Whenever you find yourself standing at the foothills of a new endeavor, remember that God created the mountain before you. He knows Your entire journey from beginning to end. And He promises to be with you every step of the way. All the Lord asks of You is to keep looking up, past the mountains and the problems ahead, and into His loving face.

Remember that your God is calling you onward with a confidence and strength in Him that cannot be shaken.

*Lord, thank You for preparing me for the journey ahead.*
*Be with me as I stand at the foothills of this new endeavor.*
*Remind me that You will be with me every step of the way.*
*Help me to keep my eyes on and my heart in You. Amen.*

# QUESTIONS

*In all this Job did not sin or charge God with wrong.*
JOB 1:22 ESV

D o you know anyone who always wears a happy face? No matter what happens, she wears a smile and has some encouraging words to say. She's always hopeful and kind. Such people are honored in the Christian world, held high as ones that truly trust God. They may leave you feeling like a "bad" Christian when you don't approach every situation the same way.

To the outside world, followers of Christ may not be allowed to grieve or express their sadness. Questioning God or being upset at what's happening in your life can be called out as a sin in some Christian cultures.

Yet God doesn't condemn His children in this way. When Job grieves and questions God, his actions aren't seen as sins against the Lord. At the end of the day, Job still holds on to the fundamental truth that God is good. In the midst of his pain, Job praises the Lord for that.

God wants your questions and your reactions. Above all, He longs for your absolute trust in Him, your knowledge that your circumstances may not reflect the truth about your God.

*Lord, when bad things happen, I will still believe that You are good. While I may not understand why things happen, I choose to trust that You have both me and my times in Your hands.*

## TURN AROUND

*God chose things despised by the world, things
counted as nothing at all, and used them to bring
to nothing what the world considers important.*

1 Corinthians 1:28 nlt

God doesn't always use the people that meet the world's standards to serve Him. The Bible is full of His daughters who started from a lowly place. Sarah was too old to have children when God announced she'd be the mother of a nation. Leah was placed second in a marriage because her sister was more beautiful. Rahab was a prostitute. Ruth was both a widow and a foreigner. Mary Magdalene was demon-possessed. And the Samaritan woman was divorced multiple times.

These women weren't important by societal standards. Some were even seen as untouchable and abandoned by the Lord. But God didn't see these sisters of God the way the world did. And each one became a major part of His story.

God takes people that are in last place and moves the finish line. With one wave of His hand, the Lord brought these women from condemnation to redemption.

God wants to do the same with you. He wants you to serve Him. All He asks is your absolute trust that at just the right time, He'll turn your situation around. And you too will be a big part of His story.

*Father, when I feel lower than low, remind me the only
standard I truly need to live up to is Yours. Amen.*

# ARMLOADS OF BLESSINGS

*Bring rains to our drought-stricken lives so those who planted
their crops in despair will shout "Yes!" at the harvest,
so those who went off with heavy hearts will come
home laughing, with armloads of blessing.*
PSALM 126:4-6 MSG

There are so many moments that can't be explained in this life. Why is it so hard to make ends meet? Why can't those who love one another stay together? Why do terrible things happen to amazing people?

The answer is that God created His children to live a joyful and fulfilling life, but this world became a broken one when Adam and Eve ate the forbidden fruit in the Garden.

Although you may not be able to figure out why certain things happen in your life or the lives of those you love, you can be sure God will use those trials for your ultimate good. To further His will. To mold you into the daughter He created you to be.

God will eventually turn your despair into delight and your tears into laughter. He's poised to fill your arms with blessings.

*Father, I realize I may not get all the answers in my lifetime.
But I know that You will use everything I go through for my
spiritual growth, and in the end I will have armloads of
blessings. In the meantime, give me faith and endurance
to keep going even when the going gets hard.*

# HE ALONE

*With the aged [you say] is wisdom, and with length of days*
*comes understanding. But [only] with [God] are [perfect] wisdom*
*and might; He [alone] has [true] counsel and understanding.*
JOB 12:12-13 AMPC

W hen Job fell into hard times, he had various people giving him
their opinions as to why he'd lost his family, servants, animals,
wealth, and health. His so-called friends described Job—a man that
"was blameless and upright, one who feared God and turned away
from evil" (Job 1:1 ESV) —as a sinner! Yet, in this confusing time, Job
was able to relate a major truth to his friend and himself: God alone
was wise and powerful. He alone had the advice and understanding
that humankind could rely on.

Distress can sometimes cloud the fact of who God is and has
been since before time began. Despair can make one temporarily
forget that it is God who holds all the answers and has all the wisdom
one could ever need.

When you come upon a hard time or you need to make a difficult
decision, you may want to go to friends and family for advice. But
God wants to be your first choice. He wants to have the final say.
Because to Him alone belongs wisdom, power, and understanding.

---

*Lord, You hold the ultimate truth and wisdom*
*in this hand. Instead of looking to others for advice*
*and understanding, I will look to You, the One who*
*holds all power, strength, and wisdom. Amen.*

# WAIT FOR THE MORNING

*I wait for the Lord more than watchmen wait for the morning,*
*more than watchmen wait for the morning.*
PSALM 130:6 NIV

Watchmen were guards who stood on the walls of ancient cities to look out for enemies. These men would sound an alarm if they saw danger approaching. This alert allowed the men of the city to prepare to protect their families.

When you were a watchman, it was important to stay awake during the night hours. But this was more than difficult. For the night was dark with no city lights to help you see off into the distance. Torch light only traveled so far. Not only was it difficult to see, but the hours seemed so long without anything to help pass the time. The watchmen were never sure what might happen in those pitch-black nights.

Many women today may feel like those watchmen of ancient days. Life may seem dark, long, and unpredictable. But just as the watchman waited for the first rays of sunshine to come over the horizon, God's daughters must wait to see their Father working.

The watchmen trusted that morning would come, and it always did. Just as it will for you. God always works and reveals Himself to His beloved at just the right time.

*Lord, when I'm in a dark place, I promise to wait for*
*Your guidance more than watchmen wait for the morning,*
*more than watchmen wait for the morning.*

# FINDING CALM

*But I have calmed and quieted myself, I am like a weaned child with its mother; like a weaned child I am content.*
PSALM 131:2 NIV

There are a couple apps you can purchase on a smartphone that promise calm. They include soft music, white noise and rain sounds, meditation and breathing exercises. The makers of these apps know what a lot of the women in this world need—a chance to escape, to relax and recharge, to find contentment. Although you may not be able to control your circumstances, you can try to get a rein on your emotions.

Like an anxious child who only wants her mother, your heart longs for a place of comfort, peace, and contentment. Although you know there are some things in this world that can give you momentary peace and comfort, where can you go for something long-lasting?

Go to God. He yearns to be that source of long-lasting calm you need. He wants you to come into His presence for comfort, peace, and contentment. This type of calm is unshakable and immovable because it comes straight from God. It will never fade away or falter.

To obtain that kind of calm, all you need to do is put your faith and trust in the Lord. When you trust that God is working in your now, you aren't anxious for your future.

*Lord, thank You for the everlasting calm You provide when I'm anxious. Amen.*

## RESTING PLACE

*For the LORD has chosen Zion; he has desired it for
his dwelling place: "This is my resting place forever;
here I will dwell, for I have desired it."*
PSALM 132:13-14 ESV

66 Resting place" in Hebrew can be translated back to many words such as *peace*, *ease*, and *sanctuary*. And that is something every woman wants, a place to call her own that is comforting and safe. From the beginning of time, God has seen that in all His people, even when they don't.

While that place of ease may not be accessible for you in the physical sense at times, you can always find a resting place in God, because Jesus Christ chose a dwelling place in you. The verse above paints a beautiful picture. The Lord has chosen you. He wants to live in you and alongside you. He calls you "peace." He calls you "sanctuary." Because Jesus, who is the very definition of those words, resides in you.

C.S. Lewis wrote about God building His children: "You thought you were being made into a decent little cottage: but He is building a palace. He intends to come and live in it Himself."

*Lord, thank You for constantly constructing me into the daughter
You intend me to be. For loving me so much that You chose to
be a part of me and my life every single day. I count it my
joy to never have to be apart from You. Amen.*

## SET IT RIGHT

*"Why doesn't the Almighty bring the wicked to judgment?*
*Why must the godly wait for him in vain?"*
JOB 24:1 NLT

Job asks the question all of God's children struggle with at some point of their lives. Why do people sometimes get away with doing bad things? No seeming consequences or punishments. Meanwhile, others who are doing life the right way, living the way they believe God is asking them to live, keep getting the short straw. It can make anyone wonder why she should keep following the Lord when it seems to get her nowhere.

Both good and bad people will have struggles, difficulties in this life, some seen and some unseen. Like Job, we must trust God is watching everyone. We must believe God will set the record straight. We may not even get to see God make it right, but we must trust anyway.

God would have you keep your mind on your own matters, not make note of wrongs and rights or to pass judgments on others. Your job is to be the best example of Jesus you can be in every circumstance. And you can be sure God will reward you for your hard work and endurance.

*God, help me to focus on myself. Quash my anger about the injustices I see. Help me trust You are setting things right.*

## WHERE IS WISDOM?

*We sometimes tend to think we know all we need to know to*
*answer these kinds of questions—but sometimes our humble*
*hearts can help us more than our proud minds. We never really*
*know enough until we recognize that God alone knows it all.*
1 CORINTHIANS 8:2-3 MSG

Job asks an important question: Where does wisdom come from? Can it be bought? Is it in the darkness or the sea? He answers no. True wisdom can only come from one source—God. "God understands the way [to Wisdom] and He knows the place of it [Wisdom is with God alone]. For He looks to the ends of the earth and sees everything under the heavens" (Job 28:23-24 AMPC). God knows wisdom because He created wisdom, so therefore He is wisdom. He knows everything about the world—and about you.

Paul is asking and answering the same question for Corinthians years later. Where can the ultimate wisdom be found? Everyone was made with that yearning to discover and a pull that leads back to God if it's followed correctly. And the answer they find was as true for them as it is for you today. Wisdom can still be found only in knowing God and being known by Him.

*Lord, thank You for always showing me true wisdom*
*in my life. When I need to make a decision, I will let Your*
*ways guide my thoughts and actions. My desire is to*
*do what's right according to Your will. Amen.*

## THE GREATEST

*"But I tell you, in this you are not right,*
*for God is greater than any mortal."*
JOB 33:12 NIV

Everyone experiences a bad day every once in a while. You know the kind, a day when you wish you'd never gotten out of bed in the morning. Imagine if that one day turned into another. . .and another. . .and another. . .and each day worse than the last. Ultimately, you're brought to your knees and cannot fathom what brought you to this place. That's the well-known story of Job.

Job lost everything. His livelihood, his children, his health. . .and did what most people would do. He tried to figure out why. Three of Job's friends offered suggestions of the cause of his misery, adding fuel to his despondency. It took a young man, Elihu, who finally offered wisdom. Job was trying to use the logic of man to rationalize a matter of God. A mere mortal could never understand God's plan. But by keeping the faith, ultimately, a person will be blessed.

Why do bad things happen to good people? We may never understand why this happens. But by keeping the faith, as Job did, God will always bring you through. Remember that next time you have a bad day. If God brings you to it, He'll bring you through it.

*Dear God, on my darkest days, help me to remember*
*that You have everything under control and will*
*see me through the good and bad times.*

## THE PRIZE

*"Do you not know that in a race all the runners run, but only
one gets the prize? Run in such a way as to get the prize.
Everyone who competes in the games goes into strict training.
They do it to get a crown that will not last, but we do
it to get a crown that will last forever."*
1 CORINTHIANS 9:24-25 NIV

P icture the starting line of the Boston Marathon, a race that
normally attracts over 30,000 runners each year. That's a lot
of people! But imagine that out of all those people, only two win the
crown—one man and one woman. Just two people out of 30,000.

Imagine all the training, sacrifice, and dedication it takes to
train for such a long race. A runner must adhere to a strict schedule
of training and a healthy diet. She must give up luxuries of social
gatherings and time with friends. And yet the end result is worth it.

The apostle Paul tells us that in the race for life in Christ, everyone
can win a prize that is eternal. The prize is yours for the asking! By
training in godliness and service to others, your victory is guaranteed.
You won't get those odds in the Boston Marathon!

*Dear God, help me in my race to win Your heavenly prize.
Help me train by eliminating those actions and habits that are
spiritually unhealthy. Help me win an unshakable crown.*

## WOE IS ME

*Then the L*ORD* spoke to Job out of the storm. He said: "Who is this that obscures my plans with words without knowledge?"*
JOB 38:1-2 NIV

I t's human nature, during tough times, to ask, "Why me? What did I do to deserve this?" When such thoughts enter your mind, consider the suffering Job. Think about what he endured and how he asked the same questions and seemed to have given up all hope. And how God answered him.

Though God never responds to Job's question of "why," He does remind Job of His infinite power and wisdom. He did, after all, create the universe without Job's assistance. So who is the all-powerful One? God. And He poses rhetorical questions, one after the other, to illustrate this point.

Rather than coming to God with the whys, Job and all humankind should remember that God is in control, and His reasons for allowing suffering is not ours to know. What *is* ours to know is that God loves us and will always take care of us, according to His plan.

Remember, no matter what you're going through or why, you're never alone. The wise and all-powerful Creator of the universe has got you in the palm of His hand.

---

*God, when I question why things happen to me, remind me that You're in control and will take care of me. Amen.*

## "TO BOLDLY GO"

*I will praise you, LORD, with all my heart; before the "gods"*
*I will sing your praise. . . . When I called, you answered me;*
*you greatly emboldened me. . . . Though I walk in the*
*midst of trouble, you preserve my life.*
PSALM 138:1, 3, 7 NIV

What a strong testament by David to the glory of God! While David was always forthcoming in his praise and gratitude to God, these strong statements of praise go that extra mile. Not only does he thank God for prayers answered, but he's obviously greatly fortified. He's endowed with the strength of spirit and the boldness to face anything.

Boldness is not necessarily strength but rather a spirit of bravery to forge ahead into the unknown. Remember the old series *Star Trek*? The tag line was "To boldly go where no man has gone before."

Physical strength is not always what's necessary to face adversity. You need that boldness of spirit that only God can bestow. Just remember that when you need boldness, it's not just yours for the asking (Matthew 7:7) but yours for the taking (Hebrews 4:16).

In today's world, you need help to cope. As you face adversities, remember David's words. Know that you too are emboldened by God. He will preserve your life. The strong spirit is within you. May you boldly go.

*God, as I call on You, it's comforting to know You will always*
*answer me, helping me to be bold.*

## WHAT'S YOUR SUPERPOWER?

*To one there is given through the Spirit a message of
wisdom, to another a message of knowledge by means
of the same Spirit, to another faith by the same Spirit,
to another gifts of healing by that one Spirit.*
1 CORINTHIANS 12:8-9 NIV

E ach of us is given talents. You might be a great singer, your
friend may have a knack for science, someone else might be a
terrific artist. Each gift granted by the Spirit is different but no more
or less important than another. It's how and when you choose to
*use* your gifts that matters.

Talents were given to be shared and for the common good. A
singer might choose to use that beautiful voice to soothe an embattled
soul; a good chef might cook for those less fortunate; a genius might
tutor a struggling student.

There is no "right" way to share your gifts. And no gift is too small
or insignificant. If your heart is in the right place and your focus is
to help others, you have succeeded in the eyes of God.

So share those gifts, which are uniquely yours. When you do,
you build up your own inner strength and confidence. Your focus
switches from me to thee. And as you find your talent uplifting others,
you become uplifted yourself.

---

*Dear God, I thank You for my talents.
Help me finda way to use them for the good of all!*

## THE MIRACLE OF YOU

*I praise you because I am fearfully and wonderfully made;*
*your works are wonderful, I know that full well.*
PSALM 139:14 NIV

Birth is often referred to as a miracle and with good reason. Each child born is so delightfully made, so perfect in God's eyes. Why? Because each child is wonderfully made in His image.

This creation and the Creator are indeed awe-inspiring. David, in today's verse, sang God's praises, overwhelmed by the majesty of his existence. God, capable of making such a biological masterpiece, is worthy of being worshipped and admired.

There's no doubt that you too are wonderfully made. Even if you may feel or have been told you are imperfect, there is no reason to be disheartened or discouraged for God sees all His children as perfect.

Today and every day, give God the praise He deserves, because He made you the incredible, unshakable person you are. Anytime you doubt your significance or relevance, just remember who made you. That unparalleled Creator, He who never makes mistakes and never takes shortcuts. As His creature, you are destined to do great things. You are God's marvel, uniquely and wonderfully made.

*Dear God, I know that by Your hands, I am*
*fearfully and wonderfully made. I stand in awe*
*of Your magnificence! When I feel unworthy or*
*downtrodden, when I'm disheartened or discouraged,*
*help remember I'm perfect in Your eyes. Amen and amen!*

## HAPPY DAYS

*When times are good, be happy; but when times are bad,*
*consider this: God has made the one as well as the other.*
*Therefore, no one can discover anything about their future.*
ECCLESIASTES 7:14 NIV

W hen things are going well, people don't need someone to remind them to be happy. No one ever asks, "Why me, Lord?" when things are on the upswing. No one ever questions good fortune! So it seems only natural that as soon as things go awry, prayers immediately go up asking, "Why me, Lord?"

The writer of Ecclesiastes says both good and bad exist in this world, and God is bringer of both. The reason behind events, good or bad, is not for us to understand. Yet there exists a ray of hope. Even though bad things may happen, "we know that in all things God works for the good of those who love him, who have been called according to his purpose" (Romans 8:28 NIV).

You've heard the saying "Behind every cloud is a silver lining." It's true, even if sometimes it's hard to identify the upside in a given situation. Just keep in mind that adversity and sadness most times leave us wiser. And the hardship you face may just enable you to help and comfort others.

*Dear God, thank You for the wonderful times in my*
*life and the wisdom I've gleaned in the darker days.*
*Help me use my experiences to help others and*
*gain a better perspective within and without.*

## MY GOD

*I say to the L*ORD*, "You are my God." Hear, L*ORD*,
my cry for mercy. Sovereign L*ORD*, my strong deliverer,
you shield my head in the day of battle."*
PSALM 140:6-7 NIV

In just two short verses, David professes his strong faith in his God and devotion to Him. He confirms his belief in God's unlimited power and His ability to keep him safe. David is secure in the knowledge that his God is his shield and his protector. There is no doubt in his mind that God will defend him against his foes as he prepares for battle. David's faith is unwavering and truly an example to all believers. What a testament to his love for the Lord!

Just as David knows that his prayers will be answered and that help is but a prayer away, you too can rest assured of this fact. You too can enjoy his level of confidence and security.

Woman of the Way, the Lord will deliver you when you declare, as David did, that He is your God! And remember: The more you confidently believe God is your shield—a fortress around you, making you impenetrable to all harm—the more unshakable you will become.

---

*Dear God, to You I pledge my devotion. To You I cry out for mercy in difficult times. Deliver me from evil, Lord. Protect me always, and I will become more and more unshakable in You.*

## FEEL THE LOVE

*[I can feel] his left hand under my head
and his right hand embraces me!*
SONG OF SOLOMON 2:6 AMPC

C an you recall a time when you felt scared and lost and perhaps all alone? It's when you are the weakest that the Lord's strength comes through to You. It's then that God sustains you, that He places His left hand under your head, supporting you and lifting you up from the depths of your despair. It's then that He places His right hand around you, embracing you and energizing you.

God's loving support, His care and attention, His strength and power will keep you from falling, even when you feel the weakest. A life-sustaining embrace from the Lord is all you need to emerge from the depths of your despair. When you feel as if you cannot even rise from your bed, all you have to do is reach out to God. He who knows you, both spiritually and physically, will uphold and strengthen you.

Today reach out for God's presence, feel His love. Allow Him to guide you, protect you, and calm you until all danger has passed. Know that He loves you, holds you, and firmly secures you. Empowered, you can and will rise stronger and do what He calls you to do.

*Dear God, I thank You for Your loving and sustaining embrace,
Your holy hand under my head, supporting and empowering me,
giving me the strength to do all You call me to do.*

# UNSHAKABLE

*Therefore, my dear brothers and sisters, stand firm. Let nothing move you. Always give yourselves fully to the work of the Lord, because you know that your labor in the Lord is not in vain.*
1 CORINTHIANS 15:58 NIV

Have you heard the phrase "My future is so bright, I have to wear shades"? This verse, which closes out the fifteenth chapter of Paul's letter to the Corinthians, is reminiscent of that sentiment. Throughout this chapter, the apostle Paul speaks of the resurrection of Jesus and the promise of our immortality in heaven with Him forever. Paul reminds us to always serve the Lord and work to His glory. The reward? A future so bright in eternal life!

Have you ever stood on the edge of the beach, letting the tide sweep over your feet as it goes in and out? Your feet sink slightly into the sand as the water flows by, offering you a firm stance. Think of the moving water as obstacles you face in life. If you stand firm and maintain your balance, you remain steady. You are immovable and unshakable, rooted in the sand of hard work and labor for the Lord. No matter what you face, you will be bolstered by God at all times!

*Dear God, encourage me every day as I strive to work hard in the labor to Your glory. Help me to serve others each day, to be loyal to You, and to stand firm in faith.*

## DIVINE GPS

*When my spirit grows faint within me,*
*it is you who watch over my way.*
PSALM 142:3 NIV

Have you ever been lost on a country road and been unable to get a GPS signal? Soon a sense of desperation sets in. You begin to feel utterly alone and afraid. Nothing looks familiar as you drive aimlessly, trying to find your way. It is an unsettling feeling, to say the least.

These emotions are common to all, especially during difficult times. When living through times of fear and uncertainty, it's easy to become disheartened, lonely, and unsettled. But when your spirit grows faint, do *not* lose hope! God is always there, watching over you, prepared to show you the path back to faith.

David was hiding out in a cave when he wrote this psalm. He was being persecuted and pursued. He feared for his life. Yet God inspired him to write these words, words that gave him comfort and hope and ultimately saved his life.

When you feel lost, helpless, and hopeless, lift your eyes to the mountains, to the source of your help, to "the LORD, the Maker of heaven and earth" (Psalm 121:2 NIV). Depend on God, using Him as your GPS as you go through this life.

*Dear God, help me as I try to navigate my journey through this life. Be with me always, guiding me through good times and bad. Sustain my spirit in times of weakness, and show me Your way.*

## SECURITY BLANKET

*Grace (favor and spiritual blessing) to you and [heart] peace from God our Father and the Lord Jesus Christ (the Messiah, the Anointed One). Blessed be the God and Father of our Lord Jesus Christ, the Father of sympathy (pity and mercy) and the God [Who is the Source] of every comfort (consolation and encouragement).*
2 CORINTHIANS 1:2-3 AMPC

There's something to be said for the feelings of serenity and security while snuggled in a plush comforter on a wintry day. You wrap yourself up in its warmth and feel at peace. Being enveloped in the loving arms of God is like that. He brings a feeling of serenity and peace to your heart that overcomes any trouble in your soul.

Each day, say a prayer of thanks for your blessings, beginning with the gift of Jesus Christ. It's His presence that warms you from the inside out. He's a gift that no one can ever take away. With Jesus in your heart, you can face and do anything.

Praise God for the gift of His Son every day. Doing so will remind you that because Jesus is in your life, you're never alone. And His compassion, His love—they are all yours. Your gratitude and faith are all that's asked in exchange.

*God, Your love and warmth are my comfort and strength. Thank You for the gift of Your Son, residing within my heart, blessing me with peace and encouragement. Amen.*

## STANDING TALL

*"If you do not stand firm in your faith,*
*you will not stand at all."*
ISAIAH 7:9 NIV

W hen toddlers first learn to walk, they have little idea of how to avoid falling. They usually try walking on their tippy toes, not yet getting the idea of maintaining a good center of gravity. The result is repeated topples and tumbles. But soon they understand that if they stand firm, they no longer waver and fall. They learn to walk. By standing firm, they achieve success.

So it is with faith. In today's verse, Ahaz, the insecure ruler of Israel, doubted his ability to rule and to vanquish his enemies. The Lord spoke these words to him, a reminder to not doubt himself but rather to have faith and to believe in God. The promise is simple —have faith and you will stand firm. What a strong and simple message for everyone, one that is repeated often in scripture. In 1 Thessalonians 3:8 (NIV) Paul wrote, "For now we really live, since you are standing firm in the Lord."

Women of the Way, plant yourself firmly in faith, using it as an anchor in your life. Only then will you stand tall, unshakable, and secure against all odds.

---

*Dear God, with each step I take, help me to remember to stand firm in faith. Help me to believe that with You, all things are possible. With You, I am strong. With You, I stand tall.*

# A GREAT LIGHT

*The people walking in darkness have seen a great light; on those living in the land of deep darkness a light has dawned.*
ISAIAH 9:2 NIV

I saiah was a well-known and respected prophet in Judah in the eighth century B.C. The people of his time were walking in darkness and despair. Isaiah's prophecies covered the reigns of many kings and leaders of the land, but nothing he'd written or spoken compared to his words in today's verse. He delivered the hopeful message the Israelites needed to hear. Just when they needed some bright news, Isaiah predicted the greatest gift of all—the coming of the world's savior, Jesus Christ.

As John wrote in his Gospel, "In him was life, and that life was the light of all mankind. The light shines in the darkness, and the darkness has not overcome it" (John 1:4-5 NIV).

Have you ever felt as if you were walking in darkness? On those difficult days, remember the words of Isaiah and John. Remember "the true light that gives light to everyone" (John 1:9 NIV), the light that was born in the little town of Bethlehem over 2,000 years ago. He alone will illuminate your darkest days.

*Dear God, what a joyful prophecy for those living in darkness years ago. Remind me that I have that Light within my heart as I journey through difficult days. I have the light of hope! Amen.*

# EVERLASTING AND UNSHAKABLE

*Your kingdom is an everlasting kingdom, and your dominion
endures through all generations. The LORD is trustworthy in all
he promises and faithful in all he does.*

PSALM 145:13 NIV

What a joy to know that God has secured the future for all believers in His everlasting heavenly kingdom! That He will fulfill all His promises to all His children and ensures His love will endure forever! That there will never be a time when His people will be left alone, for He is with us, trustworthy and faithful to us. We need never doubt that God is in charge and always will be. We can take it as fact that we will remain unshaken, protected through the generations, for all eternity!

Because of all these things, these truths, you can, without hesitation, fully put your trust in God. For He, with unlimited power and strength, cares for you tenderly, promising to be faithful. His love is unending, His power limitless, His promise forever.

Earthly kingdoms may come and go, but God's eternal kingdom is promised to you for all time. He is the ultimate and superior Being who loves you, strengthens you, and is trustworthy. Knowing your future is secure with and in the unconquerable Lord, you can be unshakable!

*Dear God, thank You for this wonderful pledge to me,
for Your love and Your eternal promises for me and
for all generations past, present, and future.*

## JARS OF CLAY

*God said, "Light up the darkness!" and our lives filled up with*
*light as we saw and understood God in the face of Christ, all*
*bright and beautiful. If you only look at us, you might well miss*
*the brightness. We carry this precious Message around in the*
*unadorned clay pots of our ordinary lives. That's to prevent*
*anyone from confusing God's incomparable power with us.*
2 CORINTHIANS 4:6-7 MSG

Decorative earthenware is certainly beautiful. It sits proudly on a mantel or shelf and is a joy to look at. However, it is delicate; a child's wayward ball or an errant elbow could send it toppling to the ground, shattering the beautiful outer shell.

That is the case of your human body. While it's a masterfully created outer shell, it's not impermeable to injury or the ravages of age. But unlike the pottery one might have in one's home, this vessel is not empty. Your body is filled with the light of God, which shines in your heart and fills you with the knowledge of His glory.

No matter what happens to your outer shell, nothing can shake this inner light with which you have been blessed. God's complete power is brilliant, as a light shining out of darkness.

*Dear God, help me to always treasure Your light,*
*which I carry within me, in my personal jar of clay.*
*May Your light—the beacon in my life—direct me always.*

# PERFECT VISION

*For we live by faith, not by sight.*
2 Corinthians 5:7 niv

How do you navigate your way through life?

Most people rely on their eyes to lead them. They don't believe things until they see them. They trust in the things before them, the things of now, the things they can touch, taste, see, hear, and smell. But...what if they let *faith in God* be their guide?

According to Hebrews 11:1 (ampc), "Faith is the assurance (the confirmation, the title deed) of the things [we] hope for, being the proof of things [we] do not see and the conviction of their reality [faith perceiving as real fact what is not revealed to the senses]." Faith is the belief in that which is unseen—the love and the promises of God. Faith is the belief in the teachings of Jesus, which gives us the blueprint of how to live a good and righteous life. Faith is stable, unwavering, and unshakable.

So, trust your faith to guide you. Trust the teachings of Jesus to lead you through your journey through life. Your eyes can deceive you, your senses may fail, but you can count on your faith to be your guide.

*Dear God, guide me through this jungle of life here on earth. Help me to rely not on my own vision, but on my faith in You and the teachings of Your Son, Jesus Christ, to lead me through. Through faith in You, I will be unshakable.*

# THE GREATEST

*Great is our Lord and mighty in power;*
*his understanding has no limit.*
PSALM 147:5 NIV

I f ever a verse inspired confidence in God's infinite power, it's this one! It is inclusive and inviting. This passage lets you know that God is "our" God. He is *your* God. And He is strong. There is no foe He cannot vanquish, no problem He cannot solve, no challenge He cannot handle.

God's understanding is limitless, well-beyond human comprehension. What does this mean for you? It means you can trust His profound wisdom has your best interests at heart. He knows you intimately, inside and out. God will always be there to pick you up if you stumble. He will always be there to lift you up when you're struggling. With His divine arms wrapped around you, you will not fall. In those arms, you are unshakable!

Woman of the Way, be secure in the fact that God knows what you need even before you need it! He knows all your concerns and your fears before they surface. His compassion for you knows no limits. And most of all, He loves you just as you are.

*Dear God, how great You are! I am comforted to know*
*that Your power is endless, your understanding unlimited.*
*You are there, ever-present in my life. I pray I will always*
*feel Your loving arms around me, protecting me,*
*and keeping me safe. With You, I can do anything!*

## A SHELTER FROM THE STORM

*You have been a refuge for the poor, a refuge for the needy in their distress, a shelter from the storm and a shade from the heat. For the breath of the ruthless is like a storm driving against a wall.*

ISAIAH 25:4 NIV

If you have ever been caught unprepared in a storm, facing wind and rain, or been walking in a parching heat, you can appreciate the importance of finding refuge. A small bus stop, the protective branches of a large tree, a cave, or even a small cabin can offer welcomed relief from inclement weather.

But for the storms of your life, there is only one true refuge —Almighty God. He offers refuge to you when you need it, both physically and spiritually. He offers shelter when you feel beat up or isolated. He protects you when turmoil around you heats up. He can strengthen your resolve, making you stronger and invulnerable. And when you face evil, which comes on like a battering storm, He will offer you His protection and be your strong shield and fortress.

Woman of the Way, with God as your refuge, no one stands a chance against you. You are unshakable.

*Dear God, strengthen my heart in times of weakness, want, and need. Protect me from the winds of life. When my enemies circle around me, be my fortress and lifeline. When I am poor in spirit and faith, fortify me with Your love. Be my shelter from the storm.*

## WISDOM OF AGES

*All this also comes from the LORD Almighty,*
*whose plan is wonderful, whose wisdom is magnificent.*
ISAIAH 28:29 NIV

I n any given task, it's always wise to seek counsel from an expert. If you wanted to invest your money wisely, you wouldn't call an electrician. Conversely, if you wanted to rewire your house, you wouldn't call a financial planner. If you want to be wise, then, listen to the words given in Isaiah, and trust in the instruction given by God. Take care to follow His steps carefully and completely. God's plans are perfect. His instruction is a gift to you.

Remember that God's plan for you is perfect and unwavering. He has laid down "a tested stone, a precious cornerstone for a sure foundation" (Isaiah 28:16 NIV). Jesus personifies that sure foundation. He brings the good news that your Father God saves as no one else can. That's why "the one who relies on it will never be stricken with panic" (Isaiah 28:16 NIV).

God will not let you fall. Through prayer, you can reach out to Him, asking for His magnificent wisdom, which is far beyond what mere mortals can comprehend.

Have faith. God has a plan for you. On that you can rely.

*Dear God, You are wise in all things. Help me to trust*
*that Your wisdom is indeed magnificent, even when it's*
*hard for me to understand. And thank You for the*
*foundation of Jesus Christ. On Him I will rely.*

## FINDING YOUR WAY

*Whether you turn to the right or to the left, your ears will hear a voice behind you, saying, "This is the way; walk in it."*
ISAIAH 30:21 NIV

Have you ever felt lost, not knowing which way to turn? You stand there, undecided, not sure if you should turn to the left or right. If left to your own devices, you could easily make the wrong choice. In times of weakness, you might react with emotion rather than with faith. You might feel alone, incapable of making a good decision.

Woman of the Way, remember that you are *never* truly alone. God is always there for you, always directing you, whispering in your ear, nudging you to go right or left. Because He has promised never to leave you, you can be assured He is in your corner, behind you, gently ushering you along the path He's laid out for you.

When you find yourself at the crossroad, unsure which way to turn, pray for God's divine directions. Then listen quietly, assured that He'll never abandon you, that He knows what you need, that He has you in His sights and watches over you day and night.

Little lamb, look to Your Shepherd. And He will guide you safely home.

*Dear God, help me to be still, to listen for Your direction, and to follow wherever You lead. I look to You, my Shepherd, to be the voice behind me, telling me which way to go.*

## SPIRITUAL VICTORY

*For though we live in the world, we do not wage war as the
world does. The weapons we fight with are not the weapons of
the world. On the contrary, they have divine power to demolish
strongholds. We demolish arguments and every pretension that
sets itself up against the knowledge of God, and we take captive
every thought to make it obedient to Christ.*

2 CORINTHIANS 10:3-5 NIV

E ach day, you might find yourself fighting a battle, not a physical
one but a spiritual one. Perhaps you are the victim of negative
thoughts, vain desires, or baseless accusations. Whatever conflict
you're facing, you can take heart! You can win any fight afflicting your
thoughts and your heart! Through obedience to Jesus and with the
knowledge of God, you can defeat any spiritual foe!

Today and every day, remember to fall back on God for strength.
He's there to empower and defend you. With the knowledge of God,
*you* have the power to demolish any evil stronghold and to free
yourself of these negative forces! You have a strong foundation, built
on God's divine love and supernatural protection.

No one can shake your faith! You are unbeatable with God on
your side!

*Dear God, help me arm myself through the knowledge
of You and my obedience to Christ, so that I might emerge
victorious in any battle within and without.*

# STEADY

*Strengthen the feeble hands, steady the knees that give way;*
*say to those with fearful hearts, "Be strong, do not fear;*
*your God will come, he will come with vengeance;*
*with divine retribution he will come to save you."*
ISAIAH 35:3-4 NIV

These words of encouragement by Isaiah are as pertinent today as they were many years ago. If you are feeling weak in the knees or feeble or your heart is afraid, God has promised to come and save you. He'll protect you and strengthen you in your weakest hour. Just as in Isaiah's day, God is present in your life. He cares deeply for you, and He longs to deliver you.

No matter what you may be going through, God encourages you to continue, to look to a future full of promise and hope. No matter what you have endured or what you fear you may encounter, don't ever lose hope.

God's promise that He'll come "with vengeance" to save you is your guarantee. And it has no expiration date! If you start to lose your balance, don't panic. He'll be there to catch you.

Remember, "God's loyal love couldn't have run out, his merciful love couldn't have dried up. They're created new every morning. How great your faithfulness! I'm sticking with GOD (I say it over and over)" (Lamentations 3:22-23 MSG).

*Dear God, thank You for Your guarantee of protection.*
*You steady my knees, strengthen my hands, and comfort*
*my fearful heart. I'm sticking with You.*

## TRUE STRENGTH

*That is why, for Christ's sake, I delight in weaknesses,*
*in insults, in hardships, in persecutions, in difficulties.*
*For when I am weak, then I am strong.*
2 CORINTHIANS 12:10 NIV

Everyone has tough days. Sometimes they expand into weeks, months, or years of trial.

The apostle Paul was given a thorn in his flesh. Although it's not known exactly what his malady was, he did plead with Jesus to remove that thorn. That's when Jesus told him, "My grace is enough; it's all you need. My strength comes into its own in your weakness" (2 Corinthians 12:9 MSG).

Those words turned Paul's life, his view of his weakness and hardships, around! Paul writes, "Once I heard that, I was glad to let it happen. I quit focusing on the handicap and began appreciating the gift. It was a case of Christ's strength moving in on my weakness" (2 Corinthians 12:9 MSG).

Just like Paul, you too can learn how to "take limitations in stride, and with good cheer" (2 Corinthians 12:10 MSG). When you feel as if you can't go on, when weakness threatens to overtake you, simply allow Christ to take over. For the weaker you get, the stronger you will become.

*Dear God, help me turn around my view of my weaknesses*
*and hardships. Instead of allowing them to bring me down,*
*help me delight in them. Help me face all things with Your*
*grace. In Jesus' name for He is my true strength. Amen.*

## SAFETY NET

*Do you not know? Have you not heard? The Lord is
the everlasting God, the Creator of the ends of the earth.
He will not grow tired or weary, and his understanding
no one can fathom. He gives strength to the weary and
increases the power of the weak. Even youths grow
tired and weary, and young men stumble and fall.*

Isaiah 40:28-30 NIV

Everyone gets tired, everyone stumbles. Little children and adults alike grow weary, trip, and fall. No one is immune. But there is always someone there to pick them up, dust them off, and ensure they are all right.

Just as a child is lifted by his parents, your almighty God, Father, and Creator lifts you when you are struggling, when you can't seem to find your feet. It is His loving arms that will gently raise you up when you feel weak. He is the One who will guide you back to safety.

God never grows tired. Day and night He watches over you. Because of His relentless love for you, you are never out of His sight. When you're weak, in despair, and helpless, He gets you back on your feet and steadies you. He, your eternal safety net, will always be there to catch you when you fall.

*Dear God, I may stumble and I may fall, but I know You are always
there to catch me and get me on my feet again. Thank You!*

## OPEN THE BLIND

*I will lead the blind by ways they have not known,
along unfamiliar paths I will guide them; I will turn the
darkness into light before them and make the rough places
smooth. These are the things I will do; I will not forsake them.*
ISAIAH 42:16 NIV

God knows who we are without His presence. We're like those who are blind, walking in darkness along stony paths upon which we can easily stumble. Yet God tells us we can live a different life—one that takes a large amount of trust, faith, and courage in a Spirit we cannot see but leads to worlds and ways we never before thought or imagined. It means following God.

When we follow the Creator of the world, He guides us through the obstacles of life, taking us by unfamiliar byways. He opens our eyes to outcomes far beyond our comprehension and shows us the way. God turns our darkness into understanding as He reveals His light. He smooths out the way for us and remains forever by our side. God removes our blinders so we can see clearly.

As you navigate through unfamiliar paths or unsteady terrain in dark times, remember that God will illuminate your journey and open your eyes so you can see clearly. He will guide you in all your stages and ages. With Him, you're never lost.

*Dear God, I once was blind, but with You, I can now see.
You make my paths straight, solid, and secure. Amen.*

## LEAN ON HIM

*Trust in the L*ORD *with all your heart and lean not
on your own understanding; in all your ways submit
to him, and he will make your paths straight.*
PROVERBS 3:5-6 NIV

If someone has had good and loving parents, she may understand what it means to trust in someone with all her heart. Good parents are reliable, wise, and loving. They have and always will have a child's best interests at heart. Because a child knows all these things from her experience with her parents, she can trust them with her present and future.

To trust the Lord with all one's heart, even when fear and doubts threaten to take over, is a little harder. That woman must have faith in God and believe that He's in charge though she cannot see Him. She must remind herself that He wants the best for her, is all-knowing, and will guide her in the very best direction. He will indeed make all her paths straight.

Though people tend to want to rely on their own ideas and intuitions, in these verses, God reminds you to trust in *His* ways, not your own, for the best possible outcome. This is true in each and every situation, even when things don't go the way you had hoped or planned.

*God, I know that with You, nothing is impossible
and that You have the best plan for me. In You alone
I trust. Please make my paths straight. Amen.*

## TRUE TREASURES

*Happy (blessed, fortunate, enviable) is the man who
finds skillful and godly Wisdom, and the man who gets
understanding [drawing it forth from God's Word and life's
experiences], for the gaining of it is better than the gaining
of silver, and the profit of it better than fine gold.*
PROVERBS 3:13-14 AMPC

Silver and gold—very valuable assets indeed. If you have an
abundance of them, you would be considered rich by many. But
are they the most important assets you can have? To have a wealth
of precious metals is, of course, a nice luxury. But not all treasures
glitter. And not all wealth is tangible.

Solomon, a wise man indeed, tells you that true treasure is found
in attaining wisdom and understanding. Wisdom is the ability to
act according to the knowledge you have gained. Understanding is
intelligence and intuition, perhaps attained by wisdom, which you
feel confident explaining and sharing with others.

Today's verses from Proverbs say that those who find these
things are blessed. To be truly happy, you should seek to find wisdom
and understanding. They will bring clarity to your life, which cannot
come from material possessions. They will bring you contentment
and peace.

*Dear God, remind me what true treasures are. Help me
to seek wisdom above all things and to understand what
You may be teaching me. Lead me to the profits of
Your Word and ways. And give me peace.*

## EQUAL RIGHTS

*There is neither Jew nor Gentile, neither slave nor free, nor is
there male and female, for you are all one in Christ Jesus.*
GALATIANS 3:28 NIV

What a wonderful concept! No one is better than anyone else,
no one is less important. All men and women are created
equal. God's template for our world is something for which we
strive. Yet each day, we hear some people falling short of grasping
this message, so it bears repeating. We are all one in Jesus Christ!
He plays no favorites.

In today's world, there are many divisions, all of which are
created by humans. While Christians seek to unite as a family, it's
sometimes very difficult to do in today's climate.

Living in a splintered world, it's helpful to remember true equality
exists and awaits us in the afterlife. But for now, we can do our part
to treat all others with respect, as equals, and to look to Jesus as
the One who unites all. It is when we stand united as one that we
become not just strong but unshakable.

*Dear God, in tumultuous as well as in peaceful times, I pray
You will help me to treat everyone as my equal, to not look
down or up to anyone, and to worship You, the one true God,
as He who will unify and strengthen us all.*

## SUNRISE

*The path of the righteous is like the morning sun,
shining ever brighter till the full light of day.*
PROVERBS 4:18 NIV

Think about a beach at dawn. As you make your way over the dune to the shore, you see the first glimmers of light appear on the horizon, over the vast expanse of ocean. You start your walk southward on the water's edge, the sand smooth and firm under your feet. Your path is straight; you know the way. No chance of getting lost on this walk. With each passing moment, the sun rises more and more, illuminating the beautiful world that surrounds you, until the full sun gives you a beautiful, bright day. You have witnessed the glory of God.

This is the path of the righteous, following the heavenly road. There are no obstacles, no snares, no turns in the road, no way to get lost. Your journey is safe, lit by God's glory, guiding you home.

Solomon used this kind of imagery to illustrate the difference between the paths of the righteous and the paths of the wicked. While the journey of the righteous is idyllic, that of the wicked is fraught with darkness and obstacles. Which path will you choose today?

*God, what a beautiful road You have set before me. Walk with me as I move closer and closer to Your heavenly light. Help me to always choose the right path, the path of Your wisdom and light.*

## BEAUTIFUL MESSAGES

*How beautiful on the mountains are the feet of the
messenger who brings good news, the good news of peace
and salvation, the news that the God of Israel reigns!*
ISAIAH 52:7 NLT

The beauty of God's creation is all around. From the explosion of jewel-toned autumn leaves to the bubbling, infectious giggle of a preschooler, we can see God's joy, peace, and harmony—if we take the time to notice it.

Appreciating God's gifts is good. It anchors us deep in His unending love and reassures us of His presence, protection, and provision. But once we've grasped hold of this truth, it's time to share it with the people around us and fully experience the good news of peace and grace. You are an influencer. Each of us—CEOs and stay-at-home moms alike—have an impact on our world. Our words and actions affect friends, coworkers, neighbors, and even perfect strangers we encounter each day.

You, lovely sister in Christ, have a beautiful message to share. Tell a friend what God's doing in your life. Talk about God's faithfulness in a difficult situation, how walking with Him made you unshakable. Encourage someone—just because. Ask God to saturate your soul with His love so that it overflows into your thoughts, conversations, and deeds.

*Father, thank You for the opportunity to be Your messenger.
Help me to live authentically, with a pure heart for Your ways.
Give me eyes to see others the way You see them—
as Your cherished children.*

## TRUE FREEDOM

*For you have been called to live in freedom, my brothers and sisters. But don't use your freedom to satisfy your sinful nature. Instead, use your freedom to serve one another in love.*
GALATIANS 5:13 NLT

"*I do what I want.*"

This tongue-in-cheek definition of freedom may sound like something from the mouth of a three-year-old, but it's essentially what the world says it means to be free.

The problem is that we will often use that freedom to satisfy our own desires. We will do whatever feels good to benefit ourselves. To indulge until we are sick. To manipulate people and situations to make them better for us. To give ourselves the edge off at any cost.

Instead, the apostle Paul encourages us to elevate our thoughts and actions about freedom, writing in 1 Corinthians 10:23-24 (NLT): "You say, 'I am allowed to do anything'—but not everything is beneficial. Don't be concerned for your own good but for the good of others."

When we use our freedom to love others, we're not only following God's second greatest command (Mark 12:31), we also experience His love for us more powerfully. Freedom that serves in love cannot be revoked. True freedom isn't found in earthly governments or constitutions; it's only found in the unending power of Christ's love for us that He demonstrated on the cross.

*I will not take my freedom for granted, Jesus.*
*Make me worthy of such a privilege. Amen.*

## REAL LOVE

*Carry each other's burdens, and in this way
you will fulfill the law of Christ.*

GALATIANS 6:2 NIV

Jesus summed up all of God's law in two simple commandments: love God; love others (Matthew 22:36-40).

But what does it really mean to *love others*? How do we take this seemingly simple command and do it?

Jesus explained practical, day-to-day love this way: love your neighbor as you love yourself (Mark 12:31). If that idea seems too abstract (because some days we're not sure we *like* ourselves, let alone *love* ourselves), Jesus says to treat others the way you would like to be treated (Luke 6:31).

Paul makes loving others even more practical in Galatians 6:2 when he tells us that we love others when we carry their burdens. That means *noticing* when someone in our sphere is having a hard time. Who in your life is stumbling under some circumstance or stress? Even if you can't solve the problem, what action can you take to ease their struggle, to help them stand firm? Maybe it's running errands, making a week's worth of freezer meals, taking a friend out for coffee and offering a listening ear. Carrying another's burden is tangible evidence of your love for others and love of God's ways.

*Father, because of Your great love for me, I want to love others the
same way. Show me opportunities to carry the burdens of others.
Make me strong in You to help in big ways and small. Amen.*

## CONFIDENT HOPE

*I pray that your hearts will be flooded with light so that you can understand the confident hope he has given to those he called— his holy people who are his rich and glorious inheritance.*
EPHESIANS 1:18 NLT

**"** I hope it doesn't rain."
"I hope the meeting today is short."
"I hope I can find a dress for the wedding this weekend."

We often use the word *hope* as a vague, "Gee, I'd like something to turn out in my favor" wish. But the confident hope Paul is praying for the believers in Ephesians 1:19 is a powerful, life-giving gift from God that's available to us today.

Faith-filled hope allows an individual to thrive in the face of a grim diagnosis. Reliance on the goodness of God's plan helps families endure financial hardships. The light of Christ keeps parents of prodigal children from despair. God's holy people know, even when the entire world is in turmoil, they have confident and unshakable hope in the Father.

Have you grasped hold of God's gift of hope? Just as Paul prayed for the Ephesians, ask God to flood your heart with light and give you greater understanding of this priceless gift. Our confidence grows when we remind ourselves of the ways He provided in the past and how He sustains us in the present—leading us to a future fully relying on Him, come what may.

*Gift-giving God, every day I choose Your confident hope.*

## EXPERT CRAFTSMANSHIP

*Together, we are his house, built on the foundation of*
*the apostles and the prophets. And the cornerstone is*
*Christ Jesus himself. We are carefully joined together*
*in him, becoming a holy temple for the Lord.*
EPHESIANS 2:20-21 NLT

YouTube is full of step-by-step how-to videos for any home project. From framing a wall to installing a toilet o-ring, any novice with an Internet connection can arm herself with information to tackle a job. But simply knowing the steps doesn't make the novice an expert, and without experience and guidance from a seasoned pro, a simple Saturday project can derail quickly.

Have you ever felt this way in your own faith? Are you hoping for growth and change but seeing little? Heart and soul renovation, like home renovation, works better alongside seasoned experts.

As the church, we are apprentices in the perfectly crafted house of God. As a work-in-progress for more than 2,000 years, Jesus Himself is not only the foundational cornerstone, He's the foreman, chief architect, and on-the-job trainer who teaches us how to build relationships, love others, and do His good work on earth. We're joined together as His crew as we continue to build and strengthen His house on the generations of believers who came before us.

*Jesus, when I feel isolated in my faith, remind me that I'm*
*an important apprentice in the building of Your church.*
*Bring mentors into my life who'll help me grow in my*
*faith and maintain an unshakable trust in You.*

## LEARN FROM THE BEST

*My son, obey your father's commands, and don't neglect your mother's instruction. Keep their words always in your heart.*
PROVERBS 6:20-21 NLT

R emember when your mom knew nothing? When she couldn't *possibly* understand what you were going through or what you were feeling?

And then, one day, she did.

Today maybe you're in the mom-who-knows-nothing role, doing your best to lovingly guide your child through the growing-up years. Even though life experience has gained you the wisdom to offer real help, that help can fall on deaf ears. (But don't give up, Mama! Keep on loving those deaf ears!)

Proverbs 6:20-21 may be directed toward a youthful reader, but each of us can learn from the wisdom in these verses. No matter our age, we can seek out godly mentors. They may be older than we are or just be further along in their faith walk, but we can learn from their experience. Do you know someone who has come through the other side of a struggle or challenge similar to your own? Ask her what she learned. Ask her what she wished she knew that she knows now and what she would change if she could do it again.

You may gain a perspective and understanding you never expected by really listening and keeping their words in your heart.

*Father, show me the mentors You've placed in my life who'll speak Your truth and wisdom into my heart. I'm listening and ready to receive. Amen.*

## PROPER ANGER

*"In your anger do not sin": Do not let the sun go down while*
*you are still angry, and do not give the devil a foothold.*
EPHESIANS 4:26–27 NIV

There's a reason we often describe anger as *fiery, white-hot, raging,* or *smoldering.* Anger can be one of the most intensely felt emotions and left unchecked can do as much damage as any wildfire. But if you read Ephesians 4:26-27 carefully, the Bible doesn't tell us that anger itself is sinful. It's what we may do *while* we're angry that may be wrong. If we react without thought, anger can injure others and wreck relationships. Anger corked up inside can cause bitterness and destroy us from the inside out.

So, what is the proper way to handle anger? Paul tells us to deal with our anger immediately—before the sun goes down—in a way that builds relationships. Dealing with angry feelings means that we're not letting ourselves stew over them. When we work through the problem, we're not giving Satan the opportunity to divide us and let grudges take root.

Are you angry with someone today? Pray, asking God to give you the steps to take to resolve those feelings. Don't wait for another day to pass by.

*God, when I am angry, help me to not react in*
*knee-jerk ways or nurse the feeling, causing it to grow.*
*Show me how to move through and move on.*

# LOVE LIKE THAT

*Observe how Christ loved us. His love was not cautious but extravagant. He didn't love in order to get something from us but to give everything of himself to us. Love like that.*
EPHESIANS 5:2 MSG

J esus loves you extravagantly. Excessively. Lavishly and without limits. Abundantly, fully, and completely. The Father's love for you goes beyond affection or infatuation. It is a deep, passionate, all-consuming love—for the authentic you (Romans 5:8). There's nothing you can do to earn His love. He *is* love (1 John 4:8 KJV).

Cautious "love" sets stipulations and limits and expectations. Jesus' reckless love knows no boundaries—even to death. How can you know what love is? Jesus Christ willingly gave up His life to save yours (1 John 3:16).

He cares about your day-to-day life. He will carry your stresses, your frustrations (Psalm 55:22) and give you the rest you need (Matthew 11:28). When the world is in turmoil, He is your shelter and safe place (Psalm 91:1-2); unending source of strength and rock (Psalm 18:1-2). Nothing can separate you from the love of the Father, the Son, and the Holy Spirit that lives and loves inside you (Romans 8:38-39).

This world needs more of that kind of love. Love like that.

*Loving God, I praise You for who You are: L-O-V-E. Your name is power and passion and patience and kindness and truth and protection and hope and perseverance. You never fail. Thank You for loving me.*

## MORE THAN WORDS

*Truth, righteousness, peace, faith, and salvation are more than words. Learn how to apply them. You'll need them throughout your life. God's Word is an indispensable weapon.*
EPHESIANS 6:13-17 MSG

Jesus died, just once, defeating death and ushering in our salvation and gift of grace. Because of what Jesus did on the cross, Satan will lose in the end. But until Jesus returns to earth, Satan's still playing his games. And we are His favorite toys.

God is our protector and doesn't ask us to initiate a battle against Satan (Exodus 14:14; Deuteronomy 3:22), but God does give us the tools we need to stand strong when we are attacked. The apostle Paul uses a powerful metaphor of a suit of armor in Ephesians 6, what's known as the Armor of God. Truth is a belt, holding our faith in place. Righteousness protects our core, guarding our heart. Peace anchors our feet to the foundation upon which we stand. Our faith is a shield against the arrows that come out of nowhere. Our salvation is the crowning glory and work of Jesus, protecting us from the top down. And the Bible—our indispensable weapon against darkness—we can pick up like a sword and illuminate any situation with the light of God's wisdom.

---

*God, thank You for arming me with the tools I need to stand strong, knowing You go before me as my protector. I do not fear the battle I face today. Amen.*

## FINDING GOD IN LIFE'S STRUGGLES

*And I want you to know, my dear brothers and sisters, that*
*everything that has happened to me here has helped to spread*
*the Good News. For everyone here, including the whole palace*
*guard, knows that I am in chains because of Christ.*
PHILIPPIANS 1:12-13 NLT

I t's possible to welcome suffering into your life.
    *Are you kidding me?* you're probably wondering. *Why would I do* that*?!*

    The apostle Paul wrote his letter to the Philippians from behind the lock and key of a jail cell. It was just one of several times in his life when he was arrested or imprisoned for preaching the truth of Jesus. But his own suffering didn't come as a surprise to him. Jesus tells us in John 16:33 (NLT), "Here on earth you will have many trials and sorrows. But take heart, because I have overcome the world."

    So, when difficult times come, find strength in the fact that no situation comes as a surprise to God. Look for His guiding hand. Ask for His intervention. Don't be afraid of tomorrow. Pray for His peace. Tap into real, lasting joy that's based on the goodness of God rather than on your circumstances. Find contentment in His love, a powerful force that remains no matter how difficult life gets. Finally, lean on Jesus, the Savior who has already conquered the darkness of the world for all time.

*Jesus, I will welcome trials and sorrows when they come.*
*You have already overcome them! Amen.*

## THE PLAYGROUND BULLY

*Don't be intimidated in any way by your enemies. This will*
*be a sign to them that they are going to be destroyed,*
*but that you are going to be saved, even by God himself.*
PHILIPPIANS 1:28 NLT

Let's call Satan what he is: a playground bully.

Playground bullies are manipulators. Some days they may seem harmless enough, but that's when they're scanning the schoolyard for weaknesses in other kids to pounce on. They plant fear in minds and hearts by their threats, physicality, picking on and making others feel inferior. But it's not what they can *do* that has any power (because playground bullies aren't in charge—adults are), it's the mental games they play that put lasting fearful thoughts inside other kids—and that fear can grow to be crippling for the child.

So when you feel the world's playground bully circling, take advice from the apostle Paul: don't be intimidated. Stand tall and confident in the knowledge that Satan's days are numbered, and he knows it. Ask the Holy Spirit to guard your heart from the lies of manipulation Satan whispers into your ear. Jesus is your Friend, and He is near. He's the One who defeated Satan, sin, and all the evil of the world once and for all time.

*Today I refuse to be intimidated by my enemies, Lord.*
*You are my daily, minute-to-minute Savior who can*
*and will save me from any situation. Thank You.*

# LORD, PLEASE BE GENTLE

*I know, Lord, that our lives are not our own. We are not able to plan our own course. So correct me, Lord, but please be gentle.*
JEREMIAH 10:23-24 NLT

We map out our route by filling up planners and calendars. We place firm but gentle grips at 10 and 2 o'clock on the steering wheel of our lives. We merge lanes as we set goals and take steps necessary to accomplish them. And then a humongous deer of a crisis bounds out of the woods into our path and we realize—in one terrifying moment—that we don't have the control over our lives we think we do.

God's expert ability to plan our lives is so much better than ours, but it's often terrifying to give up that control. Jesus, in the garden of Gethsemane just hours before His arrest, trial, and crucifixion, admitted His own desire to alter God's plans when He prayed, "If it is possible, let this cup of suffering be taken away from me. . . ." But even in His struggle, He knew God's way was ultimately the best, most perfect way when He set aside His pride and earnestly prayed, "Yet I want your will to be done, not mine" (Matthew 26:39 NLT).

"Your will, not mine" is a powerful and often scary prayer to pray. Just remember God's great love for You. Don't be afraid to ask and accept His gentle correction to your course.

*Father, take control. But please be gentle. Amen.*

## PRESS AHEAD

*I focus on this one thing: Forgetting the past and
looking forward to what lies ahead, I press on to reach
the end of the race and receive the heavenly prize
for which God, through Christ Jesus, is calling us.*
PHILIPPIANS 3:13-14 NLT

66 **I**t's called a yoga practice—not a yoga perfect!"
     If you've ever taken a yoga class, perhaps you've heard
the instructor say something like this. Every journey, every growth
opportunity takes perseverance. It takes the willingness to press
ahead and to forge through failure.

In Philippians, Paul describes the Christian life as a foot race,
and he may have understood this metaphor better than most. Paul
had good reason to want to forget his past. This former persecutor
of Christians held the coats of those who stoned Stephen, the first
Christian martyr (Acts 7:57-58). We have all done things for which
we are ashamed, and we live in the tension of what we have been
and what we want to be. But the fact remains that our hope is in
Christ, and because of that, we can let go of guilt and celebrate our
newness in Him.

Today, don't relive your past. Instead, focus on deepening your
relationship with God now. Thank Him for His forgiveness and then
move on to a life of greater and unshakable faith and obedience. You
can look forward to tomorrow.

*Father, help me to let go of my past so I can focus on
what's ahead: a glorious present and future with You!*

## REPLACING WORRY

*Don't fret or worry. Instead of worrying, pray.*
*Let petitions and praises shape your worries into prayers,*
*letting God know your concerns. Before you know it, a sense*
*of God's wholeness, everything coming together for good, will*
*come and settle you down. It's wonderful what happens*
*when Christ displaces worry at the center of your life.*
PHILIPPIANS 4:6-7 MSG

Has worry made a home in your heart? Are you so used to stomach-knotting fretting tied to anxious thoughts that getting rid of it seems impossible? Are you concerned that if you extracted worry from your life it may actually leave a hole in your heart?

Our Father, in His unending compassion for our hearts and spirits, gives us a perfect replacement for worry: prayer.

When you replace worry with prayer, God's Word promises us not just an absence of anxiety and fear but the *addition* of peace. Telling Him about your concerns brings the peace of Christ that goes beyond any understanding or rational explanation. Praising Him for what He has done in the past and clinging to the hope of what He's doing now and in your future brings wholeness that can only come from God's perfect plan. Prayer brings rest, contentment, safety, security, and confidence only found in the Savior, Jesus Christ.

Want to worry less? Then pray more!

*Worry has no home in this heart anymore, Father. Take away*
*my anxious thoughts, and assure me that You are near. When*
*worries try to creep back, replace them with the peace of Christ.*

## ANTICIPATE HIS MIGHTY WORKS

*O Lord, if you heal me, I will be truly healed; if you save me,*
*I will be truly saved. My praises are for you alone!*
JEREMIAH 17:14 NLT

What tops your list of prayer requests today? What relationship are you asking God to repair, sickness to remedy, need to meet, or circumstance to change?

It takes an incredible amount of humility to approach the throne of the King of heaven and boldly ask for. . .anything. But the truth is that we don't have to wonder *if* He will act, because scripture tells us: "This is the confidence we have in approaching God: that if we ask anything according to his will, he hears us. And if we know that he hears us—whatever we ask—we know that we have what we asked of him" (1 John 5:14-15 NIV).

Whatever need is on your heart, your loving Father invites you to lay it at His feet and know He will meet that need. When your heart is aligned with His, your desires will be in harmony with His plans. He will act according to His will—in a mighty, perfect, and powerful way!

---

*God, I need you to step in and take control of this.*
*I am struggling, and I need something to change. If You*
*choose to bring change, I know You will make*
*something beautiful and whole and perfect. I praise*
*You for Your good and perfect will for my life.*

## ROOTED

*Let your roots grow down into him, and let your lives be built on him. Then your faith will grow strong in the truth you were taught, and you will overflow with thankfulness.*

COLOSSIANS 2:7 NLT

There are few attributes more admirable in another person than a strong faith. Faith-filled individuals appear to have an inner strength that can stand in the face of any trial. They have a faith that seems to grow stronger even as their world crumbles around them.

How can this be? Their faith is rooted in Christ.

In Colossians 2, Paul uses a word picture that describes Christians as trees. These plants take nutrients from the soil through their roots, just as we take our life-giving strength from Christ. The more and longer we draw our strength from Him, the stronger our faith will grow and thrive.

How do we grow a stronger faith that's deeply rooted in Jesus?

- Read and study the Word of God (Romans 10:17).

- Pray (Hebrews 4:14-16).

- Do life with other people of faith (Proverbs 13:10).

- Trust God—especially in the difficulties (2 Corinthians 1:9).

- Thank and praise Him (Hebrews 13:15-16).

*Father, grow my roots deep into the foundation of Your Son.
I want to be that person who is immovable even when
the wind and storms of life trials beat against me.
Help me to stand tall and be an example to others of
Your true, steadfast, unshakable nature. Amen.*

## TOO MUCH TALK

*Too much talk leads to sin.*
*Be sensible and keep your mouth shut.*
PROVERBS 10:19 NLT

O ur days are filled with talk. Face-to-face, on the phone, over email, through texts, on social media. Sometimes we may feel like it's impossible to stop words from gushing out—*especially* when we have strong feelings about what we're saying.

But unfiltered talk leaves us feeling unsteady, disrupted, back on our heels, and more likely to hurt someone else. It's not the wisest way to use our words.

When your words veer out of control, shut your mouth. Simple enough, but oh, so difficult! Scripture explains in James 3:8 (NIV) that shutting up is the best option because "no human being can tame the tongue. It is a restless evil, full of deadly poison." The psalmist knew he needed help with this when he prayed, "Set a guard over my mouth, LORD; keep watch over the door of my lips" (Psalm 141:3 NIV).

But God isn't asking us to walk this earth as mute women who *never* speak. True, godly wisdom means our words are thoughtful, prayerful, and measured. They are considerate, encouraging, and helpful. Today, ask God to fill your mouth with His words and the wisdom to know when to speak so that your words are "always full of grace, seasoned with salt" (Colossians 4:6 NIV).

---

*God, be the Lord and gatekeeper of my words. With guidance*
*from Your Spirit, I will stop and think before I plow on.*

## PASS IT ON!

*Let the message about Christ, in all its richness, fill your lives.*
*Teach and counsel each other with all the wisdom he gives. Sing*
*psalms and hymns and spiritual songs to God with thankful hearts.*
COLOSSIANS 3:16 NLT

What have you learned about Jesus lately? Maybe you've been blessed by something you read in scripture. Have you received an answer to prayer? Perhaps you've heard a song lyric that touched your heart.

Whatever you're learning, don't keep it to yourself. Share it with others! Jesus explains why in Matthew 5:14-16 (MSG): "You're here to be light, bringing out the God-colors in the world. God is not a secret to be kept. . . . If I make you light-bearers, you don't think I'm going to hide you under a bucket, do you? I'm putting you on a light stand. Now that I've put you there on a hilltop, on a light stand—shine! . . . By opening up to others, you'll prompt people to open up with God."

Talk about what you've learned in conversation, send a text, post it on social media. Sound scary? Your personal experience doesn't have to be awkward or off-putting. You don't have to be a Bible scholar to share what Jesus means to you and what He's doing in your life. You never know when your story is just what someone else needs to hear.

*Jesus, show me ways to share You more intentionally. Help my*
*story encourage others to experience You more fully.*

## OPPORTUNITIES ABOUND

*Live wisely among those who are not believers, and make the most of every opportunity. Let your conversation be gracious and attractive so that you will have the right response for everyone.*
COLOSSIANS 4:5-6 NLT

E very day brings new opportunities to speak God's loving truth to the people around us. Almost every interaction, in fact, is a chance to offer encouragement. To spread some joy. To lighten a load. To be Jesus to someone who desperately needs Him. "God has given us the task of telling everyone what he is doing," Paul explains in 2 Corinthians 5:20 (MSG). "We're Christ's representatives."

Yet most days we don't even *see* these opportunities, let alone *act* on them. Why? It's not because we don't want to make the most of every opportunity. It's not because we don't care about others. It's because we're distracted by ourselves: *our* to-do list, *our* needs and desires, and *our* thoughts.

So how can you change your mindset to take advantage of these opportunities? Start your day by reviewing your calendar and pray for the individuals you'll be in contact with today. Open yourself to the possibility of unexpected opportunities as well. Ask the Holy Spirit to fill your words with grace, calm, love, and respect for others. Your Spirit-led love can plant a seed that may grow roots of a deep faith.

*God, show me how to love the hearts of the people around me. I want to make the most of every opportunity to spread Your loving-kindness.*

# GOD'S APPROVED MESSENGERS

*For we speak as messengers approved by God to be entrusted with the Good News. Our purpose is to please God, not people. He alone examines the motives of our hearts.*

1 THESSALONIANS 2:4 NLT

"Don't forget: You're representing our family." As children grow and become more independent, parents send them out into the world—often with this reminder. Do you remember what it was like to realize that your actions reflected more than just yourself? Maybe you've more recently been on the parent side of this scenario, cautiously hoping your kid makes the best choices.

God entrusts us—His children—with His message of love for the world. We don't have to be preachers or pastors or have degrees in theology. His commands are simple: love God; love others. We are His approved representatives, given freedom to share Jesus through our actions and words. What does that look like in everyday life? Begin your day in praise of the One who loves you so much that He gave up His only Son on the cross. Then let that praise inhabit the rest of your day. Share with others what God is doing in your life. When you realize the abundantly loving way God interacts with you, you'll want to let love rule your actions and interactions as well.

*I'm Your messenger, Father. Make me worthy of such a calling. Make my daily life a story of You that clearly communicates Your love, Your grace, Your strength, and Your salvation.*

## REFRESHING GENEROSITY

*Give freely and become more wealthy; be stingy and lose everything. The generous will prosper; those who refresh others will themselves be refreshed.*

PROVERBS 11:24-25 NLT

I n our efforts to be safe and secure, there's a temptation to hold on to wealth. When we feel unsafe, threatened, or unbalanced, it's human nature to want to insulate ourselves from possible (or inevitable) disaster. To hoard. To keep more than we need. Money can give us a blissful (although false) sense that we can handle any calamity that comes.

In these verses in Proverbs, we see a paradox: we become richer by being generous. The world says to hold on to as much as possible. But God blesses those who give freely of their possessions, time, and energy. When we give, God supplies us with more so that we can give more. God enriches the lives of the generous with a sense of peace about money and things. Giving also helps us gain a correct perspective on our possessions. We realize they were never ours to begin with; God blesses us with possessions that can be used to help others. What then do we gain by giving? Freedom from enslavement to our possessions, the joy of helping others, and God's approval.

*Generous and giving God, I have so much to thank You for. Show me what You want me to do with my time, my possessions, and my finances. Give me a heart that is free and ready to give. Remind me that my strength lies in You alone.*

# GOD'S GOOD CHOICE

*God chose to save us through our Lord Jesus Christ, not to pour out his anger on us. Christ died for us so that, whether we are dead or alive when he returns, we can live with him forever.*
1 THESSALONIANS 5:9-10 NLT

There's freedom in making a choice. A choice gives us a voice in a vote, allows us to follow our conscience. Decisions bring about empowerment in our own circumstances.

God, in His great love and compassion for us, *made the choice* to send Jesus to save us from our sins. No other authority told Him that's the way it had to be. He was not bound by a legal agreement or forced to act a certain way. He wasn't tricked or coerced. *He chose to save us.* The same is true for our Savior Jesus. "No one can take my life from me. I sacrifice it voluntarily," He explained in John 10:18 (NLT). "For I have the authority to lay it down when I want to and also to take it up again. For this is what my Father has commanded."

Today, thank Jesus for choosing to follow the perfect will of God, who chose to make a way for us, His children, to be with Him forever. Knowing that, you can choose to be unshakable.

*Father, You demonstrated once and for all that You love the world so much that You gave up Your Son. Thank You for choosing me. Amen.*

## ROOTED AND SECURE

*Wickedness never brings stability, but the godly have deep roots.*
PROVERBS 12:3 NLT

S in never brings security.

This may seem like an obvious statement, but we've each fallen into the trap of using deceit to try to steady our out-of-control world. *What he doesn't know won't hurt him,* we think of a lie of omission. *I'd never normally* [fill in the blank], *and I know it's wrong. . .but it'll help me out of this jam, and I'll never do it again!*

This kind of thinking may give us a false sense of security and control, but the wisdom in Proverbs 12:19 (MSG) tells us, "Truth lasts; lies are here today, gone tomorrow."

Real, forever stability and peace come from a living relationship with our Father God. Jeremiah 17:7-8 (NLT) paints a beautiful word picture of that life:

> "But blessed are those who trust in the LORD and
> have made the LORD their hope and confidence. They
> are like trees planted along a riverbank, with roots
> that reach deep into the water. Such trees are not
> bothered by the heat or worried by long months of
> drought. Their leaves stay green, and they never stop
> producing fruit."

When we put our hope in God, we're trusting Him to take care of our needs—big and small (Matthew 6:26). We're secure, knowing He loves us and will protect us (Isaiah 41:10). Are you looking for stability today? Get rooted in His Truth!

*Father, today I choose to put my hope in You.*

# WORTHY OF HIS CALL

*So we keep on praying for you, asking our God to enable you to live a life worthy of his call. May he give you the power to accomplish all the good things your faith prompts you to do. Then the name of our Lord Jesus will be honored because of the way you live, and you will be honored along with him.*

2 THESSALONIANS 1:11-12 NLT

What is God's calling on your life?

That may seem like a big, loaded question. While we're each created with unique gifts (Romans 12:6), we each have the freewill to make decisions for ourselves within the will of God. So, as Christians, our calling from God is to become like Christ. Romans 8:29 (NLT) says, "For God knew his people in advance, and he chose them to become like his Son, so that his Son would be the firstborn among many brothers and sisters."

Becoming Christlike is a gradual, lifelong process that will be completed when we see Christ face-to-face (1 John 3:2). To be "worthy" of this calling means to want to do what is right and good—to model our lives after Jesus by loving God and loving others. Not one of us is perfect yet, but we're moving in that direction as Christ and His power works in us every day.

*Father, I am worthy of Your plan for my life because You make me worthy. Lead me in the lifelong process of becoming more and more like Jesus.*

## THE LOVE OF GOD

*May the Lord lead your hearts into a full understanding
and expression of the love of God and the patient
endurance that comes from Christ.*
2 THESSALONIANS 3:5 NLT

God loves you.
    Maybe you've known this since you were a tiny child, but despite its simplicity, God's love is so vast—so wonderfully mysterious—that it'll take a lifetime (plus eternity) to understand it fully.

Today, meditate on these truths so you can understand better God's almighty love for you:

- The LORD is compassionate and merciful, slow to get angry and filled with unfailing love (Psalm 103:8 NLT).
- He heals the brokenhearted and bandages their wounds (Psalm 147:3 NLT).
- Nothing in all creation will ever be able to separate us from the love of God (Romans 8:39 NLT).
- "For this is how God loved the world: He gave his one and only Son, so that everyone who believes in him will not perish but have eternal life" (John 3:16 NLT).
- But God is so rich in mercy, and he loved us so much, that even though we were dead because of our sins, he gave us life when he raised Christ from the dead (Ephesians 2:4-5 NLT).

There is no better place for you to be and no more secure situation than resting in the love of God. When all else fails. . .His love is *more* than enough.

*God, teach me to understand Your love more fully so
that I can show that powerful love to others. Amen.*

# A GENEROUS AND GRACIOUS LORD

*Oh, how generous and gracious our Lord was! He filled me with the faith and love that come from Christ Jesus.*
1 TIMOTHY 1:14 NLT

In his letter to Timothy, the apostle Paul reminds us of his storied past. Before his encounter with Jesus in Acts 9, Paul was raised to be a zealous Pharisee like his father (Acts 23:6). His Jewish heritage, discipline, and passion were unmatched (Philippians 3:4-6). He hated and actively persecuted Christians. He had active roles in their death and imprisonment (Acts 8:1).

Yet because of God's love and compassion, Paul was forgiven much, and he knew his story was a beautiful example of the saving grace of the Father—of the transforming power of God's love. If God saved this man with such a wicked heart full of evil *and* God trusted Paul to be a messenger of Christ, then God can do the same for you too.

Today, let go of the guilt of your past. God is ready and willing to forgive and accept you. God forgave Paul and used Paul mightily for His kingdom. God can and will use you mightily too!

*Father God, today I'm releasing the shame of my past. I'm lifting my eyes to You and asking for forgiveness and freedom from the guilt I've felt for so long. Raise me up and remind me that I'm Your cherished daughter who can and will be involved in mighty things in Your kingdom.*

## ACCEPTING ADVICE

*Pride leads to conflict; those who take advice are wise. . . .*
*People who despise advice are asking for trouble;*
*those who respect a command will succeed.*
PROVERBS 13:10, 13 NLT

**❝** I was wrong."
There are few phrases in the English language more difficult to say.

Why? Because admitting we don't know everything requires humility. It's acknowledging a personal failure. It's listening to advice when our pride is already stinging.

Pride is an ingredient in every conflict. It can stir up indignant feelings and lash out. Pride is a know-it-all just waiting for someone to dare suggest there might be a better way. Pride is impatient and often rude. Pride preserves self above anything else.

Humility, on the other hand, is a calming salve in arguments and can help heal a relationship. Displaying a humble attitude takes work, but with it comes peace and a reassurance that we *don't* have to know it all or be right all the time. Humility helps us see others as Jesus sees them.

Be open to the advice of people you respect and admire. Ask for help when you need it, and be receptive to tough love, even if you don't ask for it. When we open ourselves up to wise advice from others, we're open to God's instructions. True wisdom is hearing God's guidance through His Word and following it.

*Create in me a humble heart, O God. I welcome*
*the loving instruction in Your Word and am open*
*to hearing Your wisdom from others.*

## ETERNAL BENEFITS

*"Physical training is good, but training for godliness is much better, promising benefits in this life and in the life to come."*
1 TIMOTHY 4:8 NLT

What do conditioning for a marathon, rehearsing for a performance, and purposefully becoming more like Christ all have in common? Each takes a journey, a process, discipline, a plan, and a commitment to keep making progress toward a goal.

All of these things are good, but only one has eternal benefits: training for godliness.

Spiritual training, like physical training, doesn't happen by accident. We won't spontaneously become more like Jesus in our thoughts and actions. But we do know some ways that will help us get there. First, let go of things that get in the way of that training. What parts of your schedule you could cut out to make time to spend with God? Use 1 Corinthians 10:23 (NLT) as a litmus test: "You say, 'I am allowed to do anything'—but not everything is good for you. You say, 'I am allowed to do anything'—but not everything is beneficial."

Second, choose one step to take in your spiritual walk, and then do it. Start small. Commit to opening up God's Word every day or spend a minute or two in prayer. Flex those muscles, learn the motions, and then gradually add more.

*Father, be my coach in my spiritual training. I need your encouragement and strength as I journey through this life of faith.*

# A LOVING FATHER'S CORRECTION

*Those who spare the rod of discipline hate their children.*
*Those who love their children care enough to discipline them.*
PROVERBS 13:24 NLT

No loving mom/aunt/grandma takes joy in disciplining a child. Yet when we correct the children in our lives, we show them that we love them. Even when a kid bucks and tantrums her way through discipline, a loving adult continues, knowing that discipline helps move her in a direction that will benefit her now and as she grows and matures.

Consider the words of Proverbs 24 where God is the parent and you are His child. How do you respond to God's correction? Do you scream and stomp? Whine and wail? Or can you step back and learn to see it as a deeply loving gesture of a good Father who corrects and disciplines those He loves (Revelation 3:19)? Paul puts discipline in greater context in Hebrews 12:11 (NLT): "No discipline is enjoyable while it is happening—it's painful! But afterward there will be a peaceful harvest of right living for those who are trained in this way."

God takes no joy in disciplining His children. Pray and ask God to soften your heart toward His correction. Whether it comes today, tomorrow, or sometime in the future, know that it will result in blessings on your life!

*Father, although it's a hard prayer to pray, I'll welcome*
*Your discipline when I need Your loving correction.*
*Even when it doesn't feel nice, I'll still know You love me.*

## CONTENTMENT

*True godliness with contentment is itself great wealth. After all,*
*we brought nothing with us when we came into the world,*
*and we can't take anything with us when we leave it.*
1 TIMOTHY 6:6-7 NLT

As children, we learn the difference between *needs* and *wants*. We need food, clothes, shelter, and love. Wants? Well, wants can be anything and often *everything*. Our wants can balloon into an Amazon wish list a mile long, just waiting for the day we swipe "buy now." Because those things will make us feel better, right?

After the initial jolt of dopamine that comes with the thrill of a purchase, we realize *things* don't bring peace or lasting happiness. What brings real peace and joy is contentment. The importance of this spiritual discipline can't be overlooked. Contentment coupled with godliness equals "great wealth." Why? Because when we live in a state of gratitude, trusting God will supply all we need, we realize just how immensely blessed we are. Paul writes, "Teach those who are rich in this world not to be proud and not to trust in their money, which is so unreliable. Their trust should be in God, who richly gives us all we need for our enjoyment" (1 Timothy 6:17 NLT).

Do you feel anxious, always striving for the next thing, for more? Pause. Rest, relying on God's unending strength and love.

*Father, calm my heart and help me to live every day,*
*grateful for Your surpassing goodness to me.*

## HERITAGE OF FAITH

*I remember your genuine faith, for you share the faith that
first filled your grandmother Lois and your mother, Eunice.
And I know that same faith continues strong in you.*
2 TIMOTHY 1:5-7 NLT

I f you've ever done any ancestry research, you may have uncovered connections to your family heritage that you didn't expect. Family trees often contain certain traits, careers, passions, or skills that play a big role in family histories, binding relatives together across generations.

In a similar way, our faith-family tree connects us in our common bond with other believers in a heritage that spans to the beginning of creation. It doesn't matter whether your biological ancestors passed down a faith to you. If you have accepted Jesus as your Savior, you are a part of the family tree of God. You are part of the body of Christ. You are the adopted sister of Jesus Christ and daughter of the King of kings and Lord of lords. The eternal spirit of power, love, and stability lives in you. Because of that you cannot be picked, plucked, cut out, or uprooted from this eternal tree.

If you have children, help them grow in and graft onto the tree of faith, just like Timothy's mother and grandmother did. Although it's made up of imperfect individuals, the family of God is eternal and made perfect in Him.

---

*God, I am thankful to be a part of Your family tree of faith that
spans across all borders and generations.*

# SAVE YOURSELVES

*Flee from Babylon! Save yourselves! Don't get trapped
in her punishment! It is the LORD's time for vengeance;
he will repay her in full.*
JEREMIAH 51:6 NLT

H ave you ever been in the wrong place at the wrong time? Maybe you happened to be sitting next to a friend in school who was caught cheating. Because of your close proximity, the teacher accused you as well. Or maybe your coworker ripped off the company and your boss thought you were guilty by association because you happened to be friends with her. Perhaps you were in the car with a driver who had been drinking and she caused an accident.

Sometimes God wants you to excuse yourself from a situation or relationship so that you're protected when accusations come. Then, instead of being shaken by false allegations, you're so far away from the fire that you can't possibly get burned. He wants to protect you, to guard you from any appearance of evil.

So, what relationships are feeling heated lately? What situations are sending up red flags? Maybe it's time to step back so that you're guarded against the enemy's schemes. He would love nothing more than to bring you down, by the way. But you won't let him. You're smarter than that.

*Lord, thank You for the spiritual red flags You send up! My eyes are
wide open. I don't want to be trapped in anyone else's sin. Amen.*

## DIFFICULT TIMES AHEAD

*You should know this, Timothy, that in the last days there
will be very difficult times. For people will love only themselves
and their money. They will be boastful and proud, scoffing at
God, disobedient to their parents, and ungrateful.
They will consider nothing sacred.*
2 TIMOTHY 3:1-2 NLT

Many twenty-first-century believers are accustomed to lives of
ease. We have all we could want and more. But today's verse
warns of a day—perhaps arriving sooner than we expected—when
difficult times will come upon us. We've been advised that the church
will come under attack. Religious persecution will come. During
those same days, people will shock us with their boasting—much
of it about their own sinful lifestyles. We'll be equally as stunned
by those who scoff at God and thumb their noses at Him.

The Bible says we're not to be surprised when these things
happen, but we do need to be ready, otherwise we'll be badly shaken.
We can prepare now by girding ourselves in the power of the Spirit
and donning the armor of God. We can pray in the Spirit and use the
name of Jesus to counteract the enemy's attacks.

And, in the middle of it all, we can continue to praise God. Our
songs of praise are the best weapons we have. We cannot stop, even
when the battle seems to be overwhelming us.

Keep going, friend, no matter what.

*Lord, I won't give up, no matter how difficult
the days ahead might get. Amen.*

## TEMPER, TEMPER!

*A gentle answer deflects anger, but harsh words make tempers flare. The tongue of the wise makes knowledge appealing, but the mouth of a fool belches out foolishness.*
PROVERBS 15:1-2 NLT

You're biting your tongue so hard it should be bleeding. Oh, how you want to give that store clerk a piece of your mind. She shorted you a couple of dollars and refuses to acknowledge her mistake. But you're not giving up. You'll stand here, voice raised, until you get the attention of everyone in the room.

Sure, we all have encounters like that, but are our volatile responses really pleasing to the heart of God? He has called you to be salt and light, after all, and it's hard to be a good witness when your fist is raised to the air in anger. That store clerk isn't going to see Jesus when she looks at you—she'll see an unexpected enemy, one intent on taking her down.

So, how do you squelch those feelings when they come? Start by doing what your mama told you as a kid: Take a deep breath. Count to ten. Steady your breathing. Then, as you have a moment of clear-headedness, ask the Holy Spirit to breathe through you and bring peace to the situation. He will, you know. You can trust Him to sweep in and calm the storm then give you appropriate words to speak.

*Lord, I don't want to ruin my testimony because of my temper. Cool me down, I pray. Amen.*

## WOES AND WHOAS

*"Let all their wickedness come before you; deal with*
*them as you have dealt with me because of all my sins.*
*My groans are many and my heart is faint."*
LAMENTATIONS 1:22 NIV

The book of Lamentations is heavy on woes and whoas. It's loaded with those "Why me, Lord?" moments, which often come on the heels of the woes of life.

When you're going through a season of woes (when unexpected tragedy hits or you're faced with an ongoing health crisis), it's not always easy to keep a positive outlook. Sometimes your faith is badly shaken, especially when you're not physically able to care for yourself. Instead, you're tempted to curl up in a ball and moan, "Whoa! Why me?"

God doesn't want your woes to lead to ongoing whoas. Go ahead and have that pity party, but don't camp out there for long. There's no battle you're facing that the Lord won't fight for you. Even if you're up against a Goliath of a problem, He will still sweep in and deal with your enemies, conquering them on your behalf.

The moral of the story? Don't let your heart grow heavy. Don't give up. Don't give in. Strengthen your heart in God, and trust that He will deal with both your woes and your whoas.

*Lord, may the only "Whoa!" be the one I experience*
*when I come into Your presence. Please take this heavy*
*heart of mine and turn my situation around, I pray.*

## GODLY MENTORS

*These older women must train the younger women to love their husbands and their children, to live wisely and be pure, to work in their homes, to do good, and to be submissive to their husbands. Then they will not bring shame on the word of God.*

TITUS 2:4-5 NLT

Mentors will tell you that it's always a good idea to be sandwiched between two types of people—those who are older than you (or farther along in their Christian walk) and those who are younger than you (or newer to the faith). When you have someone to mentor while you're being mentored by someone else, you all benefit. And isn't it lovely to be sandwiched between two separate generations?

There's much to be learned from those who have walked before you. They're fountains of knowledge, thanks to their many years of life experience. And you can take what you've learned—from them and from your own journey—to pour into the life of someone else who's coming up behind you.

Today, take a look at your life. Who has God placed in position to encourage you and grow your faith? Use that person as an example of who you can become to someone else. Then allow yourself to bravely reach out to a new friend, offering friendship and encouragement.

*Lord, thank You for the many mentors You've placed in my life. Please show me who I can take under my wing, I pray. Amen.*

## THINK BEFORE SPEAKING

*The heart of the godly thinks carefully before speaking;*
*the mouth of the wicked overflows with evil words.*
PROVERBS 15:28 NLT

Daylight savings time ends today. That means an extra hour of sleep. You get to "fall back" as it were. The idea of falling back an hour holds some appeal, one you may wish you could carry over to other areas of your life. Don't you wish you could fall back and fix some of the things you've said or done? Wouldn't that be great?

Here's a painful truth: sometimes we speak before we think. And when we do, we often end up regretting what we said. In fact, there are times when we're legitimately shocked at ourselves. The Bible admonishes us to think carefully before we speak, not just to avoid hurting others, but so that we don't have regrets. Those "woulda, shoulda, couldas" can really wear us down.

Are you biting your tongue right now? Wishing you could spout off on social media or let it fly in a text to a friend? Instead, channel that frustration into a prayer. Use those words to cry out to your heavenly Father. He hears you, and He understands.

---

*Lord, I confess, I don't always think before I speak. Sometimes*
*my mouth is open before the thoughts have fully engaged. But*
*today I choose to put a clamp on my mouth until my brain has*
*had a chance to catch up. Help me, I pray. Amen.*

## SWEET AS HONEY IN THE MOUTH

*Eat this scroll; then go and speak to the house of Israel.*
*So I opened my mouth, and He caused me to eat the scroll.*
*And He said to me, Son of man, eat this scroll that I give*
*you and fill your stomach with it. Then I ate it,*
*and it was as sweet as honey in my mouth.*
EZEKIEL 3:1-3 AMPC

God told the prophet Ezekiel that He was going to send him to the people of Israel, "a rebellious nation that has rebelled against me" (Ezekiel 2:3 NLT). God goes on to say, "You must give them my messages whether they listen or not. But they won't listen, for they are completely rebellious!" (Ezekiel 2:7 NLT).

At this point, you'd expect God to actually give the words to Ezekiel so he would know what to say. Instead, the Lord hands him a scroll filled with "funeral songs, words of sorrow, and pronouncements of doom" (Ezekiel 2:10 NLT). He instructs Ezekiel to eat the scroll.

Ezekiel does just that. He eats the scroll, chews on those tough words, and then delivers them to the people.

Our journey through the Word of God isn't really that different from Ezekiel's scroll-eating challenge. Sometimes what we read doesn't deliver good news to our situation. But when we chew on those words awhile, the message of hope is delivered.

What's God asking you to chew on today?

*Sometimes Your words are tough to swallow, Lord,*
*but I'll keeping chewing on them, I promise. Amen.*

## DON'T DRIFT AWAY

*We must pay the most careful attention, therefore,*
*to what we have heard, so that we do not drift away.*
HEBREWS 2:1 NIV

I f you were raised in a Christian home, no doubt you were taught the tenets of the faith—the salvation message, love your neighbors, do unto others as you would have them do unto you. And hopefully those same teachings were passed down to those in your care—your children, friends, mentees, and so on. They are principles to live by, loaded with truth.

Some people grow stronger in their faith as they age, but others drift away and begin to examine other teachings. They reject some of the biblical precepts they grew up with because they seem too narrow or don't jive with what popular culture is telling them.

Our beliefs can't change with cultural shifts, no matter how badly we're shaken by them. In Hebrews 13:8 (NIV), we read that "Jesus Christ is the same yesterday and today and forever." He's not changing with every wind, and neither does His Word, the Bible.

Today, as you head off to vote, remember the biblical principles you were taught as a child, then ask the Lord to show you the very best candidates for the job, based on what you know to be true from the Word of God.

*I will vote according to Your principles, Lord.*
*Give me wisdom from Your Word, I pray. Amen.*

## HEALING WORDS

*Pleasant words are as a honeycomb,*
*sweet to the mind and healing to the body.*
PROVERBS 16:24 AMPC

Ah, sweet words! How they soothe the soul, encourage, and offer hope amid hopelessness. And—the bonus—how they minister to the speaker as well as the hearer.

It's remarkable to think that just a few brief words could change a person's life, but they can. The woman in deep depression? She needs to hear that she's loved. That man who's just lost his job? He needs to hear that he has value and things will get better. That little girl who's feeling lonely and left out? She needs to know that she's loved by you and by God.

It doesn't take long to offer words of hope and healing to those who are in need. And when you see the expression on the recipient's face shift from despair to peace, you'll be so glad you took the time. Perhaps you'll get to watch the sparkle return to that little girl's eyes. Or maybe that woman's despair will lift as you offer words of hope.

Who can you bless today? What words can you speak (whether in person or by text or on social media)? God longs to use you to minister to the very ones who need the most encouragement.

*Show me who I can bless with my words today, Lord.*
*Ready me in offering a word of love and support.*
*I know as I bless, I will be blessed in return. Amen.*

## VIEWS ON SIN

*"Pass through the city, through Jerusalem, and put a mark
on the foreheads of the men who sigh and groan over
all the abominations that are committed in it."*

EZEKIEL 9:4 ESV

The Lord was angry over the sin in the camp in Jerusalem and decided to judge the people. He called out to a man holding a writer's inkhorn at his side then instructed him to go to the city and put a mark on the foreheads of the men who sighrd and cried for the abominations being committed. Those who did not have the seal were to be put to death immediately.

Sounds pretty extreme, but God was marking the faithful and separating them from the unfaithful. He was making sure His own were spared (much the same as in the Passover story).

When there's sin in a nation, God is always looking for a remnant. He's watching to see who still views sin the way He does.

So, where do you stand? Are you distressed over the sins of your nation? If you haven't spent time agonizing over the condition of the world around you—if sin has become so commonplace you just shrug it off—it might be time for an Ezekiel encounter. Allow God to open your spiritual eyes and to see those sins the way He does.

*Lord, I'll admit, I often don't even notice sin anymore. Separate me,
I pray. Help me care about the things that matter to You. Amen.*

## SHARPER THAN A SWORD

*The word of God is living and active, sharper than any two-edged sword, piercing to the division of soul and of spirit, of joints and of marrow, and discerning the thoughts and intentions of the heart. And no creature is hidden from his sight, but all are naked and exposed to the eyes of him to whom we must give account.*
HEBREWS 4:12-13 ESV

There's power in the Word of God. When you speak Hebrews 4:12-13 aloud, you cut through your situations with a spiritual sword, piercing them to the core. You discern the thoughts and intentions of the heart and expose evil.

How is this possible? The Word is alive. It's a living, breathing thing, as applicable today as it was when the Lord spoke through its writers millennia ago. And the same Spirit-breathed power is still resident in it (and in us), which means we can use the Word to fight our battles for us. It truly does cut between light and dark, good and evil.

All things are naked and exposed by the Word of God. You can cry out verse after verse and trust God will right the wrongs in alignment with the very words coming out of your mouth.

Speak the Word and watch the enemy flee. . .in Jesus' name.

*Lord, Your Word is powerful! It's sharper than any sword, exposing evil and separating light from darkness. Show me how best to use it, that I might be fully victorious in You. Amen.*

## GOOD MEDICINE

*A joyful heart is good medicine,*
*but a crushed spirit dries up the bones.*
PROVERBS 17:22 ESV

If you've ever dried and packaged herbs, you know they change a lot as they're drying up. They become smaller and more pungent.

Your heart is a bit like that. When you allow it to dry up, it becomes hardened to the things going on around you. In some respects, it grows smaller because it's not open to the joys of life. And the pain it encounters multiplies, becomes more potent, in much the same way those herbs become more pungent as they shrink. In other words, you react to pain more keenly.

God created you to have an open heart, one that is fully receptive to love, joy, fellowship, and companionship. You might not be able to open it all at once, but when you do peel back a layer or two, you'll experience life more fully and love more deeply. You won't be buried away behind your pain.

Would you say that your heart is more open or more shut? Perhaps this is the day to begin to nudge it open.

*Lord, I give my heart to You. I don't want to be dried up like those herbs. I don't want to be riddled with pain. I simply want to live life to the fullest and to love as You love. Amen.*

# KNOWING WHEN TO SPEAK

*Even dunces who keep quiet are thought to be wise;*
*as long as they keep their mouths shut, they're smart.*
PROVERBS 17:28 MSG

That woman at work. . .you know the one. She's always putting her foot in her mouth, saying the wrong thing (or simply saying too much when she should be quiet). Maybe she thinks she needs to keep talking to prove how bright she is. . .only, it's not working. Should you tell her?

Check out today's verse: even a fool (when he is silent) is thought to be wise. Why is that? Because it takes more self-control, more power to hold your tongue than to loosen it. It's easy to spout off what you're thinking or feeling but harder to sit in silence, yet silence is often the wiser choice.

How many times have you spoken up too quickly then regretted your words? No doubt you wished you could take them back, after the fact. But words, once flung, are impossible to retrieve. So, do yourself a favor—if you're torn between speaking and not speaking, ask yourself: Could my words come back to haunt me? If that answer is yes, you might want to cool it for a while.

*Lord, I find it hard to hold my tongue. I'll have to ask for Your help with this one! I don't want my words to come back to bite me, so I'll simmer down until I'm free to speak. Amen.*

## CARING FOR THE POOR

*"The sin of your sister Sodom was this: She lived with
her daughters in the lap of luxury—proud, gluttonous,
and lazy. They ignored the oppressed and the poor.
They put on airs and lived obscene lives. And you
know what happened: I did away with them."*
EZEKIEL 16:49-50 MSG

The people of Sodom lived in the lap of luxury. They were prideful,
ate far too much, and spent too much time lounging around
when they should have been working on behalf of others. With so
many in need around them, how could they look the other way?

Let's be honest: we often overlook the poor as well. The elderly
man on the street corner, begging for money. The woman in the
homeless shelter, wondering how she's going to get on her feet
again. Children in third-world countries who don't have adequate
food, shelter, and water. They're all around us.

Because the poor are always with us, we often overlook
them. We drive right past that man at the corner instead of offering
a bottle of water on a hot day. We see commercials about children
living in poverty and turn a blind eye.

Today, God wants you to actually see the poor. Look beyond
your own wants and wishes to the ones who are desperate for a ride
to the hospital or a hot meal. Then do what you can to help meet
those needs, either in a tangible way or in prayer.

*Thank You for opening my eyes to their plight, Lord! Amen.*

## IT'S TAKEN CARE OF

*Everyone has to die once, then face the consequences.*
*Christ's death was also a one-time event, but it*
*was a sacrifice that took care of sins forever.*
HEBREWS 9:27-28 MSG

How many sins have you committed today? Three? Five? Ten? How many sins did you commit yesterday? About the same? What about the day before? How many are you planning to commit tomorrow?

If you're like most, you've committed some doozies, probably more than you could ever add up. And if you ever *did* tally them, you would be mortified at the sheer number of times you've broken the heart of God—either with your actions or your thoughts and motivations.

Take another look at today's verse. What do you think it means when it says that Christ's death was a one-time event but took care of sins forever? Is it possible that something Jesus did two thousand years ago could take care of your transgressions today and tomorrow? The answer is a resounding yes!

No matter what you've done, no matter where you've been, Jesus' sacrifice on the cross was powerful enough to wash away your sins. There's one thing you have to do, though. . .ask. Ask Him into your heart. Ask for His forgiveness. Then accept His free gift of salvation, and breathe a huge sigh of relief as forgiveness flows freely.

*Lord, I'm so grateful You've taken care of my sin. It's washed in the*
*blood of Jesus, never to be seen again. Thank You, Lord! Amen.*

## A FORTIFIED CITY

*An offended friend is harder to win back than a fortified city.*
*Arguments separate friends like a gate locked with bars.*

PROVERBS 18:19 NLT

Old Testament cities were often built into mountains and surrounded by high walls. No one could enter, except through the gates, and the gatekeepers kept a watchful eye out for those who might want to bring harm.

The Bible says that an offended friend is harder to win back than a fortified city. When you wounded him (with your words or actions), he put up walls higher than those surrounding Jericho. And he's serving as his own gatekeeper, determined to keep you out. Why? Because he's presuming you want to bring harm to his city (his heart).

Once you've damaged a relationship like this, it can be hard to regain trust. But it's not impossible. There are twelve words that can heal any relationship, and they are usable in situations like this: "I am sorry. I was wrong. Please forgive me. I love you."

Those words, spoken in sincerity of heart, can knock down the walls of Jericho in a hurry. They can press open once-locked gates to a friend's heart and begin the process of restoration.

Who do you need to speak those twelve words to today?

*Lord, please show me who I need to reconcile*
*with today. I want to use those words to bring healing*
*to rough situations, but I will need Your help! Amen.*

## STAND IN THE GAP

*"I looked for someone who might rebuild the wall
of righteousness that guards the land. I searched for
someone to stand in the gap in the wall so I wouldn't
have to destroy the land, but I found no one."*
EZEKIEL 22:30 NLT

A re you "the one"?
In this Old Testament story, God was looking for "the one"
who might rebuild the wall of righteousness to guard the land. He
had a specific type of person in mind, one willing to stand in the
gap. One who wouldn't back down, no matter what.

So, what about you? Are you a "stand in the gap" sort of gal?
Are you willing to go the distance—to pray harder, to stand longer,
to speak up when others do not? Do you spend time in intercessory
prayer for your country, your state, your county, and your city?

A gap-stander has to be emboldened by the Holy Spirit with
courage and power. In Ezekiel's story, no one was found. Sad, isn't
it? But your story can have a hero. . .you!

Today, make up your mind to stand in the gap—not just for your
land but for all of those you love who need the extra prayer. They
will be so glad you did, and so will you.

*Lord, I won't give up. I'll keep on standing as long
as You ask me to. I'll play a role in rebuilding
the wall of righteousness around me. Amen.*

## THE EVIDENCE OF THINGS NOT SEEN

*Faith shows the reality of what we hope for; it is the
evidence of things we cannot see. Through their faith,
the people in days of old earned a good reputation.*
HEBREWS 11:1-2 NLT

**"**It's going to happen. I know it is." Maybe you've spoken those words over a situation that seemed impossible to others. But in your spirit you knew God would come through for you. . .and He did. When the impossible became possible, others marveled that you seemed to know all along things would end that way. But you just smiled and nodded.

Faith is that invisible thing that keeps you hoping even when everything around you says, "Just give up." It gives you evidence (proof) of things you can't yet see. Oh, you can see them in your spirit-man but not in real life. So, you keep going even when others say, "What's up with her? Does she know something we don't?"

"Yes, as a matter of fact," you call out, "I do know something you don't! I know that God will come through for me, just as He's done hundreds of times before."

*I have the proof, Lord! My faith is the proof—that You love me
and that You're going to come through for me. You always have,
and you always will. Have I mentioned how grateful I am? Amen.*

# AN ILL-FATED RESCUE

*A hot-tempered person must pay the penalty;*
*rescue them, and you will have to do it again.*
PROVERBS 19:19 NIV

I t's one thing to be thrown into a pit by others or even by unforeseen circumstances beyond your control. It's another thing altogether to toss yourself headlong into a pit by making poor decisions or from exhibiting a hot temper.

Maybe you've been there. You've got a family member who can't get his act together. He reaches out for help and you do your best to rescue him from his circumstances, but he turns the tables on you and blames you when things don't work out. So, you try again. The more you rescue, the more he fails, and the angrier he gets.

That's not how God intended it to work. You need to step away from the fire. You're not in the rescue business, God is. So, confidently trust the Lord to do what only He can do. Your mission, should you choose to accept it, is to step away. Pray, sure. Keep praying, even. But don't let this person's constant falls from grace consume your heart or your life.

*I'll admit it, Lord—I've been a rescuer. I've gone above*
*and beyond in the attempt to rescue folks around me who*
*seemed to be in need. Give me wisdom to step back*
*when it's not my place to help, I pray. Amen.*

## MERE MORTALS

*"This is what the Sovereign LORD says: 'In the pride of your heart you say, "I am a god; I sit on the throne of a god in the heart of the seas." But you are a mere mortal and not a god, though you think you are as wise as a god.' "*
EZEKIEL 28:2 NIV

From the time we're little, we think we're the center of our own universe. It's all about me, myself, and I. Then we enter school, where the curriculum teaches us to "discover" ourselves and to say things like "All of the answers can be found inside of me."

Are they, though? The Bible teaches us that the answers to the deep questions of life are only found in communing with your heavenly Father and looking to His Word.

So, why are we so self-focused? Why have we made ourselves gods in our own eyes, not only nudging the true God off of the throne but inadvertently placing a lot of pressure on ourselves to fix the things that go wrong in our lives?

The thing is, we don't have that kind of power. And just about the time we think we do, a situation comes along that shakes us to the core and leaves us realizing just how much we need a Savior.

Remember: He's God. . .and we're not.

*Lord, I confess I'm not You! Today, I'll commune with You and look into Your Word to find the answers I seek. Amen.*

## CONSUMING FIRE

*Therefore, since we are receiving a kingdom that cannot be shaken, let us be thankful, and so worship God acceptably with reverence and awe, for our "God is a consuming fire."*
HEBREWS 12:28-29 NIV

I f you've ever thrown a piece of paper into a blazing fire, you know it's going to be consumed right away, leaving nothing recognizable. What you're left with is only ash. Put gold into a blazing fire, however, and it melts down and is purified. It doesn't vanish into ash. In fact, it becomes even more beautiful—and more valuable—than when you put it in the fire in the first place.

Think of that analogy as it pertains to your life. God doesn't see you as paper, He sees you as gold. You might go through fiery challenges, but once you've gone through the purification process (been refined in His holy fire), your value increases exponentially. You come out stronger, more beautiful, and ready for use.

Think about the many "holy fires" you've been through. No doubt you thought they would take you down. But they didn't. They brought you to where you are today and crafted you into a holy woman—purified and ready to reach the world for Jesus.

*Lord, I'll admit. . .I don't like fiery trials. I'd rather do without them, thanks. But You're teaching me that I'm simply going through the purifying process. I submit myself to that, Father. Amen.*

## YOUR AVENGER

*Do not say, "I'll pay you back for this wrong!"*
*Wait for the LORD, and he will avenge you.*
PROVERBS 20:22 NIV

U gh! Someone went behind your back and spread a rumor that isn't true. Worse still, there's no way to prove that what she said *isn't* true. So, now everyone thinks you're in the wrong, even though you're completely innocent. You feel trapped, like there's no way out. And it really bugs you that all of this is happening publicly. How can you defend yourself when no one seems to believe you? It's impossible.

What do you do in situations like these? Do you retaliate? Do you return evil for evil? If you take a closer look at today's verse, you'll see that God promises to duke this one out for you. No, really. You don't have to do anything but wait on Him.

Waiting isn't easy, but it will pay off. Knee-jerking will get you nowhere, and you'll just have regrets later. So, patience! Rest in Him and this story will end well. He will (as Romans 8:28 says) work all things together for your good. That's a promise you can take to the bank.

*Thank You for avenging me, Lord. I don't have to put my dukes up and take swings at anyone today. I simply have to rest in the knowledge that You are taking care of everything for me. Amen.*

# WATCHMEN ON THE WALL

*So you, son of man, I have made you a watchman*
*for the house of Israel; therefore hear the word*
*at My mouth and give them warning from Me.*
EZEKIEL 33:7 AMPC

Have you ever been to an event where you were met at the door by a bouncer? Usually he's a big guy, intimidating in size and disposition. You stare up at him, wide-eyed, and hope he doesn't take issue with you.

Our modern-day bouncers are the equivalent of Old Testament watchmen and gatekeepers. The role of the watchman was to watch for incoming bad guys and to warn the people with a trumpet blast. This would immediately mobilize the residents, and they could put protective measures in place and gather their weapons of choice.

God has called you to be a gatekeeper for your family. He has asked that you pray for the safety of your loved ones and to stand in the gap in prayer for those you love. With your prayers, you can guard them from unsuspecting attacks of the enemy. So, keep your eyes and ears open, and be diligent in prayer.

You might not look like a bouncer, girl, but that's exactly what you are!

*Lord, I will do the job You've called me to do—to pray,*
*to stand, and to protect those You love. Help me*
*to be a watchman on the wall. Amen.*

## GIVE THANKS WITH
## A GRATEFUL HEART

*If indeed you [really] fulfill the royal Law in accordance*
*with the Scripture, You shall love your neighbor as [you*
*love] yourself, you do well. But if you show servile regard*
*(prejudice, favoritism) for people, you commit sin and are*
*rebuked and convicted by the Law as violators and offenders.*
JAMES 2:8-9 AMPC

Happy Thanksgiving! What a wonderful day to celebrate family and friends and to pause to give thanks for all God has done. When you think of giving thanks, what comes to mind? What are you most thankful for this year? Your family? Your friends? Your job? Your relationship with Jesus?

No doubt the word *love* factors in. Are you grateful for the love of the Lord and the love of those amazing people He has placed in your life?

Today, be reminded that God is in love with you too. He sees great value in you because you're created in His image. Just as you are grateful for so many things on this important day, God is grateful for you! Isn't it amazing to think that the Creator, Sustainer, and Maintainer of the universe cares about you so much? He's celebrating Thanksgiving today too, by the way. In fact, He's celebrating *you*!

*Lord, thank You for giving me a heart of gratitude today.*
*There are so many things I'm grateful for, for Your strength*
*and grace, but mostly Your amazing love for me.*
*How I praise You for that today! Amen.*

## JOY TO THE RIGHTEOUS

*When justice is done, it is a joy to the righteous*
*(the upright, in right standing with God), but to the*
*evildoers it is dismay, calamity, and ruin.*
PROVERBS 21:15 AMPC

Do you ever wonder why the bad guys always seem to get away with everything? It feels like there's no justice at times. Crime rates continue to rise. Evildoers get away with all sorts of mischief. Politicians scheme and plot behind our backs. When will they pay for what they've done—or don't do?

Oh, but when justice does come—when you get your day in court or you're exonerated from a crime you didn't commit—what sweet relief floods over your soul. Finally! Someone sees the truth! True justice brings peace and joy to the one who's suddenly off the hook.

Now think about the evildoers in this world. They live to create chaos. And when they get justice (time in the penitentiary, for instance) it brings dismay, calamity, and ruin. They're devastated and often surprised at the outcome. Why? Because as the Bible clearly mandates, justice will reign.

No matter what you're standing for and believing today, just know that God will shed His light on it. You can count on it. And when He does—when justice comes—it will be a joy to you and the others who've been believing with you.

*Lord, I won't give up. I'll keep standing and believing until*
*justice comes. Shine Your light, I pray. Amen.*

## THERE'S COMING A DAY

*"My holy name I will make known in the midst of my people Israel, and I will not let my holy name be profaned anymore. And the nations shall know that I am the LORD, the Holy One in Israel. Behold, it is coming and it will be brought about, declares the Lord GOD. That is the day of which I have spoken."*
EZEKIEL 39:7-8 ESV

E ver feel like the whole world's gone crazy? Maybe you wonder if anyone even cares about God anymore or His church. All around you, people are behaving in shocking ways, making you wonder if things will ever turn around.

God says, "There's coming a day." On that day He will make himself known in the midst of the people. He won't allow people to speak profanely (with evil, vile intent) on that day. Romans 14:11 (NIV) says that "It is written: 'As surely as I live,' says the Lord, 'every knee will bow before me; every tongue will acknowledge God.' "

When will that day happen? Only God knows. But hold on tight. Remain strong in Christ. That day is coming. Maybe not in your lifetime, but you have His promise that all will be made right on that amazing day.

*Lord, I know every knee will one day bow to You, and that gives me hope. Even if some people don't recognize You now. . . they will. There's coming a day when all will know, and I look forward to that with great hope! Amen.*

# THE CURE

*Is anyone among you suffering? Let him pray.*
*Is anyone cheerful? Let him sing praise.*
JAMES 5:13 ESV

God's formula for powering through rough times doesn't always make sense, does it? Take a look at today's verse. When you're suffering, pray. When you're cheerful, bump it up a notch and sing a song of praise. In other words, never be content to stay where you are. Always shoot for the next highest level and keep going.

We're not usually wired that way. When we're suffering, we tend to pull inward. And when we're happy, we don't always make a big deal about it. But when we step out of our comfort zone, we see there's a bigger God-way to deal with life's circumstances, and it requires something more of us than what we're used to giving.

It's not good to grovel in the pain, so bump it up to prayer. And when things do resolve, don't be content to just be happy about it—begin to shout a praise to the Lord at the top of your voice. In other words, keep going, even when you don't feel like putting one foot in front of the other. When you stay in perpetual motion, you're acting in faith.

*Lord, I'll keep going. The cure is in perpetual motion forward.*
*So, I'll pray. I'll sing. I'll keep taking steps of faith,*
*and I won't quit. Amen.*

## BETTER THAN SILVER OR GOLD

*A good name is to be chosen rather than great riches,*
*and favor is better than silver or gold.*
PROVERBS 22:1 ESV

Hundreds of years ago, names (particularly surnames) had a lot more value (and stigma) than they do today. A family name was meant to be cherished, treasured, and protected at all costs. If you study ancient history (for example, Scotland and England), you'll see the pride in family lineage.

You have a name too: Christ-follower. Because you carry His name, Jesus wants you to protect it at all costs. That means you have to make sure there's no hypocrisy in your walk. It gives Him a bad name when you espouse one thing but live another.

To Jesus, wearing His good name is better than having all the money in the world. There's no silver or gold that can buy you what His name can. So, don't strive after the things of this world or the pleasures they (supposedly) afford. Seek Him. Be like Him. Wear His name proudly, as a daughter of the King.

One final thought: Don't be shaken (or surprised) if the world hates your name. They hated Him, after all. And don't relinquish that name when you feel pressured by those who disagree with you. Keep on keeping on, Woman of the Way. You're a Christ-follower, loaded with both earthly and heavenly value.

*Lord, I love wearing Your name.*
*May I represent You well. Amen.*

# GOODBYE QUARRELS

*Throw out the mocker, and fighting goes, too.*
*Quarrels and insults will disappear.*
PROVERBS 22:10 NLT

Y our fists are doubled up. Your blood pressure is rising. You can feel the heat in your cheeks. You've had enough of this gal who's always mocking your friends, and you're ready to take her down.

Deep breath, girl! It might be time to separate yourself from her, but do it God's way. Once you've had a chance to get control of your emotions, you'll be in better shape to take a step back.

Maybe you're thinking, *Does God really want me to separate myself from people? Isn't He all about forgiveness and reconciliation?* God does want reconciliation when possible, but let's be honest: it's not always possible. There really are situations where that other person is toxic, and you must be separated from him or her. Perhaps this is why Jesus said, "If any household or town refuses to welcome you or listen to your message, shake its dust from your feet as you leave" (Matthew 10:14 NLT).

There are times when separation is a good thing, so don't hesitate to protect yourself and others so you can remain safe and strong.

*Lord, please give me wisdom! I don't want to pull away from people until I know for sure You're calling me to. But I'm done with the mockers and fighters, Father! I won't let them destroy those I love any longer. Amen.*

## STAY AWAY FROM WORLDLY DESIRES

*Dear friends, I warn you as "temporary residents
and foreigners" to keep away from worldly
desires that wage war against your very souls.*
1 PETER 2:11 NLT

You're inundated with commercials, tempting you with everything from laundry soap to fancy cars. And just about the time you think you're above temptation, your neighbor gets new living room furniture. Or puts in a swimming pool in her back yard. Or announces a trip to Europe with her husband.

Ugh. It's hard not to want all of the things, isn't it? "You deserve it!" we're told. "You should have it, no matter the cost. Buy it now and pay it off later in three easy payments!" And when we start to give in to that temptation, it leads us down a twisted road with an unexpected dead end.

You don't need all of the things, sweet girl. Maybe you want bigger, better, shinier, newer, but—in the grand scheme of things—is it all really necessary? Can't you be just as grateful for what you have—right here, right now?

Set your heart, your thoughts, and your desires on the Lord. He has great plans for you. And He's already made provision for all you will ever need, so put your trust in Him.

*Lord, I won't give in to the temptation to want "all the things."
I'll begin to praise You for what You've already provided.
You've been so good to me, Lord, and I'm so grateful. Amen.*

# THE GOOD SHEPHERD

*This is the kind of life you've been invited into, the kind of life
Christ lived. . . . He used his servant body to carry our sins to
the Cross so we could be rid of sin, free to live the right way.
His wounds became your healing. You were lost sheep. . . . Now
you're named and kept for good by the Shepherd of your souls.*
1 PETER 2:21-25 MSG

Once you have accepted Christ into your heart, you are invited into a different kind of life—one that follows in the sure steps of the heavenly Father. And this, dear one, is the purpose of your calling.

Because of Christ's sacrifice on the Cross, you are free from sin so you can live "the right way." And with Christ as your Savior, you are healed! Not only are you His—He's the actual Keeper of your soul! No matter what happens today or in the days to come, if you follow the Good Shepherd, you can rest assured He will never lead you astray. Following in His footsteps will lead to a life of confidence and joy. Who wouldn't want that kind of life?

Can you imagine anything more freeing than this unshakable life in Christ?

*Father, Keeper of my soul, thank You for inviting me into a
better life—a life where You lead the way for me each and
every day. I don't want to do life without You. Amen.*

## INHERITED BLESSINGS

*Be like-minded, be sympathetic, love one another, be compassionate and humble. Do not repay evil with evil or insult with insult. On the contrary, repay evil with blessing, because to this you were called so that you may inherit a blessing.*

1 PETER 3:8-9 NIV

In this all-about-me culture, we're encouraged to think about what we "deserve." A bigger house. . . A nicer car. . . A larger balance in our bank account. . . The world tells us that we should have it all. But the truth is, things will never satisfy; they'll only leave us wanting more. God's Word says in 1 John 2:16-17 (MSG): "Practically everything that goes on in the world—wanting your own way, wanting everything for yourself. . .has nothing to do with the Father. It just isolates you from him."

So what truly satisfies and promises unshakable, lasting contentment? God's Word has the best answer: *think of others*. Put others first. Even when it's hard. Even when it's inconvenient. The heavenly Father knows that being sympathetic, loving, compassionate, and humble isn't always easy. But if you say "yes" to God and embrace this challenge, then you will experience God's blessing—that's a promise!

A life blessed by the heavenly Father is something you don't want to miss!

*Heavenly Father, make me more like You each day.
I want to think less of me and more of others.
And I can't do that without Your help. Amen.*

## EVEN IF HE DOESN'T. . .

*Shadrach, Meshach, and Abednego answered King*
*Nebuchadnezzar, "Your threat means nothing to us. If you throw*
*us in the fire, the God we serve can rescue us from your roaring*
*furnace and anything else you might cook up, O king. But even*
*if he doesn't, it wouldn't make a bit of difference, O king. We still*
*wouldn't serve your gods or worship the gold statue you set up."*
DANIEL 3:16-18 MSG

Can you even begin to fathom the deeply rooted faith these men—Shadrach, Meshach, and Abednego—must have had? When King Nebuchadnezzar ordered every person to bow down to the golden statue, these three refused, knowing that in refusing, the fiery furnace would be their ultimate fate. Talk about an unshakable faith!

In their response to the demanding king, the men readily acknowledged that God might not choose to deliver them from the flames. And yet they knew He *could* save them—if He chose to do so. Either way, they would obey their heavenly Father and not the earthly king. In life—or death—they believed in God's saving power.

Do you have this kind of faith? Do you believe it in your head *and* your heart? If your faith is falling short today, ask your heavenly Father to give you an unwavering faith now and for eternity!

*Heavenly Father, I do believe. But I need Your*
*help connecting my head knowledge with my heart.*
*Give me an unshakable faith! Amen.*

## A LIFE ON FIRM FOOTING

*Friends, confirm God's invitation to you, his choice of you.*
*Don't put it off; do it now. Do this, and you'll have your life on*
*a firm footing, the streets paved and the way wide open into*
*the eternal kingdom of our Master and Savior, Jesus Christ.*
2 PETER 1:10-11 MSG

Have you accepted the Savior's invitation? Or have you been putting it off—waiting for just the "right time"?

The truth? No matter what decision you might be considering, there will likely never be the perfect time. Life is messy. . .and without Jesus, it will likely get messier with each passing day. And, as this scripture from 2 Peter says, there's no better time than right now! So don't put it off!

Sure, you can wait one more day, but one more day without Jesus means one less day of comfort and assurance, one less day of knowing what the future holds for you. Wouldn't you rather have a lifetime of joy with Jesus rather than years of insecurity and doubt?

The invitation is right there. God's waiting for you to accept Him. And with your acceptance come the promise of "firm footing" and a sure path to eternal life.

*Thank You for this invitation, Lord. I accept! Please come*
*into my life and give me the assurance that only You can*
*provide. . .a certain, firm footing as I approach each*
*new day with a heavenly perspective. Amen.*

# HOW SWEET IT IS!

*My child, eat honey, for it is good, and the honeycomb is sweet
to the taste. In the same way, wisdom is sweet to your soul.
If you find it, you will have a bright future,
and your hopes will not be cut short.*
PROVERBS 24:13-14 NLT

Perhaps you prefer a drizzle of honey to sweeten your hot tea; or maybe you enjoy the flavor of honey on a warm, buttered biscuit. Did you know that in addition to being used as a sweetener, honey is also used for its anti-inflammatory and antibacterial properties? Honey can soothe a sore throat and even help ease the pain of a mild burn.

In the above verses from the book of Proverbs, Solomon is making a connection between honey and wisdom. He observes that both honey and wisdom are sweet and beneficial. Just as honey sweetens whatever it touches, wisdom sweetens your life!

If you have a relationship with God, you're already on the right track to finding wisdom. In addition to spending quality time with Him and reading His Word, all you need to do is ask for wisdom, and He'll provide it for you (James 1:5). "Eat up" every bit of wisdom the heavenly Father provides!

*Father, give me the wisdom Solomon writes about
in the Proverbs. I long to have a life abundant in
unshakable hope and a bright future too! Thank You
for keeping the promises in Your Word. Amen.*

## THE LIVING GOD

*"I decree that everyone throughout my kingdom should tremble
with fear before the God of Daniel. For he is the living God, and
he will endure forever. His kingdom will never be destroyed,
and his rule will never end. He rescues and saves his people;
he performs miraculous signs and wonders in the heavens and
on earth. He has rescued Daniel from the power of the lions."*
DANIEL 6:26-27 NLT

Darius made a decree that for thirty days, no one in his kingdom could pray to anyone or anything other than himself. But Daniel, who trusted God with his life, decided to keep praying to God just as he always had. When his disobedience was discovered, Daniel was tossed into a den of hungry lions.

Imagine Darius's amazement the next morning, when he found Daniel alive and well—without a single scratch from the lions. This unbelievable miracle caused Darius to have a complete change of heart. And so he made a proclamation that everyone in his kingdom should fear Daniel's God—Darius knew there was no power like the power of the living God.

How wonderful that Daniel's God is still our God today. He still rescues. He still saves. He still performs miracles. He is King forever!

*Miracle-worker, my King, thank You for being the
same God today that you have been since the beginning
of time. Your unwavering love, Your promise-keeping,
help to create an unshakable faith in me! Amen.*

## UNSHAKABLE FOCUS

*Don't love the world's ways. Don't love the world's goods.*
*Love of the world squeezes out love for the Father. Practically*
*everything that goes on in the world—wanting your own way,*
*wanting everything for yourself, wanting to appear important—*
*has nothing to do with the Father. It just isolates you from*
*him. . . . Whoever does what God wants is set for eternity.*
1 JOHN 2:15-17 MSG

D o you love the world? Do you love the "things" of the world? Do you desire your own way? Do you want to be important or appear important in the eyes of others? There's no denying that the world pulls at each one of us with a super strong force!

There's a reason these verses from 1 John begin with a single command from God—*Do not love the world!* God knows it's impossible to keep our sights on worldly things and on Him at the same time. One will ultimately win our heart—but *only One* can truly satisfy our souls. . .Christ Himself!

Who—or what—will win the battle for your heart? Don't push God aside for the "treasures" of this world that will pass away. Choose Him first. . .every single day!

*Father, I want to keep a steady focus on You and You alone!*
*Help me to avoid the temptations of this world. . . . I want to stay*
*close to You today and for all my days to come! Amen.*

## NO SHRINKING VIOLET HERE

*And now, dear children, remain in fellowship with Christ so that when he returns, you will be full of courage and not shrink back from him in shame. Since we know that Christ is righteous, we also know that all who do what is right are God's children.*
1 JOHN 2:28-29 NLT

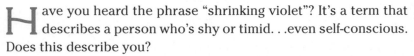

Have you heard the phrase "shrinking violet"? It's a term that describes a person who's shy or timid. . .even self-conscious. Does this describe you?

If you are deluged with insecurities and could use a heavenly boost of courage, sister, re-read the scripture above from 1 John. This passage holds the secret for standing tall and confident as you await the day of Your heavenly Father's return. The secret is abiding in Christ. Abiding in Him means that you maintain a strong connection with Him, you depend on Him. . .you fully rest your soul in Him, trusting in His promises! Now doesn't that sound like a beautiful way to live?

Daughter of God, you have no reason to be a shrinking violet when you're a child of the one and only King! Ask Him to walk alongside you every step of your journey. He won't let you down!

*Father God, I come to You today with an insecure heart. Help me to see that You are with me in every moment and that I have no reason to be timid or self-conscious when I have You in my life. Amen.*

## KNOWING CHRIST

*Everyone who sins is breaking God's law, for all sin is contrary
to the law of God. And you know that Jesus came to take away
our sins, and there is no sin in him. Anyone who continues to
live in him will not sin. But anyone who keeps on sinning does
not know him or understand who he is.*

1 JOHN 3:4-6 NLT

There is no stability in the sinful life. Sin is complete and utter lawlessness. When we sin, we're ignoring God's rules—we're behaving as though they don't exist. We're acting as if God's commands are of no consequence.

It's tempting to write off each and every sin as innocent "mistakes"—missteps that we didn't mean to take. But the truth? When we sin, we Christ-followers are usually making a conscious decision to disobey God. We know in our heads and our hearts that we're entering into sin—and yet we do it anyway.

The good news is we're fully equipped to win the battle against sin by knowing God's truth and practicing it every day. Set aside daily time to read the Bible and spend time in the heavenly Father's presence. Truly get to know Him—He's on your side and will help you battle any temptations that come your way.

*God, I want You to have ultimate authority over
my life. Help me to know You better every day and
understand the truths of Your Word. Amen.*

## THE PRACTICE OF LOVE

*My dear children, let's not just talk about love;
let's practice real love. This is the only way we'll know
we're living truly, living in God's reality. It's also the way
to shut down debilitating self-criticism, even when there is
something to it. For God is greater than our worried hearts
and knows more about us than we do ourselves.*
1 JOHN 3:18-20 MSG

I t's easy to say we "love" something. "I love the color blue." "I love the beach." "I love my neighbor." "I love my kids." "I love my spouse." Words are easy to come by.

But, sister, are you in the business of *practicing* love? Truly genuine love is made evident through our actions. So instead of saying, "I love my neighbor," *show* your love for your neighbor. Mow her lawn. Cook a meal and hand-deliver it. Just check in to say hello.

The fantastic thing about showing your love is its "cause and effect" relationship—actively practicing love causes wonderful things to happen in others *and* ourselves! When we practice love, not only do we shine light into the souls of others, it floods our very own souls with light. And through our love, others will see the unchanging, unshakable love of the Father!

*Father God, remind me today that my actions are
often more important than the words I speak. I want
others to see You through me. Help me to show love
to someone who needs Your light. Amen.*

## SO THAT YOU MAY KNOW. . .

*I write these things to you who believe in the name of the Son*
*of God so that you may know that you have eternal life.*
*This is the confidence we have in approaching God:*
*that if we ask anything according to his will, he hears us.*
*And if we know that he hears us—whatever we ask—*
*we know that we have what we asked of him.*
1 JOHN 5:13-15 NIV

When you know Jesus. . .when You've trusted Him as leader of your life, you gain a fantastic gift—the gift of confident assurance. As a child of God, you can trust and truly "know" that:

You are forgiven.

You have eternal life.

You can have freedom from fear and anxiety.

God hears your prayers.

When you pray according to God's will, He will give you what you've asked of Him.

And so much more!

Every day of your life, you can trust in His precious promises. What makes this beautiful assurance even better? It comes with an abundance of joy!

What about you, friend? Are you living joyfully through Jesus? Have you fully trusted in the saving power of Jesus? Are you becoming more and more unshakable every day?

*Heavenly Father, thank You for the confident assurance*
*I have because of Your precious promises. I trust You, Lord, as*
*leader of my life today and for all my days to come! Amen.*

## NOTHING HAS CHANGED

*I can't tell you how happy I am to learn that many members of
your congregation are diligent in living out the Truth, exactly as
commanded by the Father. But permit me a reminder, friends,
and this is not a new commandment but simply a repetition
of our original and basic charter: that we love each other.
Love means following his commandments, and his unifying
commandment is that you conduct your lives in love. This
is the first thing you heard, and nothing has changed.*
2 JOHN 1:4-6 MSG

One of the most beautiful things about God and His Word is
consistency. God and His Word are unchanging. What was true
yesterday is still true today. . .and will be true tomorrow. When it
comes to God, there's never any guesswork.

So it should be no surprise that today's scripture ends with
the phrase "and nothing has changed." Living in love? Check! *Still*
God's commandment. It's both comforting and reassuring to know
that what's essential in the Christian life doesn't change from day
to day, week to week, or year to year.

So today, Woman of the Way, let's keep it simple. Love others.
Follow God's commandments. If you stay true to these things, you'll
be living your best life. And that's a promise!

*Lord, there's nothing I love more than the unchanging
nature of Your character and Your Word. Thank You for
being a Promise Keeper. I love You! Amen.*

# THE ONE AND ONLY GOD

*"I'm still your GOD, the God who saved you out of Egypt. I'm the only real God you've ever known. I'm the one and only God who delivers. I took care of you during the wilderness hard times, those years when you had nothing. I took care of you, took care of all your needs, gave you everything you needed."*
HOSEA 13:4-6 MSG

Think about this: Are you *too* comfortable?

If we're completely honest with ourselves, we would admit that we tend to get comfortable when life is going just as we'd hoped it would. As a result, we begin to take God for granted, and before we know it, we lose our faith focus and end up wandering away from Him.

If you notice that you're getting too comfortable in your faith, just remember today's scripture. The same God who delivered the Israelites and met all their needs is the very same God who cares for us today! And if you keep moving forward—taking all the steps you can to build your relationship with the One who loves you most—then you can maintain sure steps on the path to an unshakable Christian life.

Refuse to get comfortable. Accept the challenge to keep moving closer to God, the Giver of all good things. Keep that faith focus, friend!

*Lord, I'm so sorry for losing my focus on You.*
*Help me to keep pressing closer to You. Amen.*

## SAFE IN GOD'S LOVE

*But you, dear friends, must build each other up in your most*
*holy faith, pray in the power of the Holy Spirit, and await the*
*mercy of our Lord Jesus Christ, who will bring you eternal life.*
*In this way, you will keep yourselves safe in God's love.*
JUDE 1:20–21 NLT

Take a good look around, and you'll see it's undeniable: the world is full of deception and rebellion against God. It's overflowing with false teachings and ungodly temptations. So what's a woman to do to safeguard her heart and mind?

To keep from falling prey to the ways of the world, it's never been more important to remember the simple truths of God's Word. So each day make the choice to:

Soak up the God-breathed scriptures.

Encourage your brothers and sisters in Christ.

Pray according to God's will.

Seek to do only those things that are pleasing to Christ.

Believe the promises of scripture.

Take each opportunity to share the light of the Savior.

As you choose to live each day with your focus on Jesus, you'll find yourself safe in His love—and there's truly no better place to be than that!

---

*God, help me to keep Your will in mind as I pray.*
*When I struggle with the messages of uncertainty in the world,*
*bring Your very certain Word to the forefront of my mind.*
*Thank You for the unshakable faith foundation that*
*is mine—all because of You! Amen.*

# ALWAYS!

*"I am the Alpha and the Omega—the beginning and the end," says the Lord God. "I am the one who is, who always was, and who is still to come—the Almighty One."*
REVELATION 1:8 NLT

We humans have a tendency to put our hope and trust in the temporary things of this world. We have a laserlike focus on our dreams and plans for the future. And so we spin our wheels and spend our days working so hard to have a perfect family, a lovely home, a rewarding career, and more. We want it *all*!

The "all" should be everything we'd ever want or need. . .right?

Truthfully? The "all" can only be found in *one* perfect being. . .and His name is Jesus. Jesus—who came to save you and me! Jesus—who is the beginning and the end. . .and everything in between! Jesus—who made all things. Jesus—who controls all things. Everything is in His very capable hands.

If you find yourself exhausted and searching for the "all" in this world, give yourself a break. Slow down. Look and listen for the Almighty One. He has a lot to say to your uncertain heart. Let Him fill it up with His assuring love and promises today.

*Jesus, thank You. You are the only steady, reliable thing in this world. Help me to depend on You—and You alone!—for all of my days. I look forward to a forever life in heaven with You. Amen.*

## HIS WILL. . .TO THE END

*"To the one who is victorious and does my will to the end,
I will give authority over the nations—that one 'will rule them
with an iron scepter and will dash them to pieces like pottery'—
just as I have received authority from my Father. I will
also give that one the morning star. Whoever has ears,
let them hear what the Spirit says to the churches."*
REVELATION 2:26–29 NIV

What happens once you receive Christ as leader of your life? If your answer is "I become a changed person," you're right! Once we accept Jesus as leader of our lives, it's true. . .we are changed humans. However, this transformation doesn't happen overnight.

A true transformation takes time and persistence. We should persevere in our faith so, over time, we grow closer to Jesus every single day. And as we grow closer to Him, our thoughts, attitudes, and actions begin to change. But we can't grow and change all on our own. . .not without Jesus' help! He is our example and guide for a faith-filled life. Following in His steps will help us to change from the inside out.

How have you transformed since meeting Jesus? Tell Him "thank You" today!

*Heavenly Father, I commit today and the rest of my
days to You. I want to live in Your will and Your way.
I long for a steadfast faith foundation and a transformed
heart. Make me more like You, Lord! Amen.*

# GOD SPEAKS

*"Look! I stand at the door and knock. If you hear my voice and open the door, I will come in, and we will share a meal together as friends. Those who are victorious will sit with me on my throne."*
REVELATION 3:20-21 NLT

The heavenly Father speaks to you. Do you hear Him?

If you're unsure if God has ever spoken to you, ask yourself a few questions:

- Do you ever feel a small nudge in the depths of your soul to do something good or right?

- Have you experienced a hardship? A job loss? The inability to pay the bills? An illness?

- Or have you ever been through a season when you encountered blessing upon blessing?

Sometimes God speaks in small whispers, but He also will sometimes use more drastic means to get your full attention. When He speaks, He leaves it up to you to respond. He'll never force Himself into your life.

Open your ears and your soul to His voice today. And when you hear it, open the door to your heart and invite Him in. He desires an intimate relationship with you, dear one. Don't you desire the same?

One thing is certain: when you say yes to the heavenly Father, your life will never be the same. You'll be on your way to a victorious life in Christ!

*Father, I hear You knocking on the door
of my heart. And I am saying, "Yes!"*

## CREATOR GOD

*"You are worthy, O Lord our God, to receive glory and*
*honor and power. For you created all things, and they*
*exist because you created what you pleased."*
REVELATION 4:11 NLT

What's your favorite part of God's creation?
A fiery summer sunset?
A sparkling blue-green ocean?
A glistening snowflake?
A multicolored carpet of wildflowers?

Whatever you delight in, know that the Creator God is worthy of your praise for His incomparable artistry and creativity. Without Him, *nothing* would exist. In fact, everything is dependent on Him—including you and me! And the God who created all things also sustains all things.

Can you think of anything better? What worries and concerns do you need to carry if God is in control? If all of creation is entirely up to Him, what do you need to stress and fret about?

Not one single thing! You don't need to have a care in the world when you have complete faith and understanding that God has it all—the entire world and everything in it—in His very capable hands.

So let go of your worries today, and give the Lord glory and honor for His beautiful and wonderful creation.

---

*Creator God, although I sometimes take Your creation*
*for granted, I know You are worthy of my daily praise*
*every time I enjoy the beauty of a sunset or take pleasure*
*in the colorful landscape of autumn. I want to have*
*a grateful heart always. Thank You, Father.*

# REMEMBERING THE PROMISE KEEPER

*"As my life was slipping away, I remembered the Lᴏʀᴅ. And my earnest prayer went out to you in your holy Temple. Those who worship false gods turn their backs on all God's mercies. But I will offer sacrifices to you with songs of praise, and I will fulfill all my vows. For my salvation comes from the Lᴏʀᴅ alone."*
Jᴏɴᴀʜ 2:7-9 ɴʟᴛ

Jonah, likely overwhelmed by sorrow, had all but given up hope on life. He had made some not-so-great decisions and had tried to run away from God, and poor Jonah was feeling the full weight of his sinful and shortsighted consequences.

And yet Jonah "remembered." Although his remembering of the Lord appears to be quite late, remember God, he did. He remembered God was the ultimate Promise Keeper. He remembered God was gracious and full of mercy. He remembered God was Healer and Forgiver and Savior. And after his prayer to God, Jonah received Christ's blessing.

No matter what mistakes you've made, know this: there is beauty in your remembering who God is. And while we might treat God badly for a time or even try to run away from Him, He is *always* waiting and ready for us to seek Him again. Still, He cares. Still, He loves.

*Heavenly Father, I'm sorry for ever trying to run away from You. I need You—today and every day. Please keep my thoughts focused on You and Your steadfast goodness and mercy.*

## FOREVER AND EVER

*Meanwhile, all the other people live however they wish,
picking and choosing their gods. But we live honoring GOD,
and we're loyal to our God forever and ever.*

MICAH 4:5 MSG

L ook around you, and you can readily see people "picking and choosing their gods" and living "however they wish." To Christ followers, this is both sad and alarming. When you've trusted God as the Lord and leader of your life, it doesn't make sense to see so many people putting their faith and trust in temporary treasures and pleasures and even in other people. And it's even more difficult to understand when these people seem so lost and unhappy.

What about you? Have you made the choice to live a life that honors God? Have you given Him your loyalty? If you have, God has promised you a better life, a longer life, a peaceful life, and the best thing: everlasting life in heaven with Him (Proverbs 3:1–2 and John 3:16)!

When you compare a life with Jesus to a life without Him, there's no denying the best choice. There's no life like the life of a Christ follower. With Him, your future is secure!

*Father God, I give You my loyalty and love and my whole heart.
May I live each day to honor You. I pray others would
see the joy and hope You bring into my life so they will
want to know You as their Lord too. Amen.*

# THREE THINGS

*O people, the LORD has told you what is good, and this*
*is what he requires of you: to do what is right,*
*to love mercy, and to walk humbly with your God.*

MICAH 6:8 NLT

W hat three things does God require of you?

1.  to do what is right
2.  to love mercy
3.  to walk humbly with Him

Now, an even more important question: *How* can you accomplish these three things in your life? Are there any prerequisites? First (and most importantly), a right relationship with God as your Father. From this, all else will flow. Without this relationship, it's impossible to meet all of His requirements.

So today, focus on this one thing: your connection to the heavenly Father. Ask Him for His help, and then commit to doing the work it takes to make your relationship stronger than it is right this very moment. Once you've established a firm and unshakable faith foundation, you'll see just how naturally the three requirements of God come to you. And truly, there's no better example to follow than Jesus for a life well-lived!

*Father God, I want to please You today and all my days. It's my*
*desire to meet Your requirements and to do all things well. Help*
*me to stay strong in my commitment to You, Lord. With You by my*
*side, I can accomplish all You expect and ask of me. Amen.*

## A HIDING PLACE

*God is good, a hiding place in tough times.*
*He recognizes and welcomes anyone looking for help,*
*no matter how desperate the trouble.*
NAHUM 1:7-8 MSG

Think about some of the most troublesome things in your life. What do you stress over and worry about the most?

Your health?

Your finances?

Your relationships?

Your career?

Your family?

No matter what troubles you may encounter in this life—big or small—remember that in all of it, God is good. He is compassionate and kind. And in the uttermost darkness, God is your light. He protects His children—and that's a promise you can count on! With Him in your life, you can overcome any hardship. The Bible says to "Give all your worries and cares to God, for he cares about you" (1 Peter 5:7 NLT) and "Don't be discouraged, for I am your God. I will strengthen you and help you. I will hold you up with my victorious right hand" (Isaiah 41:10 NLT).

Isn't it wonderful? God recognizes what you're going through—*and* what's more, He's standing by, ready to offer His help. In fact, He *welcomes* you and all your troubles. So hand over your worries and cares to Him today, and then be sure to thank Him for His unending goodness!

*God, You are so, so good. Thank You for rescuing me from my troubles. I give You all the glory. Amen.*

## EVEN IF. . .

*Though the fig tree does not bud and there are no grapes on the vines, though the olive crop fails and the fields produce no food, though there are no sheep in the pen and no cattle in the stalls, yet I will rejoice in the LORD, I will be joyful in God my Savior.*
HABAKKUK 3:17-18 NIV

The fig tree mentioned in today's scripture produced fruit that was a food staple in ancient times. Grapes were picked from the vine and used to make wine. Sheep and cattle provided meat. With these things in scarce supply, it would have made sense if Habakkuk had written "and so I will be unhappy." Rejoicing just doesn't make sense in this situation, does it?

What about you? Have you ever suffered a momentous loss? Have you invested time and labor into something important to you, only to have it all fall apart? Have you experienced a tremendous disappointment? How did you react to life's let-downs? Were you joyful? Or did you spiral into a dark, emotional abyss. . .angry, sad, hopeless?

God's Word says, "Rejoice always, pray continually, give thanks in all circumstances; for this is God's will for you in Christ Jesus" (1 Thessalonians 5:16-18 NIV). No matter what life brings your way—good or bad—*rejoice*! Because you have Jesus!

*Father, some days are just hard. It's comforting to know that because of You, I can have joy despite my circumstances. Amen.*

## WHO BUT GOD?

*Who but God goes up to heaven and comes back down? Who
holds the wind in his fists? Who wraps up the oceans in his
cloak? Who has created the whole wide world? What is his
name—and his son's name? Tell me if you know!*
PROVERBS 30:4 NLT

No person has gone to heaven and returned to earth to tell us
mortals what they've seen. Sure, Enoch and Elijah were taken
into heaven while they were still alive (Genesis 5:24 and 2 Kings
2:11)—but heaven is where they stayed. Their tickets to heaven were
one-way only. Going up to heaven and coming back down? God is
the only One who has this power.

And it's certainly not within the realm of human possibility for
any man or woman to set the winds free to blow or to bring them
to stillness. The power lies with the heavenly Creator alone, who
has complete control over the winds and the seas that obey Him
(Psalm 135:7; Matthew 8:26-27).

God—and only God—has the ability to create the entire world
and everything in it. All of creation is in His powerful, capable hands.
Who but God, indeed?

---

*Lord God, I can go to sleep in peace each night,
knowing that You alone are in control of the entire
world and everything in it. Thank You for calming my
heart even as You calm the winds and waves. Amen.*

## CONTENTMENT WITH
## "JUST ENOUGH"

*O God, I beg two favors from you. . . . First, help me never to tell*
*a lie. Second, give me neither poverty nor riches! Give me just*
*enough to satisfy my needs. For if I grow rich, I may deny you*
*and say, "Who is the LORD?" And if I am too poor, I may steal*
*and thus insult God's holy name.*

PROVERBS 30:7-9 NLT

W hat do you pray for? Do you ask the heavenly Creator for "more"? . . . Perhaps more money in the bank? More food in the refrigerator? More stuff than what you really need?

If so, you're not alone. In today's culture, we're trained to think we need more of one thing or another. Surely without "more," we'll never be happy and satisfied. But is this true? Or does "more" just make you crave even. . .*more?*

The author of this selection from the Proverbs, Agur, gives us some wisdom on what really brings true contentment and lasting satisfaction—ask God for just *enough*. . ."neither poverty nor riches." Agur knew there is danger in growing rich and having so much that you quit depending on God for His provision. Agur also knew that were he poor, he might be tempted to steal what he needed, which would reflect badly on the Savior.

Woman of God, trust God to provide your "just enough" today.

*Father, thank You for Your provision.*
*May I rely on You and You alone. Amen.*

## SONGS OF PRAISE

*"Great and marvelous are your works, O Lord God,
the Almighty. Just and true are your ways, O King of the nations.
Who will not fear you, Lord, and glorify your name? For you
alone are holy. All nations will come and worship before you,
for your righteous deeds have been revealed."*

REVELATION 15:3-4 NLT

Where is your focus? Are you distracted daily by your own thoughts—does your brain swirl with uncontrolled worries, cares, and stresses? Is your glass half-empty today, friend? If so, give your spirit a much-needed holy pause.

Refocus your thoughts on your heavenly Father—the One who makes all things possible (Matthew 19:26). When you turn your thoughts on Him—and not yourself—you'll be amazed at the transformation of your mindset. Just try it. . .and see what happens.

Repeat today's song of thanksgiving and praise from the book of Revelation.

The words of wonder and admiration will turn your heart to praise. Every sentence is an intentional focus on God and His mighty works! This song is a joyful celebration of His infinite power and wisdom and His righteousness!

Aren't you blessed to know the one and only Miracle-Worker, Truth-Teller, and Promise-Keeper? You are blessed indeed!

*Promise-Keeper, I am so blessed to have a growing relationship
with You. Please refocus my thoughts. I want to think less of
myself and more of You every day. I praise You! Amen.*

# UNCHANGING MESSAGE

*"The Message hasn't changed. GOD-of-the-Angel-Armies said then
and says now: 'Treat one another justly. Love your neighbors.
Be compassionate with each other. Don't take advantage of
widows, orphans, visitors, and the poor. Don't plot and
scheme against one another—that's evil.'"*
ZECHARIAH 7:9-10 MSG

Is it possible to be right with God if your relationships with people are a complete and utter mess? The short answer. . .no! God's Word says in Matthew 5:23–24 (MSG), "This is how I want you to conduct yourself in these matters. If you enter your place of worship and, about to make an offering, you suddenly remember a grudge a friend has against you, abandon your offering, leave immediately, go to this friend and make things right. Then and only then, come back and work things out with God."

With this knowledge, it's so important to be compassionate, show mercy, help the needy, be kind and loving to our neighbors—all the things that make for fantastic relationships with others. These things aren't easy. In fact, most days they're downright challenging—especially when you're interacting with someone who's hard to love.

Is there someone you need to make things right with today? Ask the unshakable God to give you the courage and strength to start the conversation—and then do it!

*God, thank You for Your unchanging message.
I desire to obey You for all my days. Amen.*

## THE ONE YOU DEPEND ON

*Ask the LORD for rain in the springtime; it is the LORD who sends the thunderstorms. He gives showers of rain to all people, and plants of the field to everyone.*
ZECHARIAH 10:1 NIV

Did you know there's a direct connection between prayer and God's promises? It's true! Just read God's Word, and you'll see for yourself. Here are just a few scriptural truths:

- Ask, and it will be given to you (Matthew 7:7-11; Luke 11:9-13; Matthew 21:22; John 14:13–14).

- Call on God, and He will rescue you (Psalm 50:14-15).

- The Lord listens to the humble (Psalm 10:14).

- The Lord answers His people (Zechariah 10:6; Isaiah 41:17).

In the Bible, you'll also discover that we humans are dependent on the heavenly Father for our every need (John 15:5; John 14:6; Romans 8:28). And prayer is our expression of that dependence. Whether we have needs and wants, praises or pleas, when you talk, He listens—and He'll answer!

How beautiful to know, without a doubt, that the same God who controls the winds and the rains also listens to your prayers (Psalm 135:7). Never stop praying!

---

*Father God, I am so thankful that You are the One who always listens, always understands, always answers, always knows exactly what I need. Thank You for being the One I can always depend on—no matter what! You are my everything! Amen.*

## SPEAK UP!

*"Speak up for the people who have no voice,
for the rights of all the misfits. Speak out for
justice! Stand up for the poor and destitute!"*
PROVERBS 31:8–9 MSG

The heavenly Father is concerned for those who are weak and can't speak up for themselves. He cares deeply for those in society who are easily forgettable.

Jesus' directive is to be His hands and feet to the people who need our help the most. The elderly. The mentally challenged. The beat-down and bullied. The unborn. The poor and destitute. We can bless these people with God's love and provision.

Sadly, our reason for helping others is often selfish. It's tempting to do for those who can do something for us in return. We think, *How will this benefit me?* We certainly don't help others because it's difficult, complicated, and sometimes downright miserable.

If you think about it, it's only because of someone else that you are where you are today—God and His amazing grace, who brought us out of darkness and into His glorious light!

Take a look around. Who in your world needs you right now? Ask God for His strength and the courage you need to speak up today.

*God, You have transformed my life, and You continue
to bless me day by day. Now help me to have Your heart
for others. To reflect Your love and grace to those in need
today. To be Your hands and feet, Father! Amen.*

# GOOD NEWS!

*"But for you who fear my name, the Sun of Righteousness will rise with healing in his wings. And you will go free, leaping with joy like calves let out to pasture. On the day when I act, you will tread upon the wicked as if they were dust under your feet."*

MALACHI 4:2-3 NLT

I f it seems like you're constantly bombarded with bad news. . . If you ever find yourself in a difficult place. . . If your faith is faltering and your heart is hopeless. . . If you feel alone and abandoned. . . There's good news for you, dear one!

If you're a faithful follower of Jesus, you're on the receiving end of bountiful blessings. And they're yours for the taking. Part of those blessings include ultimate healing, joy, and freedom in Christ. How can you know this for certain? Because the promises of God's Word are unfaltering and trustworthy. If His Word says it, you can believe it! "GOD always does what he says, and is gracious in everything he does" (Psalm 145:13 MSG).

Today, thank God for making you one of His own. Praise Him for His saving grace. He is the one and only Redeemer!

*Father God, because of Your steadfast love and grace, I am free. I have joy in my heart even when life is hard. You give me hope not just today but for the future. I choose to follow You all the days of my life. Thank You! Amen.*

## UNCHANGING, CONSTANT

*"I am GOD—yes, I AM. I haven't changed. And because*
*I haven't changed, you, the descendants of Jacob, haven't been*
*destroyed. You have a long history of ignoring my commands.*
*You haven't done a thing I've told you. Return to me so*
*I can return to you," says GOD-of-the-Angel-Armies.*
MALACHI 3:6-7 MSG

I n our human relationships, it's virtually impossible to find a person who will never let us down. . .someone who follows through on every single promise. . .someone who always shows up. . .someone who loves us on our good days and our "difficult to love" days. No human being is perfect—including us. And imperfect people make for imperfect relationships.

In a world of all this imperfection, what a relief to know that we can have a beautifully secure relationship with the Father! He is steadfast and true to His Word. We never need to wonder where He stands or how He feels about us, because He is unchanging.

When you're feeling unsure, wrap your soul in these comforting scriptures:

- Hebrews 13:8
- James 1:17
- Numbers 23:19
- Isaiah 40:8
- Psalm 119:89
- Psalm 33:11

Praise the unchangeable God! The One who is faithful and true. His mercies are everlasting!

*Great is Your faithfulness, Lord. And I am forever grateful*
*that I can know You and that Your love and expectations for*
*me never change. Your constant presence and unconditional*
*love are sources of peace, comfort, and joy. Amen.*

# CONTRIBUTORS

Born in Paraguay, **Terry Alburger** grew up in Levittown, Pennsylvania. She has always had a passion for writing, which blossomed in her position at Brittany Pointe Estates. Terry is a columnist for a local newspaper, is currently working on her twelfth play, and is the editor of Brittany Pointe's newsletter. Terry's devotions appear in the months of September and March.

**Linda Hang** is a freelancer from Ohio. She enjoys old movies, kayaking, and discovering each day what God has planned for her—like writing. Her unexpected writing projects include *3-Minute Prayers for Women* and *Unfinished: Devotions and Prayers for a Heart Under Construction*. Linda's devotions appear in the month of June.

**Donna K. Maltese** is a freelance writer, editor, and writing coach. Mother of two adult children and grandmother of a little one, she resides in Bucks County, Pennsylvania, with her husband. When not playing with words, Donna is knitting, journaling, reading, or exploring landscapes within and without. Donna's devotions appear in the months of February and July.

**Kelly McIntosh** is a wife, twin mom, and editor from Ohio. She loves books, the beach, and everything about autumn (but mostly pumpkin spice lattes). Kelly's devotions appear in the month of December.

**Valorie Quesenberry** is a pastor's wife, mother, musician, editor of a Christian ladies' magazine, and a writer. She periodically contributes devotionals to a Christian literature provider. Her first book released with Wesleyan Publishing House in April 2010. Valorie's devotions appear in the month of May.

**Janice Thompson** is the author of over 100 books for the Christian market—including inspirational romances, cozy mysteries, and devotionals. She lives in Spring, Texas, with her three ornery pups and spends her days writing and baking up cakes and cookies. Her tagline "Love, Laughter, and Happily Ever Afters" sums up her take on life. Janice is strong in her faith and does her best to keep the Lord at the center of all she does. Janice's devotions appear in the months of January and November.

**Annie Tipton** made up her first story at the ripe old age of two when she asked her mom to write it down for her. Since then she has read and written many words as a student, newspaper reporter, author, and editor. Annie loves snow (which is a good thing because she lives in Ohio), wearing scarves, sushi, Scrabble, and spending time with friends and family. Annie's devotions appear in the month of October.

**Ellie Zumbach** is a freelance writer and actor in northeastern Ohio. She earned a BA in Creative Writing from Malone University. Her writings have been awarded the Malone Writers Prize in areas of Fiction, Creative Nonfiction, and Poetry, and presented at Taylor University's Making Literature Conference in 2017 and 2019. She has been published in *30N* and *The Cobalt Review* and is a contributor to *Memoirs of a Virtuous Woman*. She believes stories are some of the most important things in the world and spent her years growing up on a dairy farm reading as many as she could. Ellie's devotions appear in the months of April and August.

# READ THRU THE BIBLE
# IN A YEAR PLAN

| | | | | | |
|---|---|---|---|---|---|
| 1-Jan | Gen. 1-2 | Matt. 1 | Ps. 1 |
| 2-Jan | Gen. 3-4 | Matt. 2 | Ps. 2 |
| 3-Jan | Gen. 5-7 | Matt. 3 | Ps. 3 |
| 4-Jan | Gen. 8-10 | Matt. 4 | Ps. 4 |
| 5-Jan | Gen. 11-13 | Matt. 5:1-20 | Ps. 5 |
| 6-Jan | Gen. 14-16 | Matt. 5:21-48 | Ps. 6 |
| 7-Jan | Gen. 17-18 | Matt. 6:1-18 | Ps. 7 |
| 8-Jan | Gen. 19-20 | Matt. 6:19-34 | Ps. 8 |
| 9-Jan | Gen. 21-23 | Matt. 7:1-11 | Ps. 9:1-8 |
| 10-Jan | Gen. 24 | Matt. 7:12-29 | Ps. 9:9-20 |
| 11-Jan | Gen. 25-26 | Matt. 8:1-17 | Ps. 10:1-11 |
| 12-Jan | Gen. 27:1-28:9 | Matt. 8:18-34 | Ps. 10:12-18 |
| 13-Jan | Gen. 28:10-29:35 | Matt. 9 | Ps. 11 |
| 14-Jan | Gen. 30:1-31:21 | Matt. 10:1-15 | Ps. 12 |
| 15-Jan | Gen. 31:22-32:21 | Matt. 10:16-36 | Ps. 13 |
| 16-Jan | Gen. 32:22-34:31 | Matt. 10:37-11:6 | Ps. 14 |
| 17-Jan | Gen. 35-36 | Matt. 11:7-24 | Ps. 15 |
| 18-Jan | Gen. 37-38 | Matt. 11:25-30 | Ps. 16 |
| 19-Jan | Gen. 39-40 | Matt. 12:1-29 | Ps. 17 |
| 20-Jan | Gen. 41 | Matt. 12:30-50 | Ps. 18:1-15 |
| 21-Jan | Gen. 42-43 | Matt. 13:1-9 | Ps. 18:16-29 |
| 22-Jan | Gen. 44-45 | Matt. 13:10-23 | Ps. 18:30-50 |
| 23-Jan | Gen. 46:1-47:26 | Matt. 13:24-43 | Ps. 19 |
| 24-Jan | Gen. 47:27-49:28 | Matt. 13:44-58 | Ps. 20 |
| 25-Jan | Gen. 49:29-Exod. 1:22 | Matt. 14 | Ps. 21 |
| 26-Jan | Exod. 2-3 | Matt. 15:1-28 | Ps. 22:1-21 |
| 27-Jan | Exod. 4:1-5:21 | Matt. 15:29-16:12 | Ps. 22:22-31 |
| 28-Jan | Exod. 5:22-7:24 | Matt. 16:13-28 | Ps. 23 |
| 29-Jan | Exod. 7:25-9:35 | Matt. 17:1-9 | Ps. 24 |
| 30-Jan | Exod. 10-11 | Matt. 17:10-27 | Ps. 25 |
| 31-Jan | Exod. 12 | Matt. 18:1-20 | Ps. 26 |
| 1-Feb | Exod. 13-14 | Matt. 18:21-35 | Ps. 27 |
| 2-Feb | Exod. 15-16 | Matt. 19:1-15 | Ps. 28 |
| 3-Feb | Exod. 17-19 | Matt. 19:16-30 | Ps. 29 |
| 4-Feb | Exod. 20-21 | Matt. 20:1-19 | Ps. 30 |
| 5-Feb | Exod. 22-23 | Matt. 20:20-34 | Ps. 31:1-8 |
| 6-Feb | Exod. 24-25 | Matt. 21:1-27 | Ps. 31:9-18 |
| 7-Feb | Exod 26-27 | Matt. 21:28-46 | Ps. 31:19-24 |
| 8-Feb | Exod. 28 | Matt. 22 | Ps. 32 |
| 9-Feb | Exod. 29 | Matt. 23:1-36 | Ps. 33:1-12 |
| 10-Feb | Exod. 30-31 | Matt. 23:37-24:28 | Ps. 33:13-22 |
| 11-Feb | Exod. 32-33 | Matt. 24:29-51 | Ps. 34:1-7 |
| 12-Feb | Exod. 34:1-35:29 | Matt. 25:1-13 | Ps. 34:8-22 |
| 13-Feb | Exod. 35:30-37:29 | Matt. 25:14-30 | Ps. 35:1-8 |
| 14-Feb | Exod. 38-39 | Matt. 25:31-46 | Ps. 35:9-17 |
| 15-Feb | Exod. 40 | Matt. 26:1-35 | Ps. 35:18-28 |
| 16-Feb | Lev. 1-3 | Matt. 26:36-68 | Ps. 36:1-6 |
| 17-Feb | Lev. 4:1-5:13 | Matt. 26:69-27:26 | Ps. 36:7-12 |
| 18-Feb | Lev. 5:14 -7:21 | Matt. 27:27-50 | Ps. 37:1-6 |
| 19-Feb | Lev. 7:22-8:36 | Matt. 27:51-66 | Ps. 37:7-26 |
| 20-Feb | Lev. 9-10 | Matt. 28 | Ps. 37:27-40 |
| 21-Feb | Lev. 11-12 | Mark 1:1-28 | Ps. 38 |
| 22-Feb | Lev. 13 | Mark 1:29-39 | Ps. 39 |
| 23-Feb | Lev. 14 | Mark 1:40-2:12 | Ps. 40:1-8 |
| 24-Feb | Lev. 15 | Mark 2:13-3:35 | Ps. 40:9-17 |

# SCRIPTURE INDEX